THE BORZOI
HISTORY OF ENGLAND
VOLUME TWO
1154-1485

The Borzoi
History of England

General Editor
ARTHUR JOSEPH SLAVIN
University of California at Los Angeles

ANGLES, ANGELS,
AND CONQUERORS
Volume I: 400–1154
Joel T. Rosenthal
State University of New York at Stony Brook

THE COMMUNITY
OF THE REALM
Volume II: 1154–1485
Michael R. Powicke
University of Toronto

THE PRECARIOUS BALANCE:
English Government and Society
Volume III: 1450–1640
Arthur Joseph Slavin
University of California at Los Angeles

A CERTAINTY IN THE SUCCESSION
Volume IV: 1640–1815
Gerald M. and Lois O. Straka
University of Delaware

Volume V: 1815–the Present
J. B. Conacher
University of Toronto

THE BORZOI
HISTORY OF ENGLAND
VOLUME TWO
1154-1485

THE COMMUNITY OF THE REALM

ALFRED A. KNOPF   NEW YORK

MICHAEL R. POWICKE
University of Toronto

THIS IS A BORZOI BOOK
PUBLISHED BY ALFRED A. KNOPF, INC.

First Edition
987654321

Copyright © 1973 by Alfred A. Knopf, Inc.

All rights reserved under International and Pan-American Copyright Conventions. No part of this book may be reproduced in any form or by any means, electronic or mechanical, including photocopying, without permission in writing from the publisher. All inquiries should be addressed to Alfred A. Knopf, Inc., 201 East 50th Street, New York, N.Y. 10022.
Published in the United States by Alfred A. Knopf, Inc., New York, and simultaneously in Canada by Random House of Canada Limited, Toronto.
Distributed by Random House, Inc., New York.

Library of Congress Cataloging in Publication Data

Powicke, Michael Rhys.
 The community of the realm, 1154–1485.
 (The Borzoi history of England, v. 2)
 Bibliography: p.
  1. Great Britain—History—Plantagenets, 1154–1399.
2. Great Britain—History—Lancaster and York, 1399–
1485. I. Title. II. Series.
DA26.B65 vol. 2   942 [942.03]   72-11839
ISBN 0–394–47950–5
ISBN 0–394–31140–X (textbk.)

Typography by Jack Ribik

Manufactured in the United States of America

To Hilda

Foreword

The volumes making up the Borzoi History of England spring from the desire the authors share to preserve for the present the excitement of the English past. To a somewhat smaller degree we also share a prejudice against the writing of a history unified artificially by an allotment of "factors" and "forces." We do not think a good consecutive history of England between the coming of the Anglo-Saxons to Britain and the British entry into the Common Market can be made by such stinting of work.

This is not to say that we dismiss the need for a concern over how five volumes by as many historians go to make one history. It is to say that we began by admitting the diverse character of our assignments. We recognized at the outset that what might be central to the history of Anglo-Saxon England might be eccentric, if given the same weight by another author, to a history of industrial England. Moreover, we began in agreement that our own gifts and interests, if followed in a disciplined way, could bring out of many volumes one book.

Professor Rosenthal's history of early English society employs a narrative technique around a political center. Yet his most basic concern is to give the reader a sense of the rudeness of life in Anglo-Saxon England.

Because Professor Rosenthal had so firm a base on which to work in Volume I, Professor Powicke agreed to concentrate his work in another direction. He set out to tell how the medieval realm was ordered. While not altogether abandoning traditional narrative, he thought it profitable to examine in detail the shape and character of the various communities that constituted the medieval realm—royal, ecclesiastical, urban, and manorial.

The aim of the medievalists was thus to establish and explain the institutions and culture in a broad way, while telling how they worked. Their working order was profoundly challenged over a period of time stretching from

Chaucer's age to that of Milton, or, reckoning politically, from Edward III's time to that of Charles I. It was my concern to describe and explain how a series of shifts in the social basis of politics led the English to reorder a turbulent commonwealth.

The efforts at establishing political, religious, and social stability undertaken by the Tudors proved more daring than durable. Professor and Mrs. Straka wished to deal with the undisputed establishment of political stability between the Puritan Revolution and England's wars to contain the expansion of revolutionary France in Napoleon's time. Where Volume III sought to base an analysis of government and society in the economic and religious life of the era, the Strakas thought it essential to tell how stability was achieved in terms narrative and political at heart. They felt they could build confidently on the descriptions already achieved in Volume III, just as Professor Powicke thought to thicken the texture of the society whose shape was defined by Professor Rosenthal.

This alternation was acceptable to all because we accepted in principle the existence of three great revolutionary situations in English history—that surrounding the Norman Conquest, another focused on the Reformation, and a third based on the transformation of a mixed commercial-agrarian society into an industrial one. It fell to Professor Conacher to take forward into our time the account of the revolution that made aristocratic England into the liberal, industrial democracy of the empire and the welfare state.

Hence this History has taken shape around two concerns: giving scope to narrative, where the story of change was itself dramatic in social terms rather than in dynastic ones; and allowing room for more analytical work, where this seemed to point to an understanding of why changes took place rather than merely what changed and how.

Our historical assumptions reveal a pluralism rather than the ideas of a "school." Our concerns and styles differ, and we hope this difference is appropriate to our problems. We felt we would work best if we marched to the drum each heard best, whether it was the steady one of ordinary people working the land and the common rhythm of factory pistons or the subtler one beating to political tunes in high places. It has been our hope thus to avoid the mere repetitious noise of texts cut to cover uniformly every aspect of society. Philosophers say nature does nothing by leaps. History, however, is constantly surprising; it is alive precisely because of its variety, its stubborn refusal of any lockstep.

Between the extremes of Alfred's tight little island and the august empire ruled by Queen Elizabeth I's heirs and successors, English history lies, a polyglot thing, nurturing our own civilization and its discontents. Since the time when Ranke spoke of national histories as a perfect guide to people's consciousness, the sense of history has profoundly altered. Yet narrative—description and analysis centered in political life as widely defined to make room for religion, economics, and popular culture—has not yielded its central place. We therefore offer this History: of a country bound in by her triumphant sea; a sepulchre for famous men; an often bleak workshop; a place that sent blacks into slavery in 1562 in a ship named *Jesus;* frankly political.

ARTHUR JOSEPH SLAVIN

Contents

LIST OF ILLUSTRATIONS

Chapter One
APPROACHES TO ENGLISH MEDIEVAL HISTORY

Until recently, the literature about medieval England has not been conspicuously self-conscious. Few pages have been devoted to the rationale of a particular interpretation. Yet each generation has had its own purposes, and any student embarking on the study of the English Middle Ages is well advised to think about his presuppositions and expectations. For most periods the scholar has gone about his ways without too much reflection on his particular intention: the inculcation of virtue, the celebration of national glory, the strengthening of national liberties, or the furthering of the class war. Yet by and large the force of the motive has varied directly with the skill and volume of the output.

Beginning perhaps with the flurry of controversy about the value of Bishop Stubbs' writings, there has been a marked increase, which can be expected to continue, in the examination of viewpoints and methods. This examination has been greatly advanced by Norman Cantor's brilliant, if idiosyncratic, survey of English historical scholarship and history, *The English*. Mr. Cantor has given us all an added awareness of where we stand in the currents and crosscurrents of historical writing.

The study of medieval history by postmedieval man began with an emphasis on dynastic struggle and personal heroism or wickedness. Such was the stream of writing beginning with Polydore Vergil and Sir Thomas More and culminating in Shakespeare's historical plays. The main contributions of sixteenth-century historians to our knowledge of the Middle Ages were literary richness and dramatic interest.[1]

Polydore Vergil, an Italian émigré in England (he came as a taxcollector but

---

[1] For what follows, see F. J. Levy, *Tudor Historical Thought* (San Marino, Calif.: Huntington Library, 1967), and M. McKisack, *Medieval History in the Tudor Age* (Oxford: Oxford University Press, 1971).

stayed for over fifty years before returning in old age to his beloved Catholic Italy), was able to see through the fantasies of Geoffrey of Monmouth (see page 155) and made use of English chroniclers, and to a lesser extent state documents, to construct a *History of England* that would please his royal patrons. His book was organized around the biographies of English kings. Like his medieval chronicler sources, he was guided in this enterprise primarily by notions of divine providence and of the lessons of history as to right and wrong, and only to a slight degree by the exploration of human personality and other rational causes. Nevertheless, he incurred odium for his attack on the Arthurian legend put out by Geoffrey of Monmouth and was regarded by many as a papalist Romanizer.

Sir Thomas More, in his biography of King Richard III, was another exemplar of protohumanist history. Thought by many to be the greatest man of his age, More was brought to an untimely death by his Catholicism. His *Richard III* carried the biographical approach of Vergil to extremes. Richard emerges as the tyrant *par excellence*, and this classical motif (also prudential for a servant of the early Tudors) has colored most subsequent thought on the subject. It was from Tacitus and Suetonius, the classical Roman biographers, rather than from any valid historical references, that More drew his picture of the last Yorkist king.

At the same time a contrary current of inquiry emerged—the collection of source materials by antiquarians. The confrontation of these two themes—the dramatically interpretative and the patiently accumulative—was not to take place until the nineteenth century and is in many ways still the critical question behind modern medieval studies. From the sixteenth to the nineteenth centuries the two streams tended to flow side by side, intermingling only at times of acute crisis.

With the Tudors a new sense of national history developed, and eventually it became a flood. Dynastic pride in the ruling house was closely linked to pride in the unity and prosperity of the realm, while the establishment of a national Anglican church under the rule of the monarch added a new spirit of nationalism, as well as a new search for a historical base, to the labors of scholars. No one was to match the brilliant literary endeavors of Polydore Vergil and Thomas More, though it was later writers such as Edward Hall and Ralph Holinshed who supplied Shakespeare with his medley of information and misinformation.

Under Elizabeth a new range was achieved. For this the vast labors of John Leland had provided a firm foundation: his *Itinerary* marks a new stage, an altogether new dimension, of patriotic antiquarianism. Leland's work, which remained in manuscript until the eighteenth century, has been called the *fons et origo* of all that followed. Leland defended the Geoffrey of Monmouth's

Arthur against humanist skepticism. Yet his topographical account of England was to be the basis of all subsequent studies of this nature. His detailed recording of all he could lay hands on with regard to the history and topography of England was a treasure house from which his better-known successors drew much of their outlook and material. The late sixteenth century abounded in intensive studies of counties and towns, such as William Lambarde's survey of Kent and John Stow's study of London. They remain the starting points for students of medieval England. Another related development was the science of cartography. The two approaches—historical and geographical—were united in the greatest product of Tudor historiography, William Camden's *Brittania*.

Camden combined a sharp insight into surviving material with a sound historical sense.[2] He was inspired by the classicist Abraham Ortelius, an Anglo-Dutch cartographer, who had long sought an English scholar to put in order the antiquities of Britain. Camden's predecessors—the Welshman Humfrey Lluyd prominent among them—had laid the groundwork. He used classical sources as a base and added the careful study of coins, inscriptions, and archeological remains. Starting with the *Antonine Itineraries*, a late-third-century guide to Roman roads, Camden, with some knowledge of Welsh and Anglo-Saxon, sought to reconstruct the early history of Britain. With a classical and patriotic base, he used Leland's *Itinerary* and medieval chronicles to fill out a general archeological history of England. Camden's work introduced England to Europe, and for England constituted a veritable essay in self-discovery. In this he was assisted by an army of local antiquarians who were intently investigating the origins of their localities. The move from Roman to genealogical interest in later editions of *Brittania* laid the basis for the great seventeenth-century county histories.

John Stow's *Survey of London* was closely inspired by Camden's work. His approach was more "present-oriented" than that of Camden. Meanwhile, inspired by Elizabeth's prelates and courtiers, libraries were being assembled, archives catalogued, dictionaries of old languages written, and editions of chronicles and new histories prepared. Shakespeare's historical plays owed much to this work, and their spirit tells us of the new national self-appreciation that drove the pens of the antiquarians.

The first Society of Antiquarians (1590–1607) came together to pool and to spread the learning of such men as Camden and Stow. Heralds, lawyers, and recordkeepers filled its ranks; learned papers were read and lecture courses arranged. That it did not perpetuate itself after the dispersal or death of its original membership should not detract from its contribution to the more

2 F. J. Levy, *op. cit.*

advanced antiquarian researches of the seventeenth century. Possibly one reason for its "suspension" was the fact that the national and local pride typical of Elizabethan England gave way in the following century to powerful partisanship in political and religious affairs.

The seventeenth century saw the study of the Middle Ages enter the political arena in a more fundamental way than the sixteenth. Now royalists and parliamentarians vied with one another in pillaging the medieval sources for arguments and documents to buttress their claims. Hence a preliminary fusion between antiquarian and historian was made. William Prynne's great collection of parliamentary documents (*Parliamentary Writs*) was a case in point. So, in a less lasting manner, was Sir Edward Coke's invocation of medieval precedent to support opposition to the king's authority in his *Inventories of the Laws of England*. As David Douglas has shown, there was a great advance in the knowledge of the Middle Ages under the pressure of the seventeenth-century political and religious controversies.[3] No period has been more self-conscious —and blind—about its presuppositions. In spite of all the bias and misunderstanding, in the sense of apologetics for the monarchy, for the opposition, for Canterbury, or for Rome, the seventeenth-century political antiquaries set in motion a movement of inquiry that is still with us.

The heroic achievements of the Elizabethan historians and antiquarians in mapping the past led, through the work of such giants as John Selden, Sir Henry Spelman, and Prynne, to the glorious flowering of the Restoration and revolutionary era. In the latter period, driven more by sectarian enthusiasm, local pride, and continued patriotism, scholars in historical and allied fields reached a peak and produced a volume of learned material—notably dictionaries and editions of medieval charters, chronicles, and records—that was to be used by the new wave of scholarship in the nineteenth-century revival. It is unfair to single out particular studies for mention, but one thinks naturally of those still in use today, such as Henry Wharton's *Anglia Sacra,* Thomas Madox's *Exchequer,* and Rymer's *Foedera.* The scholar might be a hunted nonjuror (a cleric who would not take the oaths of allegiance to the Orange monarchy) like George Hickes, whose *Treasury of Northern Tongues* was a miracle of linguistic, especially Anglo-Saxon, knowledge; or a hopelessly underpaid editor, like Rymer, whose *Foedera* was one of the few works produced by national rather than prelatical or aristocratic patronage. William Dugdale's *Warwickshire* may be singled out from the large number of county and town histories that, spurred by the pride of the local gentry, limned for the first time the story of manor and family. Mere religious and political enthusiasm produced, of course, a variety of worthless tracts; yet it somehow combined with

[3] D. Douglas, *English Scholars, 1660–1780* (2nd ed., London, 1951).

herculean diligence and more or less exacting scholarship to create, by 1730, a new library of scholarship—a giant leap forward in learning. By the dawn of the eighteenth century auxiliary sciences like grammar, paleography, genealogy, and ancient law had been transformed from amateurish beginnings into a formidable critical body of knowledge.

Perhaps the best example of brilliant scholarship harnessed to the fiery steeds of religious partisanship was Henry Wharton, who before his untimely death in 1695 at the age of thirty had not only published the magnificent folios of *Anglia Sacra,* still an essential source of medieval church history, but also contributed extensively to William Cave's *Historia Literarie,* edited James Ussher's *Historia Dogmatica,* and written learnedly (if neurotically) on celibacy and clerical marriage. His greatest work, begun at Cambridge, was done in the service of the learned William Sancroft, archbishop of Canterbury, and he found time to make an early catalogue of the manuscripts in Lambeth Palace. In precocity, partisanship, and productivity, Wharton was a fine example of the immense energies of this golden age of medieval scholarship.

The historians of the eighteenth-century Enlightenment were not particularly interested in the Middle Ages. Their eyes were focused on the more distant and seemingly sympathetic vistas of ancient Greece and Rome; to them the Middle Ages was a period of Gothic darkness and barbarism. The flood of seventeenth-century antiquarianism was reduced to a trickle. Yet the instruments of interpretation and expression were refined to a point that once again, as in the sixteenth century, made history a branch of literature.

In the nineteenth century two major movements brought medieval history to the summit of its prestige. First, the romantic revival, ranging all the way from Gothic romance to popular " Merry England," led to a new appreciation of—and distorted empathy with—medieval chivalry, art, and daily life. Second, the rise of historical science, with its strong German inspiration, gave historians new tools and skills in the editing and interpretation of difficult documentary sources. To some historians, successive publications of the Record Commission, begun systematically in 1800, and similar bodies are the greatest achievements of this century.[4]

With the Record Commission the prosperous governments of the late eighteenth and early nineteenth centuries entered the historical scene with a brief burst of generosity. Costly folio editions in type that approximated the original edition were issued. The Public Record Office as we now know it was built, and at last a staff capable of indexing its vast holdings was hired. As the century progressed, record type printing gave way to ordinary printing in extenso, and this in turn led to abbreviated calendars in summarized and

[4] For this development, see V. H. Galbraith, *An Introduction to the Use of the Public Records* (Oxford: Oxford University Press, 1934).

often translated versions that are still being published. It has long been apparent that the idea of making available in print the main British records is a totally impossible undertaking. It is with all the more awe that we regard such early pioneers as Frances Palgrave and Joseph Hunter and their grandiose dreams.

The greatest of English medievalists, William Stubbs, successively parish priest, librarian, professor, and bishop, was himself involved in one of these government undertakings, the Rolls Series, to which he contributed some of the finest editions. A loyal High Churchman, he was deeply indebted to the German scholars who had already begun the great *Monumenta Germaniae Historica*. In fact, Stubbs' Germanism has been his undoing among certain modern Germanophobes. The compass of his work was universal, ranging from editions of church documents (perhaps his finest work, scientifically speaking) to his brilliant (a few would say notorious) *Constitutional History of England*. Perhaps his *Select Charters* was the most representative of his works, for here his editorial and interpretative skills were joined, and a century of England's best scholars have been nurtured on its treasures.

F. W. Maitland, regarded by many as the true founder of modern historical scholarship in Britain, had nearly all the virtues of Stubbs, including brilliant editorial skill and a capacity for both analysis and synthesis, together with an added clarity and pungency of style. His writings showed a tendency that most scholars will applaud today, and few will regret—the rejection of any dominant sense of purpose in history. Thus history began to be freed of the Stubbsian and pre-Stubbsian concern with the evolution of democracy and the special mission of English civilization in the realm of order and liberty. Undoubtedly, to the extent that this enabled Maitland to correct Stubbs' inaccuracies— notably on such topics as the English church and the origins of Parliament— this new "scientific" approach was a great step forward. The emphasis on royal initiative in the formation of national institutions prepared the way for a vast body of new research. To some, the task since Maitland has been simple: the exploration in ever greater detail and with steadily increasing science of the whole of English history. The milestones are worth mentioning: T. F. Tout's *Chapters in the Administrative History of Medieval England;* H. G. Richardson's and G. O. Sayles' work on legal records; the enormous amount of work on the Norman Conquest period—from J. H. Round to V. H. Galbraith and D. Douglas, W. Hollister, and R. A. Brown; W. E. Lunt's and A. Steele's studies of financial matters; and K. B. MacFarlane's and R. L. Storey's research on the fifteenth-century sources. Most of these scholars have worked as craftsmen, hewing the raw materials out of the various archives and reassembling them in greater or lesser, better or worse, narratives and analyses. Most have almost entirely rejected as irrelevant the questions "What is it all for?"

"What does it mean?" "Why are we doing it?" Yet a certain iconoclasm, an irreverence or downright hatred of Victorian beliefs—already apparent in Maitland—too often mars their pages. It takes the form of ill-tempered denunciations (usually of Stubbs and of any with the temerity to respect him) or of sarcastic asides. On the positive side, there has been a strong sense of the importance of economic and family self-interest, but the prevailing negativism has done much to discredit medieval studies.

A minority of modern historians have stayed faithful, in differing degrees and in differing ways, to Stubbs' vision of history with a grand purpose. Few of these writers would like to be lumped together in the same category, yet what they have in common is of the greatest significance. Such scholars as F. M. Powicke and his disciples have sought, in the manner advocated by the philosopher-historian R. G. Collingwood, to enter empathetically into the minds of medieval men and women. Helen Cam has written with clarity and warmth on the humbler men of the localities and their institutional life. J. G. Edwards, while bringing Stubbs "down to earth," has stayed loyal to the great bishop's vision in a series of brilliant studies. B. Wilkinson, the latest great constitutionalist, has added a new vitalistic insight into the way the struggle for a reasonable balance between liberty and order has had to be renewed in every generation. In all these writers there is a happy combination of a more scientific approach with a view of history as meaningful and purposeful.

In America a great series of constitutionalists tended on the whole to follow Maitland and Tout and to show how English institutions laid the foundations of American liberties. The latest of these scholars, Bryce Lyon, has nicely blended the two great traditions stemming from Stubbs and Maitland. But in America, as in Britain, the stress has been on specialized studies of royal institutions, with no apparent purpose other than the increase of knowledge, and the American studies generally lack the polemic negativism of English scholarship.

The pioneers of local history—the gentlemen antiquarians of the sixteenth and seventeenth centuries—have had successors in the *Victoria History of the Counties of England,* in the course of whose majestic progress, achieved over nearly a century, a shift is to be detected from genealogical interest to local history in the study of agricultural and commercial societies. Hence a new "science" of local history, headed by two brilliant scholars, H. P. R. Finberg and W. G. Hoskins, has arisen. This local history is closely allied to economic studies of manorial life, industry, and trade. A useful, indeed crucial, marriage of legal and economic understanding of the daily lives of ordinary medieval man is arising; this will certainly bring about a new appreciation of Stubbs' vision of England as a fruitful union of authority and local self-direction. Some historians, notably R. B. Pugh, see local history as a key to the understanding of national development. Others, notably those at the University of Leicester or working on the same lines, see it as an end in itself.[5]

Of archeological studies one noted practitioner has written: "Whether it consists of pieces of pottery, broken implements, bones, pins, boots, manuscripts, huts, and towns, or merely of disturbances in the ground, it is essentially material evidence—visible, tangible, and free from duplicity."[6] Although the work of the archeologist is of primary interest to the student of prehistory (i.e., history before the time of written evidence), it can add vast stores to our knowledge of a given period, even of advanced civilization. Another "visual" approach—iconography—can throw vivid light on men's attitudes and beliefs and even on the extent of an individual's authority. Tombs and churches not only tell of artistic development; they also shed light on family and social history. Aerial photography adds immensely to our knowledge of field systems and town layouts, as well as communications. Finally, the study of coins is an obvious and fruitful source of knowledge about economic history.

Intellectual and literary history have rightly been disciplines in themselves. Only in this way could the great critical indexes and editions of medieval lawyers, theologians, classicists, chivalric writers, dramatists, and so on, have been prepared. The relating of these writings to one another and to the institutions in which they were conceived has still a long way to go. Tentative work on the influence of ideas on institutions has been done by Gaines Post (canon law and politics), A. B. Ferguson (chivalry and politics), G. R. Owst and M. H. Keen (sermons and ballads in their influence on social attitudes), and G. Matthew (the court and culture). In a class apart is F. R. H. Du Boulay's brilliant essay on the late Middle Ages, *An Age of Ambition*, perhaps the first really mature sociocultural history of medieval England. This is not to exhaust a long and inspiring list. If this field of study were not so appallingly difficult and hazardous, it would be the most promising area of growth for medieval studies in the latter half of the twentieth century.

A final word should be said about the approach taken in this volume. It seems that the greatest justice can be done to the body of historical knowledge that has been acquired over the past centuries by looking at English medieval history as the history of communities. Beneath the overarching community of king and court (including the higher aristocracy) was a diverse constellation of communities that embodied the lives and aspirations of the people. The key questions of authority and liberty, of exploitation and emancipation, had to be worked out, usually without self-conscious purpose, by these groups of men and their leaders. Through their efforts civilization was advanced or

[5] H. P. R. Finberg, "Local History," in *Approaches to History*, ed. H. P. R. Finberg (Toronto: University of Toronto Press, 1962).

[6] F. T. Wainwright, "Archaeology and Place-Names," in *ibid.*, pp. 200–1.

retarded. Each community also nurtured a culture, a form of conscious expression of attitudes and ideas. How this culture was a reflection of the community's economic and political life and how it influenced that life are matters admitting of no general laws. Here the historian will elucidate, with the possibility of infinite refinement, whereas the sociologist tends to overschematize. The following pages should help the reader to understand the richness and subtlety of the story of an emergent civilization; with the appended note on sources and the selected reading list, they should lead him to inquire further and more deeply for himself.

Chapter Two
THE MONARCHY AND THE COMMUNITY OF THE REALM

Kings were indisputably the active rulers of medieval England. They had three main functions: defense of the church, administration of justice, and military leadership. Perhaps their foremost responsibility was the maintenance of their "estate"—that worldly wealth which good husbandmen nourish and pass on to their heirs. In the course of medieval times the king's power over the church described an inverted parabola. Starting in the twelfth century with a challenge to virtually total control, it descended to a low point under Henry III (1216–72) and then rose steadily, via Provisors and Praemunire (statutes that limited papal appointments and appeals to Rome) and the state's onslaught on Lollardy, toward the Reformation supremacy.

A brief narrative of the reigns of kings between 1154 and 1485 may serve as an introduction to the survey of royal government, justice, and taxation. The personality of the king was always of major importance; hence it is all the more pity that biography was a rarely cultivated art during this period, and that other contemporary sources of insight, such as letters or autobiographical writing, are either absent or unrevealing. Hence perhaps the variety of opinions on medieval kings and the lack of good modern biographies of them: who can embark on a biography when it means sifting the abuse and near-hagiographical praise that remains to us or making deductions from official documents whose authors we rarely know? Only with the coming of "humanism"—faintly visible in the twelfth, and in full spate from the end of the fifteenth, century—do we begin to get vivid (though highly biased) portraits of any significance. The centuries between are indeed barren; however, this narrative may serve as a chronological frame on which to hang the more analytical studies that follow. The kingship of this period may be divided into "Angevin Despotism" (1154–1216), "The Great Century" (1216–1327), "The Hundred Years' War, and Postlude" (1327–1485).

The Angevin Despotism (1154–1216)

Henry II (1154–89) had, for most of his reign, tremendous personal drive, mounting at times to miraculous bursts of energy; a sound judgment of men (one may ask, What of Becket, the man he picked to lead the English Church and who turned against him? But could Henry possibly have anticipated Becket's *volte-face*?); good but not great military leadership; and a personal interest in government (notably justice). Such a combination gave him a claim to be the greatest of English kings.

It is hard to conceive today the daunting problems faced by an early medieval king in keeping control of, let alone reforming, vast territories which included most of Britain and half of France. Fortunately, the furious energy with which Henry II met this challenge has been recorded by keen observers of his court. One of these observers, a vain and witty Welsh clerk named Gerald of Wales, wrote: "In time of war . . . he gave himself scarcely a modicum of quiet to deal with those matters of business which were left over, and in times of peace he allowed himself neither tranquility nor repose." Walter Map ruefully observed that "he was ever on his travels, moving by intolerable stages like a courier, and in this respect showed little mercy to his household which accompanied him."

One result of the growth of royal activity and business at this time was the need for a secretariat and a seal that were more immediately at the service of the king than the increasingly cumbersome great seals of Chancery and Exchequer whose use was set about with elaborate routine. This need came to be met by the Chamber ("the king's private treasury," as it has been called, though in fact it has a far wider, national significance) and by the introduction of the king's privy seal.[1] Evidence for the use of the latter dates from the reign of John.

Henry's quarrel with Becket should not lead the student to dub Henry "anticlerical"; he genuinely planned to go on Crusade at the end of his reign (although wars with France prevented his setting out), his foundations and devotions were exemplary, and he never had a serious quarrel with the pope. But it is as a great architect of English government and law, not as a warrior or patron, that he has rightfully won fame in English annals. In this respect he shares honors in the Middle Ages only with Edward I. Yet his cruelty, his arbitrariness, and his preference for France over England serve to remind us of the fact that he was still a primitive French-speaking and French-reared leader in an age of exploding renaissance and of semibarbarous manners.

[1] Seals were the normal way of guaranteeing the authenticity of medieval documents. The privy seal was smaller than the great seals, and was kept by an official in the king's immediate entourage.

His son, Richard "Coeur de Lion" (1189–99), was hardly an English monarch at all. He was, however, a great warrior capable of holding a French king (the brilliant Philip II "Augustus," 1180–1223) and English rebels at bay while going on Crusade and spending over a year in a foreign prison. His English politics consisted largely of continuing (through his regents) the policies of his father; intervening for brief moments, in person or by letter and emissary (even from prison), in the sharp clashes of personality among the various "regents" and princes; and raising vast revenue for his far-flung "foreign" enterprises—including his ransom. Owing to his absences, the government of the realm tended to devolve upon a small council of officials and barons. In this way Richard's reign foreshadowed the governmental developments of the following century.

Richard's younger brother John succeeded. He will probably never live down the harsh vilification of thirteenth-century chroniclers; even if he does emerge as a literate, constructive ruler, much will always remain enigmatic in his character. That he was a despot there is no doubt; but this characteristic he shared with his father and brother. But in John arbitrary cruelty and prejudice were carried to greater lengths, at a time when French and papal politics made such behavior dangerous for himself and his realm. His loss of Normandy by 1202 made him the first king, and his barons the first "community of the realm," to have an absolutely dominant interest in English (and British) affairs. The popular view of him focuses on his two titanic struggles, both culminating in surrender—with Pope Innocent III (1198–1216) over the appointment of Stephen Langton to be archbishop of Canterbury and with a large group of his barons and their allies over royal, baronial, and local rights. The first quarrel ended with acceptance of Langton as archbishop and of the pope as feudal overlord. The second, of course, culminated in Magna Carta, which was followed by civil war. Some modern scholars have tended to show that John was as great an administrator as, if not greater than, Henry II. Although his savage acts of injustice (some invented) were stigmatized by the St. Albans chroniclers of the next reign,[2] John seems to have been regarded by most contemporaries as a just man. Certainly the great series of government documents (mostly in the form of rolls of parchment), one of the glories of English history, begins to be extant (if it didn't actually begin) with his reign. Perhaps John's tragedy was that he, a typical Angevin despot, was ruling at a time when England was outgrowing despotism, a valuable but primitive form of government.

It is instructive to compare the various baronial revolts against the first three Plantagenets. The rebellion of 1173–4 seems to have been largely nega-

[2] See the Appendix for the attitude of the St. Albans chronicles, and the caution with which they must be used.

tive—an unholy alliance of foreign kings, royal princes, and great earls aimed at carving out greater holdings and privileges for themselves. Uncoordinated, and without any national program, it was put down by the ruthless energy of Henry II and his officers and mercenaries. Henry even received the occasionally active support of townsmen and peasants during the rebellion, and in any case could count on their passive loyalty. The only hint of a positive purpose was Henry's promise (not kept) to relax the forest laws.

The two revolts of Richard's reign—one against Longchamp, an overbearing chancellor, and the other against Richard himself (led by John)—were politically motivated. Their aim was control of the kingdom. The former led to the displacement of Longchamp on Richard's orders; the latter, in which Philip of France was deeply implicated, was easily put down by Richard's regents.

The rebellion against John which led to Magna Carta began with sectional resistance to the king's military and fiscal demands, escalated through a series of especially willful and stupid attacks by the king on individual barons, and finally became an almost national movement with a positive, though conservative, program of reform. Perhaps the unique combination of John's failures in France and a new spirit of the "community of the realm," guided by statesmen of high caliber such as William the Marshal and Stephen Langton, explained the remarkable advance in the political consciousness of the leading classes. While it would be premature to write of a "national consensus" at so early a date, it is something approaching such a consensus that distinguishes the English from similar contemporary movements on the continent of Europe. From that time on, a king, in order to be successful, had to act as head of a commonwealth, not as a supreme feudal overlord.

The Great Century (1216–1327)

Henry III (1216–72) is the sort of king whose record tends to please us today, in that his devotion and cultural patronage outshone his military and political acumen. He, like John, has had to be rescued from the abuse of the St. Albans chroniclers and of their nineteenth-century students. We know, thanks to the researches of Sir Maurice Powicke, that he was a much more effective leader than used to be thought. After a relatively peaceful minority, he built on the work of both the Angevins and their opponents to create a new kind of monarchy. New institutions, such as Council, Parliament, and the court of King's Bench, arose. English law had its greatest medieval commentator in Justice Bracton during this reign. Failures in France and a foolish commitment to finance the reconquest of Sicily by the pope delivered Henry over to the barons in 1258. Among these barons emerged Simon de

Montfort, Earl of Leicester, a brilliant but egotistical leader who practically ruled England for lengthy periods between 1258 and 1265, notably from 1264 to 1265. The central domestic issue was the power of Henry's Lusignan and Savoyard relations: but no mere personal quarrel ensued. Great questions concerning Council and Parliament, as well as local government, were raised.

In the struggle for the Provisions of Oxford of 1258, the goals of the baronial opposition and its supporters advanced from legal to political or constitutional issues. With these provisions the opposition secured, for a while, a dominant voice in the king's Council and the establishment of triennial parliaments,—that is, assemblies of Council by a selected group of magnates. They also set in motion commissions of inquiry into abuses by local officials, even extending the investigation into misdoings of the barons' own officers. The attempt to control the king was probably doomed to failure in view of the lofty notions of royalty held by his contemporaries, but the insistence on more regular consultation with the "community of the realm" and the curbing of oppressive officialdom was to bear fruit in the future. Thanks largely to Lord Edward, Henry III's eldest son and heir, all ended in a royal triumph on the field of battle (Evesham, 1265), but it was a triumph of a moderated and chastened monarchy.

Many would select Edward I (1272–1307) as the greatest of English medieval rulers. Unlike his father, he was both a great military commander and a great lawgiver. He gave England the conquest of Wales; but he also gave her the greatest single body of statute law of the Middle Ages. To achieve the former Edward completed the evolution of the feudal and communal army into a paid, year-round force. Pay was the key factor, but there were also "technical" innovations, probably including the use of the longbow, extended use of light mounted troops, and the specialization of the war "departments" within the household. Involved in both achievements, probably, was the rise of Parliament as a place where great matters could be resolved upon and the necessary taxes levied. (Not that all great decisions in the Middle Ages were made there, or that all its resolutions were of great moment.) Wales was partly included in the system of English government after the second war, that of 1282–3 (Statute of Wales, 1284), but large areas remained as the "liberties" of the Marcher (border) lords, and some Welsh law survived. The statutes of Edward I were largely concerned with land and government. Despite the fact that Edward ruled with vigor and intelligence, embroilment with the papacy and with France and Scotland made his last years expensive and turbulent. The loss of two great supports, Queen Eleanor and Chancellor Robert Burnell, must have contributed to this state of affairs. Yet he never lost his courage; and the contrast between the two ailing kings, John losing his treasure and crown in a futile march, and Edward dying in one last effort to subdue Scotland, is not without force.

Edward II's (1307–27) reign is both a sequel to that of Edward I and a prologue to that of the great Edward III. Personal indulgence (in favorites and in ignoble pastimes such as swimming and playacting) and failure in war—notably a disastrous defeat at Bannockburn, Scotland, in 1314, another costly failure in Scotland in 1322, and the fiasco of the Saint-Sardos war with France—combined to give political opponents a series of opportunities to humiliate him and eventually depose and murder him.

Some important administrative reforms were promulgated during Edward's few years of domestic victory, but the most notable political advances of the reign lay in the new coronation oath of 1308, which required the king to promise to observe laws and customs enacted by the community of the realm,[3] the Ordinances of 1311 (abrogated in 1322), and the lords' declaration separating king and crown. The ordinances represented a great step forward in baronial thinking. The key element was now Parliament—more precisely, the magnates in Parliament. Through this now established institution, the peers of the realm were clearly determined to establish their incontrovertible right to consent to all the major activities and interests of the king. The new interest in the household instruments of government illustrates the growing insight of the baronial leaders, while the emphasis on consent rather than control showed a true grasp of their proper function. The declaration separating loyalty to the king from loyalty to the crown was in accordance with sophisticated theological thought, and, if maintained, could have provided the theoretical framework for a "loyal opposition."

The king and his supporters were responsible for what was in some aspects the most significant promulgation of the reign, the Statute of York, which followed the defeat and death of the great rebel Thomas of Lancaster in 1322. This document has been analyzed from a truly astonishing variety of viewpoints. On balance, it would seem best to regard it as expressing the constitutionalism of a victorious but chastened monarch. While reserving the full powers of government to the monarch, and outlawing opposition thereto, it accepted the duty of the king to consult the lords and commons alike in weighty matters—basically, we may infer, in lawmaking and taxation. Thus the need for a harmonious relation of crown and community was recognized, even if in watered-down terms; and this recognition was never to be entirely lost.

All these proposals and measures put Parliament, as the supreme expression of the community of the realm, in a far stronger position. The statute protected the king from any unlawful attacks on his power, but gave a consulta-

---

[3] See page 28 for further explanation.

tive role to the lords and commons alike. The deposition, though carefully framed to be by the "estates" rather than by Parliament, completed the process. It is not easy at first to see why this deposition was necessary. One can turn to the intrigues of the king's ambitious queen and her lover, the escaped prisoner Mortimer, for a romantic explanation. But that would hardly explain the rallying of so many sections of the nation to the conspirators. After all, the English were hardly a romantic people. The avarice of the Despensers, now undisputed advisers of the king; the death of Pembroke; and the disaffection of stout loyalists such as Andrew Harclay, Earl of Carlisle (due to Edward's Scottish policies), and of an important group of bishops were all part of the story. Oppression of the church and denial of her liberties were charged against Edward and his supporters. Further, the cult of the "martyred" Thomas of Lancaster provided an anti-Edwardian myth. As in nearly all medieval constitutional crises between king and subjects, London's disaffection was of great importance. Yet personal reasons must take second place to the fact that the nation assembled as a whole rejected a king who could not win foreign wars, who was vengeful and unkingly, and who had violated his sacred oath of office.

The 100 Years' War and Postlude (1327–1485)

Edward III (1327–77) overthrew the rule of Isabella (his mother) and Mortimer (her paramour) in 1330 with the aid of powerful magnates, notably Lancaster. He showed little interest in combating the new forces in English politics. Instead he sought to harness them to his main preoccupation, war. His reign saw almost continuous warfare with Scotland, then France, then both together. He, with the Black Prince, with Henry of Grosmont, Duke of Lancaster, and with a new breed of professional captains including Chandos, Manny, Loring, and Knollys, achieved a series of smashing victories over Scots and French alike, and almost won the throne of France. For Edward, it was a great age of chivalry, with tournaments and round tables and a new English chivalric literature; the Order of the Garter for a while made Edward the leader of European chivalry. Yet his warfare was scientific and plebeian; the English archer and the dismounted knight fighting in close cooperation, not the glamorous cavalry charge, were the secret of his stunning victories. These victories were usually accompanied by fearful and deliberate devastation of the French countryside and towns lying on the route of march. The French were taught in brutal fashion the futility of relying on the protection of the ruling Valois king. At home he gave away a great series of powers to lords and commons in Council and Parliament. Parliamentary consent to, and even appropriation of, taxation became normal, and was extended to the wool

21

customs; the crises of 1341 (brought on by Edward's heavy expenditure on continental allies) and of 1371 and 1376 (in which, as so often with medieval crises, the sickness of an aging king was a factor) advanced parliamentary judicial authority, and the birth of the process of impeachment.

The men who brought about these great advances in English constitutional practices were barons, justices, and ordinary councillors, most of whom remain anonymous. Occasional individuals, like Archbishop John Stratford in 1341 and Sir Peter de la Mare in 1376, figure as constructive leaders. But the achievement was a common one; the "nation" was finding itself, increasingly English-speaking, curbing papal powers or claims, and glorying in English arms and their triumphs. The qualities of the English such as military prowess, proud yeomanry, and peasant piety were celebrated in verse and prose. All this cultural transformation was reflected in the actions of Parliament, Council, and courts. In this movement, embracing and transcending all classes, many subtle transformations came about. The clauses of Magna Carta concerning "free men" came to be applied to all; while on the other hand, Parliament passed laws which regulated the standards of dress for the different segments of society. The last years of the reign, in which the king's younger son, John of Gaunt, Duke of Lancaster, was the dominant force, brought military futility (great destructive but ineffectual marches back and forth across France) and political crisis. Yet out of it all, between 1327 and 1377, the commons had emerged as a major partner, and often an initiating force, in the affairs of the kingdom. The Black Death of 1348 (and frequently thereafter), so momentous to contemporaries, had strangely little influence on England's development.

Richard II (1377–99), like Henry III, appeals to moderns because he made peace abroad and cherished the arts. His was a turbulent reign, with the Peasants' Revolt (1381), the heresy of Wycliffe, the impeachment, attainder, and political murder, first of the king's men (1386, 1388) and then of his opponents (1397), and finally the king's bid for power culminating in his deposition (1399). Yet with all it was the greatest age of medieval English literature and art, with the royal court at the very heart of the renaissance: the age of Chaucer.

The years of Richard's minority were characterized by essays in continual councils and commissions elected in Parliament which on the one hand circumscribed royalty and on the other issued class legislation detrimental to the lower orders of society. John of Gaunt, Duke of Lancaster, Edward III's third son and Richard's uncle, kept his distance. He allowed himself to be represented by followers but did not seize what appeared to be a great chance of personal power. Richard was being educated by men with a high notion of royal authority.

Financial difficulties beset the minority government and led eventually to the adoption of the ill-fated poll taxes. It was the third of these new taxes, exceptionally unjust in its incidence, that sparked the Peasants' Revolt. This revolt, or series of partially coordinated revolts, had political and idealistic as well as social causes. After a brief triumph, involving the occupation of London and the execution of the most hated ministers, it was easily put down. The king's authority was itself never questioned, and he showed precocious skill in bringing about the peasants' downfall. This, his first major political achievement, must have confirmed Richard's partially formed views of a personal royal mystique. He began to build up a following of loyal and able men who would control the nation. Among the important princes and magnates he excluded were Gloucester, Warwick, and the Arundel brothers, who felt they had superior claims to royal confidence. These "appellants" mustered support enough from lords and commons to bring about the downfall of the royal ministers—notably Michael de la Pole, Earl of Suffolk—abortively in 1386 and finally in 1388. In so doing they stepped well beyond the powers of any subject or institution, however mighty; but when challenged by the judges, they brought these men down too. Out of this melée, which involved little actual fighting but much bloodletting, emerged two polarities—royal authority in enhanced glory versus the quasisovereignty of Parliament as the high court of the realm with its own law.

The years 1389–97 were ones of compromise. Richard asserted his leadership, but he did not undo entirely the work of the appellants. So sudden was his revenge in the parliament of 1397, when he secured the condemnation and death of his chief opponents, that it has been thought that his mind had become unhinged by the experiences to which he had been subjected. This in particular seems the case in his handling of the young Henry Bolingbroke. Bolingbroke was deprived of his vast inheritance in a way that threatened all great lords. The Court itself was never more splendid—in fact an attack by the Commons on this body had sparked Richard's violence. Richard was but following out the lessons of royal majesty that he had early imbibed. The whole nation felt threatened by Richard's behavior, and his absence in Ireland in 1399 enabled the exiled Bolingbroke to bring about his deposition and to seize power for himself. The quasiparliamentary assembly of estates, which achieved this second deposition of the century, greatly enhanced the stature of Parliament itself in the following decades.

The House of Lancaster (1399–1461), a cadet branch of the Plantagenets, hardly forms a unity. Its "constitutionalism" is now discredited, but for periods Parliament or Council (now a Council largely of lords) dominated politics as never before and as never again for centuries to come. Otherwise, the period has many marks of decline. Shrinking towns, toppling thrones, corruption and crime, the loss of France, and cultural flabbiness have all been noted. Yet probably the average Englishman had "never had it so good."

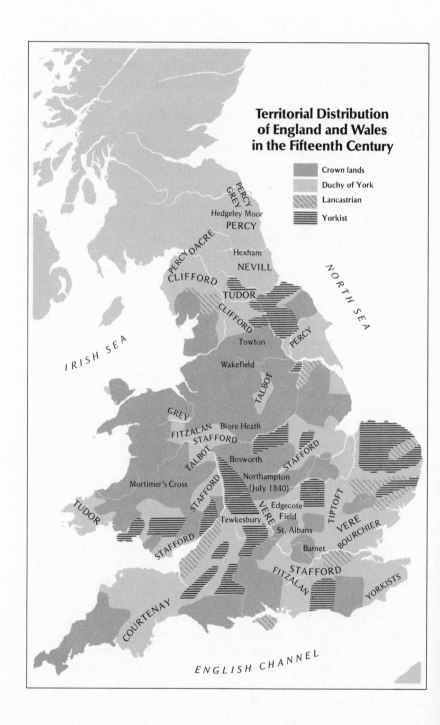

**Territorial Distribution
of England and Wales
in the Fifteenth Century**

Crown lands
Duchy of York
Lancastrian
Yorkist

NORTH SEA

IRISH SEA

PERCY
GREY
Hedgeley Moor
PERCY
PERCY DACRE
CLIFFORD
Hexham
NEVILL
TUDOR
CLIFFORD
Towton
PERCY
Wakefield
TALBOT
GREY
FITZALAN Blore Heath
STAFFORD
TALBOT Bosworth
STAFFORD
STAFFORD
Mortimer's Cross
Northampton
(July 1840)
STAFFORD
VERE TIPTOFT
Tewkesbury Edgecote
Field VERE
St. Albans BOURCHIER
TUDOR
STAFFORD
Barnet
STAFFORD
FITZALAN
STAFFORD
YORKISTS
COURTENAY

ENGLISH CHANNEL

Moreover, in Henry V (1413–22) England produced a mighty conqueror, and in Bedford, his brother and regent in France (1422–35), a great administrator, diplomat, and soldier. Political corruption was rife, it is true, especially in the 1450s, the last sad years of the occasionally insane Henry VI, who as a result of an extraordinary alliance of Queen Margaret and her bitter enemy the earl of Warwick, engineered by that master diplomat Louis XI of France, enjoyed a brief return to "power" in 1470.

The student has two principal choices in searching for the causes of the civil wars, romantically and unhistorically known as the "Wars of the Roses," between 1455 and 1485. One school of historians would stress the feebleness of Henry VI's government, his reckless generosity at the expense of the crown and the corruption of his ministers, especially in the southeast. This school would also stress military failure—that is, the loss of France—as a factor. The other school stresses the mounting local civil wars in the provinces, especially the conflict of the two great northern families, the Percies and the Nevilles; the "national" civil war, in this view, was but the product of the local conflicts in which the protagonists sought the aid of differing groups at the center. However, there is little doubt that the local warfare could have been contained and even eradicated by firm and wise direction at the center. Moreover, "crime" has been grossly exaggerated by the partisan pamphleteering of the opposing factions and by the fact that a considerable volume of correspondence of the people at last emerges to tell us something of the realities of medieval social life. It was not a great age for England, except perhaps for Henry V's victories, but it was an age of the little man, of peasant wealth, of prosperous farmers, of ballads and carols, of mysteries and moralities.

The brief period of Yorkist rule (Edward IV, 1461–83; Richard III, 1483–5) did not bring a sharp break with Lancastrian rule. True, the feeble hand of Henry VI was replaced on the tiller by the masterful, although gross and cruel, hands of Edward IV and Richard III. But the tradition of Edward's despotism and luxuriousness has been modified,[4] and Richard, whose responsibility for the murder of his young nephews has been challenged without convincing many scholars, was not the monster painted by Tudor historians. The Yorkist age was chiefly notable for the restoration of medieval monarchy, which, though it was still as fertile in new devices as it had ever been, did not depart markedly from the medieval combination of king, household, Council, Parliament, and the great departments of administration and law. Perhaps it was the peace (of defeat) brought on by Henry VI's hated ministers, Suffolk and Somerset, that enabled the Yorkists to win a popularity not even destructible by hostile Tudor biographers.

---

[4] J. R. Lander, "Edward IV: The Modern Legend and a Revision," *History*, XLI (1956).

The two Yorkist kings, Edward IV and his brother Richard III, differed much in personal character. Yet they had qualities in common. They had inherited from the propagandists for York a passion for "good governance." This they gave. Edward IV's contribution was marred increasingly by a passion for good living, but recent scholarship has shown that he never forsook the aim of restoring peace and prosperity to the land. In fact, at times he harnessed even his ebullient high spirits to the cause of the country, as when he won grants from reluctant tax contributors by his flirtation with their wives. Richard must stand as a cruel and vicious man, anticipating the even greater personal atrocities of the early Tudors, but he was nevertheless dedicated to the good of the realm. The two Yorkist monarchs reveal the divorce of private from public morality, intrinsic in medieval governance, that was just beginning to arouse comment in the humanist circles of the pre-Renaissance period.

This brief narrative will have shown how important war, finance, and justice were in the government of medieval England. With this in mind, it will be well to turn to the various organs of authority through which these purposes were achieved or frustrated.

The monarchy has come to be recognized by all scholars as the key institution in the growth of the English nation from at least the time of the establishment of the Anglo-Saxons until the early nineteenth century. Our knowledge of such matters as coronations, household, lands and revenues, and other instruments of the crown grows yearly greater. Moreover, the monarchy is now seen to be the key to the evolution of what were once distinguished as "national," as opposed to "royal," institutions, such as Parliament and the common law. Yet the king never acted as a totally free agent. The forces that played upon him were many and various, and have been summed up here in the phrase so frequently heard from the thirteenth century onward, "the community of the realm."

The coronation, and in particular the anointing of the king, established what was to be called the king's "majesty," if not his very authority, and at the same time included the terms of his contract with the whole community. Both the religious and the political aspect of the ceremony had evolved, with intermittent continental influence, from the first extant rite in the tenth century.[5] The summary by Wilkinson in a pamphlet of the Historical Association (1953) gives the most stimulating overview. He states that the coronation shows how "the English state moved, unevenly and precariously, though in the end successfully, to the practice of parliamentary monarchy . . ." (p. 9). Schramm had written in similar vein that "in those three chief acts (anointing, election

[5] The fundamental study by P. Schramm has been heavily qualified, though in contradictory directions, by many researchers, including H. G. Richardson, R. S. Hoyt, T. Sandquist, and B. Wilkinson.

THE CORONATION OF EDWARD I.
*An illumination from a fourteenth-century manuscript. Courtesy the New York Public
Library Picture Collection.*

and oath) we find a reflection of constitutional history," and that "It is the history of the oath which most clearly reveals how England . . . grew to occupy a special place in the world" (pp. 228, 229). Yet the fundamental act of sacring (anointment), with its early indication of *dominus Christi,* and a high peak of claim to priestly lordship at the end of the eleventh century gave the English monarch both an untouchable dignity (including magical healing powers) and a lofty responsibility. These claims conflicted with the older *primus inter pares* ("first among equals") outlook of Germanic kingship, and contained the seeds of that "oriental" despotism which so often threatened the English as it did other European states.

The "elective" element in the coronation was first dramatically recorded in the chronicler's account of William the Conqueror's coronation in Westminster Abbey on Christmas day 1066, although this element had indeed existed in Anglo-Saxon times. But at this time of conquest and its temptations, the addition of "acclamation" to the ceremony was a guarantee of its continued vitality. It is not so much the actuality of election, even at times of change of dynasty as in 1066, 1399, and 1461, that deserves emphasis, as the implications of the act for the establishment of the relationship between king and subjects. The Londoners' desire for popular endorsement should warn against dismissing "acclamation" as mere ceremony.

Closely connected, in principle if not in the actual *ordines* (written forms of ceremony), was the older oath of office. In this oath were spelled out the very rudiments of royal duties: to keep the peace, to suppress evildoers, and to enforce justice. First known in the tenth century, the oath developed and changed significantly over the centuries. From it, probably, sprang the "Coronation Charters" and hence, eventually, Magna Carta itself. The most famous of these developments was the "fourth clause," first actually used at Edward II's coronation in 1308. The origins and significance of this clause have been hotly disputed. It went as follows:

Sire, do you grant to be held and observed the just laws and customs that the community of your realm shall have determined . . . ?

I grant and promise them.

Interpretations of this clause vary. Some see it as a natural evolution of the thirteenth-century practice, some as a part of the whole antiroyalist atmosphere of Edward II's succession.[6] The latter of these views, besides having contemporary support, accords with the turbulent events that followed (see below).

[6] See the references in B. Wilkinson, *Constitutional History of Medieval England,* vol. II, chap. 1 and vol. III, chap. 1 (New York: Barnes & Noble, 1958).

Yet while a modern student is liable to underemphasize the significance of such matters as ceremonials and oaths in early politics, there is the contrary danger of reading too much into the words of a formula-loving age.

When we look at the exercise of kingship, we are faced with the fact that the medieval king initiated and controlled almost all of the central, and a large part of the local, institutions. The inspiration of this monarchical development can only rarely be discovered. It is almost certainly true that, first, there was the slow accumulation of precedents from the first days of Anglo-Saxon kingship; second, the irregular flow of ideas from abroad—from the papacy, France, and the empire in particular; and third, the demands of subjects or groups of subjects.

Kingship: War

Of the instruments of war at the king's disposal, revenue and troops were of primary importance. Half the history of medieval politics has to do with these two needs. Ferdinand Lot, in a book in other ways inferior to Oman's "Art of War" studies, recognized this duality. It can be asserted of England, as of no other country, that the kings had an exclusive right to the military service of their people, from mighty magnate to humblest peasant. The defense of existing territories (medieval war was nearly always "defensive") and the making good of new claims demanded much of the time, and more of the resources, of every medieval king. Even with the codification of "laws of war" in the fourteenth century, the authority of the prince remained unquestionable justification for fighting. Now, while leaving a study of military service till later, it may be proposed as an axiom here that the success of a medieval ruler at home varied directly with his success in arms "abroad." Even the least military of medieval kings, Henry VI, took an occasional interest in the business of war. English kings were lucky (or had to give thanks to precocious internal development), in that their wars were mostly external. On the one hand, the "successful" kings were military commanders of high competence—Henry II, Edward I, Edward III, Henry V; all these men contributed, during their military success, to peace at the least and to constructive growth at best, in domestic politics. The most extreme cases of military failure leading to domestic discomfiture were John, Henry III, Edward II, and Henry VI. It is not a fixed rule, but a useful rule of thumb.

The military "machine" was always largely dependent on royal revenues. We have a rich, if patchy, secondary literature on this subject; the impact on politics has only been fitfully broached.[7] The household, the immediate and

[7] W. Stubbs, *The Constitutional History of England* (Oxford: Oxford University Press, 1874–98); M. R. Powicke, *Military Obligation in Medieval England* (Oxford: Oxford University Press, 1962).

personal organ of the king's will, was constituted principally of Chamber and Wardrobe offices with varying financial and clerical duties. From its limited peacetime establishment to its vastly enlarged war footing, the household is now generally recognized as having provided the core of the army, from the royal thanes of Alfred's day to the retainers receiving royal expenses and clothing of the later Middle Ages. The household also functioned as a pay-master's office for most of the period—certainly for the thirteenth and four-teenth centuries—a fact that has led scholars to differ about where the line between household and other offices should be drawn. It is probably wise, in the interests of clarity, to use the term in a fairly restricted way.

The "feudal" army, so dear to older historians and to the popular mind—that medley of uncoordinated private contingents under baronial leaders anxious to prove their prowess—has been shown to have had a relatively short life. By 1154 its days were numbered. It shrank drastically, by either royal wish or baronial evasion, until it could be counted in the hundreds by the thirteenth century. The establishment of a paid feudal army, begun by Henry III, was consolidated by Edward I.[8] When paid, the shrunken contingents could once more expand and of course could be kept in the field for a longer period.

The local militia, with its defense and police duties, was incorporated in the main army of the monarchy twice in medieval history—in the early Norman period and between the years 1250 and 1350. In these years it contributed to victories in France, Wales, and Scotland. "Selective service" replaced uni-versal obligation in these wars; even so, such "foreign" service was not popu-lar, and the general obligation sank again to local defensive activity in the last medieval century.

One of the most intriguing features of English history, the persistence and adaptability of the hereditary aristocracy, is well illustrated in the military sphere. In the twelfth century the lords secured a drastic reduction in their feudal dues, and in the thirteenth they established themselves as paid leaders of expanded contingents. They fought side by side with professional captains and with yeomen in the Hundred Years' War on the basis of written contract. What happened was a move from hereditary to life contracts, supplemented by annual or other short-range indentures.

In this process, the hereditary contracts between king and lords and between lords and vassals that were typical of the feudal age (in the eleventh through thirteenth centuries) gave place to lifetime contracts in the fourteenth century. These new contracts did not supply an adequate amount of service, so they were heavily supplemented by short-term contracts, by which an individual undertook to serve in a given campaign for periods of various lengths (six

[8] J. E. Morris, *The Welsh Wars of Edward I* (Oxford, 1908).

months was the most typical length). The lords were thus able to maintain their dominant role in war (helped by the royal policy of marrying the royal children into their ranks) and hence acquired a partial control of war-making decisions, whether in political counsel or on the field of battle. Politically, the lords came to think of themselves as the "community of the realm," thus leading the way to a parliamentary monarchy.

The trappings and mythology of warfare are not a neglected area—witness the flourishing state of Arthurian and heraldic studies.[9] Their exact relation to the business of war itself is a challenging subject. A good deal of light on one major aspect of this question has been shed by the students of the "laws of war," while modern writers on chivalry have indicated the yawning gulf between precept and practice.[1] Of course, the increasingly heavy armor as well as the cost of a knighting ceremony tended more and more to change the old standard "knight," or ordinary mounted warrior, into a somewhat exotic and ceremonial figure, a trend encouraged by the founding of such honorary orders as the Garter (1349) and the Bath. As for the chivalric "codes" of behavior, with their mingling of tradition and pre-Renaissance classicism, they seem to have been a base more of bitter attacks by moralists on the actualities of knightly behavior than of any notable activities. Besides, the English seem to have been far more ready than their Franco-Burgundian counterparts to regard the whole notion of knighthood as a literary or cere-monial game.

The dissolution of the short-lived feudal and communal militia seems, on the whole, to have left the monarch with greater rather than less control of the military arm. Pay, of course, became a perennial problem, as revealed by the diversion of the wool customs at Calais to the maintenance of the garrison, the murder of Bishop Moleyns by unpaid soldiers, the revolt of the Percies, occasioned in part by lack of pay, and the increasingly long intervals between major expeditions. But the feed retainers and contracted companies of the fifteenth century were royal servants no less (and no more) than the feudal and county contingents of the period 1150–1350.

Kingship: Finance

The "national pie" of productivity was of course basically in the form of land and appurtenant services. It increased in size with the spread of technology (in milling, mining, and to a limited extent grain and stock raising);

---

[9] For introductions to these studies, see R. S. Loumis, *The Development of Arthurian Romance* (London, 1963) and A. R. Wagner, *Heraldry in England* (London, 1953).

[1] M. H. Keen, *The Laws of War in the Later Middle Ages* (London, 1965); S. Painter, *French Chivalry* (Baltimore, 1940).

the development of secondary industries, notably cloth manufacture; and the growth of population. Prosperity and economic viability depended on an efficient currency, and England was fortunate to have the most centralized and stable of medieval currencies. The division of the pie tells us a lot about the structure and values of society. No attempt has yet been made to study this distribution in depth and continuity. The following review is tentative.

We have to go back to the *Domesday Book,* the great survey of England's resources completed in 1086 on the order of William the Conqueror, for even a rough picture of the king's and others' share of the wealth. It has been estimated from that source that out of a total revenue of approximately £73,000, the king and household took £19,400; the church £19,200 (including £11,000 for the monasteries); and the lay tenants in chief, who held land by military service directly from the king (about 170 in number) £30,350. The remainder was taken up by individual officers and dependents. The story of medieval royal finance consists largely of the king's efforts to encroach on the other figures.

The royal revenue was by no means confined to the receipt of the royal demesne, though the constant demands of the baronial opposition that the monarch "live of his own" show that it was a strongly held view that it should be. "Demesne" itself is not a simple term. It encompassed all the yield derived from the royal lands, which could vary in kind and quantity almost as much as the supplies coming in from "extradomainial" sources. Taken together, this income was included at first in the annual accounting of the sheriff at the Exchequer. In Henry II's time the individual items were lumped together in a "farm," a fixed amount due from each sheriff; to keep pace with rising prices, this amount was increased from time to time by additional charges and what were called *proficua*. In John's reign the yield of these county farms was 17,000 marks[2] per annum.

Other revenue has sometimes (and in France, normally) been called "demesnial." This is what S. K. Mitchell calls "ordinary" revenue.[3] It included such items as judicial fines, borough farms, feudal incidents, and special fines and charges for royal favor, royal charters, and so on. The yield of these items was slightly higher than that of the county farms—22,000 marks in John's reign. This gives a total demesnial or ordinary revenue of 39,000 marks per annum. It was on this, presumably, that the people expected the king to live and rule.

---

[2] The mark was not a coin but a money of account, used for reckoning purposes. It was worth 13 shillings 4 pence (i.e., two-thirds of a pound).

[3] S. K. Mitchell, *Studies in Taxation Under John and Henry III* (New Haven, Conn., 1914), chaps. 1–4, esp. p. 16.

The mention of feudal dues and borough farms may suffice to underline the fact that the distinction between ordinary and extraordinary, between demesnial and extrademesnial, revenues cannot be clearly drawn. Moreover, it has been shown that there was a close interrelationship between military and fiscal obligations. In the matter of scutage the royal demands came in conflict with the interests of the lords. Scutage was payment by tenants in chief for commutation of military service, of special, though not unique, interest to ecclesiastical tenants in chief who as clergy naturally did not wish to lend military assistance. The king faced two problems: the unreality of the military service quotas on which scutage was based to the number of knights of each lord and the escalating costs of hiring household or mercenary troops. The famous *Carte Baronum* of 1166 (the returns to Henry II's inquiry into knights' fees) reflected the young Henry's biggest effort to exact the highest quantity of service the land would bear; it is also our major source of information about the feudal service quotas established, according to most historians, by William the Conqueror. Henry attempted to make scutage rates equal to the wages of soldiers. But he never received the extra assessment he sought, and scutage failed to keep up with wages. Nevertheless, because of John's exactions, the barons of Magna Carta succeeded in shifting scutage from the area of " custom " to that of " consent " : it lost its association with demesnial or ordinary revenues.

Borough farms, our other example of the "twilight zone," also undoubtedly included demesnial and extrademesnial revenues. On the one hand, there were the rents due the king from boroughs as part of the royal demesne and the profits of justice due him from the local courts, both of which were comparable to the sheriff's farm and at first included in it. On the other hand, there were the extra dues accruing from special borough justice, from the monopoly of markets and tolls, and from other similar rights granted in charters.

Certain revenues were unmistakably " nondemesnial," and it was over these that the struggle for consent, and with it the rise of Council, of representation, and of an element of nonroyal sovereignty, emerged. The greatest of these taxes was, of course, the tax on movables. There were also *dona,* ostensibly free gifts raised from religious houses (and after the middle of the thirteenth century from diocesan clergy), and the customs revenues initiated by John but not of great consequence until Edward I's reign. Shorter-lived experiments included carucages (taxes levied on the carucate—land plowed by one ox team —and descendent of England's oldest tax, the Danegeld), the tallages (a demesne tax of great importance until 1300), and various ingenious poll and income taxes and benevolences (supposedly voluntary), devices typical of the last medieval century.

Kingship: Government

The enforcement of rights in land or money or military service, the exaction of judicial dues and privileges, and the manifold relations these involved constitute medieval government. This is a far saner approach than "home and foreign policy" or "church and state," terms to which medieval realities but barely correspond.

The machinery of enforcement, together with the whole apparatus of delegated and representative government, adds up to "administrative and constitutional history." To the study of this subject the greatest of English historical minds have been bent. The tension between order and liberty that developed in the Middle Ages and the successful resolution of that tension underlie the claim of English medieval history to a large place in the story of civilization.

The years 1154–1216, the period of "Angevin despotism," form a convenient first unit of study. It was in this period that the administrative and legal structure of England took a "great leap forward." The key figure in this structure was the king himself. After him came the great justiciars, who occupied almost prime-ministerial status, for this was the period when this office was at its height; then came the other royal officers—chancellor, treasurer, and so on. One might also include the members of the royal family in this list, but they are perhaps best considered as the first subjects rather than agents of the king. As such, they were often called on to share in political power.

The apportionment of responsibility for the reorganization of government between king and officers under the Angevins is a difficult task. That Henry II and John were extremely able, if highly different, men seems to be generally accepted. That their justiciars, men like Richard de Luci (1167–78), Ranulf Glanvill (1180–89), Hubert Walter (1193–8), and Peter des Roches (1214–15), shared in the molding of government cannot be doubted. We should do well to look at the developments themselves, apportioning responsibility where it is possible to do so.

The primary "institution" of Angevin government was the Curia Regis (literally, the king's court), and the chief arm of the Curia was the Exchequer, a complex institution that did justice, heard accounts, and dispensed and collected revenues. Credit for the establishment of this arm probably belongs to Henry I and his justiciar, Roger, Bishop of Salisbury. Our first full knowledge of its working is derived from its accounts, the Pipe Rolls—the first continuous public records of England—later to be joined by the Memoranda Rolls and a congeries of related and subordinate rolls. The famous *Dialogus de Scaccario*, a handbook of administrative practice under Henry II, is the greatest description of government in the high Middle Ages and should be read by any student of English medieval politics. Ranulf Glanvill's *De Legibus,* England's first lawbook, written later in the same reign, should be placed alongside it, for it also was, of necessity and by explicit acknowledgment, concerned with the proceedings of the Exchequer.

The Curia Regis, usually meeting *ad scaccariam* (i.e., at the Exchequer), dealt with all manner of business, whether disguised as "king's" or "kingdom's" (the important distinction began to be made in the twelfth century and had considerable political results). Here undoubtedly the king deliberated on such matters of policy as defense and claims involving war, papal initiatives, relations with other kings, and the behavior of great vassals. More specifically, great trials and changes in law were deliberated and decided in the Curia. Such matters would naturally call for (though we can't say require) the greatest counsel, and so it is here that we have the origins of Parliament.

Twice a year the Curia had to meet *ad scaccariam* to audit the royal finances. Under the presiding king or justiciar, the barons of the Exchequer (i.e., the chief officials of state) met as a sort of fiscal court to review the performance of the local officers, notably the sheriffs, in the collection of revenue. It was the checkered cloth on which the calculations necessary for the audit were made that gave the name to these sessions. The procedure is characterized in the following way in the *Dialogus:* ". . . just as on a chessboard, battle is joined between the kings, here too the struggle takes place, and battle is joined . . . between . . . the Treasurer and the Sheriff who sits at his account. . . ."[4]

The actual handling of the money at these great semiannual accountings was in the hands of the treasurer, chamberlain, and lesser officials (treasurer's clerk, chamberlain's knights, and so on) in the Lower Exchequer, or Treasury of Receipt. Here the money was received, counted, and assayed (i.e., samples melted to determine their silver content), and receipts (wooden tallies) were issued.

The importance of the Chamber as the household organ of financial administration, closer to the king than the Exchequer, with its own rolls, probably its own seal, and its own direct revenues based on "Chamber manors," has long been recognized.[5] We now know that the Chamber was the primary arm of twelfth-century finance. "Of the dominant role of the Chamber in financial administration," it has been written, "there can be no doubt."[6] We may suggest the virtual absence, for this era at least, of any distinction between "household" (and therefore royal-controlled) and "state" (and therefore potentially baronial-controlled) departments.

---

[4] *Dialogus* (ed. and trans. C. Johnson, London, 1950), p. 7.

[5] T. F. Tout, *Chapters in Medieval Administrative History,* chap. 3 *et passim* vol. I.

[6] H. G. Richardson and G. O. Sayles, *The Governance of Medieval England* (Edinburgh, 1963), chap. 12.

The Chancery, emerging from the clerks of the king's chapel, was a highly organized body, and a very efficient one, by the reign of Henry II. Its officers were at work in the Exchequer and in all other departments of government. The key to its role was the custody of the great seal. In short, the Chancery was the source of all official documents. Whether it be a lawsuit, a military summons, a tax, or an appointment, the affixing of the king's seal by the chancellor, or keeper of the seal, was the official public act. This clerical practice (an aspect of which—that concerning official documents—is considered diplomatic) had two main sources: the fertile precedents and simple efficiency of Anglo-Saxon rule and the elaborate sophistication of the papal government. It was both simple and subtle in its practice. Original and confirmed charters (the more formal and elaborate of its documents, important for the conveyancing of lands and privileges) have survived in considerable numbers. Its judicial writs are conveniently classified by Glanvill in the *De Legibus*. At some time in Henry II's reign Chancery, following the Exchequer, began to keep enrollments of its charters and writs. These are not extant until Richard I's reign, however. From then on not only the methods of Chancery but the whole operation of government is known in a continuous way, with few breaks, down to the present day. The principal categories of document were charter and writ. Ordinary letters known as writs could be either patent or close—according to their purpose, or indeed the whim of the Chancery staff. This simple pattern was capable of indefinite expansion: like the Pipe Rolls of the Exchequer, the records of Chancery spawned subordinate rolls for special subjects.

The problems posed by these developments in government practice were twofold: complexification and control. The former meant the proliferation of offices and documents, often with heavy overlapping—for example, between the financial offices, Chamber and Exchequer, or between the clerical offices, Wardrobe and Chancery. The second concerned the hierarchy of decision making and leads straight into constitutional history. For the students of administrative, or "diplomatic," acts, it means the question of seals, warrants, and endorsements. Thus the emergence of a small "privy seal," in the custody of a household official, to "move" (authorize the use of) the great seal of Chancery in John's reign testifies to the determination of the king and his intimate advisers to retain that control of the bureaucracy for which personal presence or word of mouth had previously been sufficient. The frantic scurryings of Henry II's court, who through inheritance and conquest had vaster lands to control, and the inevitable creation of "appanages" and "liberties" territories given usually to members of the royal family with large elements of sovereignty are sure signs of the pressures that led to the small or privy seal, the development of "warrants," the founding of a sworn Inner Council of officers and the king's confidants, and much else. If, as Yeats has it, the "centre cannot hold," then indeed "things fall apart"! For John the center held all too well: he was able to control England, and even Scotland, Wales, and Ireland, in a way no previous king had done; even his abuses of this power only led to a definition of his rights in Magna Carta, and not to any arrest in the rapid evolution of the central administration.

The thirteenth century saw further elaboration of administrative office and documents and some shifts of departmental power, but no deep change of course. The notion of a division between household and state departments, that is, between Wardrobe and Chamber on the one hand, and Chancery and Exchequer on the other, arises during this period, but more from the barons' ultimately unsuccessful attempt to control the appointment of state officers than from any evidence yielded by the operation of these departments. The ideal of conciliar government, with the chief officers answerable to a baronial council, was in the air, and by the Provisions of Oxford in 1258 briefly achieved.

The elaboration of the Angevin government during this period was the result not so much of steady growth as of spasmodic efforts by the king or some royal agent to strengthen or rationalize the operation of a department. The actual drive behind these actions can rarely be discovered. An outstanding royal servant in this regard was Henry III's faithful supporter Peter des Rivaux, who gathered into his hands a great range of affairs. He seems to have been instrumental in two major developments between 1220 and 1250: the establishment of the Wardrobe as the right arm of royal fiscal and military power and the reform of Exchequer procedure in the years after 1232.

The Wardrobe emerged as the leading household office in the early 1220s, when "the chamberlain of 1219 became the clerk of the Wardrobe of 1223."[7] It developed a staff consisting of keeper (or clerk or treasurer), controller, and subordinate lay or clerical officials. It was very flexible, with expenditures soaring in time of war. Its principal revenue was at first derived from the Exchequer, to which it accounted (this was the reason for the controller), but it could and did draw substantial moneys directly from the source, and even raised loans. It produced offshoots—the Great Wardrobe, the Privy Wardrobe, the Queen's Wardrobe, and so on—and was copied by many of the great lords. The custody of the privy seal in the Wardrobe was a potential, but under Henry III undeveloped, step toward a new chain of command; moving the great seal by warrant of privy seal was still an embryo process.

The reforms at the Exchequer, of which Peter des Rivaux also appears to have been the guiding intelligence, consisted of improving the machinery for bringing in the royal revenues (particularly the "bad debts" that figured so

[7] T. F. Tout, *op. cit.,* vol. I, p. 191; quoted in S. B. Chrimes, *Introduction to the Administrative History of Medieval England* (New York: Barnes & Noble), p. 102.

prominently in the Pipe Rolls), of giving the responsibility for the royal demesne (previously that of the sheriffs) to new officers, and of rationalizing the bookkeeping. From 1234 on the "foreign" accounts (those accounts outside, that is, foreign to, the sheriff's responsibility) and the subordinate rolls are both more important and more intelligible. The sheriff became more a paid administrator with greatly restricted power (for example, the loss of responsibility for escheats and demesne revenues) and less a universal director of local business. The goal was to keep the complex organization already developed functioning—in particular, to keep up with royal needs and check lazy or rapacious local officials. The task was made easier by the more complete emergence of the King's Bench as a separate court and of the sworn Inner Council from the general Curia.

Under Henry III Chancery also took a step forward as an organized body: with the suspension of the office of chancellor in 1244, the opportunity was taken to convert the profits of office by which officials lived into salaries and to establish Hanaper (named from the hamper in which documents were kept until paid for) as a separate department of Chancery in charge of receiving fines and profits. It is possible that the existence of a separate Chancery office, in a fixed place not yet at Westminster—rather than totally with the king—dates from this time.

It is not surprising that in reviewing these thirteenth-century developments modern historians have concluded that Henry III must have been a more effective ruler than older critics have allowed. Behind the religious and military incompetence of Henry there was a calculating administrator, just as behind John's ferocity there was something of an executive genius.

Edward I's governmental reforms now seem overshadowed by those of Henry III, just as Henry II's have been seen as less original than those of Henry I. Edward's major achievement was perhaps that of renewing with force the measures initiated in the 1220s and 1230s, but most effectively because this time the administration had the cooperation of the nation's leaders in a way that it had not had under Henry III.

Administrative development under Edward I consisted mainly in the further elaboration and expansion of those trends already set in motion by his father. The privy seal, still located in the Wardrobe and in the care of the controller, began to assume its obvious function of moving Chancery by means of warrants. The role of the Wardrobe, initially the war and finance office, emerges more clearly as its books begin to survive in great numbers; during Edward's reign it collected and spent enormous sums on Welsh, French, and Scottish wars. Later, the Wardrobe became the instrument for setting up field commands and pay offices, as Edward I's military genius forged the typical late medieval paid army machine, which was to score such brilliant successes in the Hundred

Years' War. To a certain extent, both Chancery and Exchequer were over-shadowed by the Wardrobe expansion. Yet it was a period of great chancellors and treasurers, who probably played an important role in the evolution of Council and Parliament, as well as in administration. No Wardrobe official had a standing with Edward I comparable to that of his great chancellor Robert Burnell (1274–92). Chancery became located at Westminster, with lengthy stays at York during the Scottish wars later in the reign. It is hard to believe that the baronial opposition did not see this separation from the king as a threat to orderly government, as the more recent offices remained at the king's side.

The elaborate machinery of the Exchequer was to a certain extent circum-vented by the use of "assigned tallies" (the assignment of certain revenues in advance to certain persons by giving them the tally stick, or receipt, normally given to an officer when he paid his dues). This device helped military or financial officers to collect money directly from the source and enabled the sheriff to produce a much reduced "profer" (his submission of financial dues) at his biannual accountings. The contracting of loans by the Wardrobe grew apace, as Italian bankers found in England a ready source of profit. Thus the crown began that slide into chronic indebtedness that was to plague it in the last two centuries of the medieval period. The bad debts of the Exchequer, already a plague in John's reign, were now transferred from the Pipe Rolls to special records of debt known as the *rotulus pullorum* and the Exannual Rolls.

The major reform of Edward II's reign, the Ordinances of 1311,[8] made no distinction between household and state offices: the barons were to have a share in the control of all alike. Yet baronial opposition, especially when in-telligently directed as under the earl of Pembroke during the brief supremacy of the "middle party" (c.1317–20),[9] did undoubtedly force the king and his ministers to revise the working of the system. What, then, were the principal administrative developments of Edward II's reign? First, the directing of the whole machine, while remaining flexible, was made more effective by the large-scale use of the privy seal to move the great seal of Chancery and the duplicate Exchequer seal. Second, the emergence of the keeper of the privy seal as a separate office emphasized its new importance. Third, the Chamber, the first household department to emerge under the Angevins but long secondary to its lusty offspring the Wardrobe, was greatly strengthened as a personal office of the king's. Quite apart from internal evidence, the fact that it was thought worth "controlling" in 1318, but not in 1311, dates the sudden revival of this department. Besides acting as a new fiscal body, particularly

---

[8] See p. 54.

[9] The whole question of whether a "middle party" with definite ideals did in fact exist is now being debated.

useful for the administration of confiscated lands and the raising of loans, the Chamber also had custody of a new "secret seal," which partially displaced the privy seal in the moving of the great seal and in the direction of government.

Chancery and Exchequer also underwent important developments under Edward II. The chancellor continued his rise to the position of "first minister," though we must not call him that. His department was less important in promoting this growth than his position on the Council. But though Chancery had no "independence"—it was still an instrument to be moved by regal orders, verbal or written—the fact that it retained and increased its position as the major source of all writs going out to the people, whether judicial or administrative, gave it the gravity and weight of a great department of state comparable to those of modern government.

The Exchequer once again became bogged down in the multiplicity of its operations; notably, it had still not solved the problem of bad debts. To the improvement of this situation Treasurer Walter Stapledon, Bishop of Exeter, and others less prominent, promoted long-lasting reforms in the years after Edward had routed Thomas of Lancaster and his other enemies at the battle of Boroughbridge and at last given the king's servants a free hand. The reform ordinances of these years (1322–6) established the foreign accounts and Ex-annual Rolls as clearly defined subsidiaries to the great rolls of the Pipe. Personnel was increased, and the judicial activities of the Exchequer were restricted to financial matters. At the same time, the Wardrobe's accounting system was made less rigid, and therefore more workable, and its supervision of foreign accounts (e.g., the financial aspects of Hanaper and the Great Wardrobe) was transferred to the Exchequer. Hence by the time of Edward II's overthrow his officers had achieved one of those periodic prunings and rationalizations of government that were to keep English administration in working order for centuries. It was in part the absence of such a "revival," which led to a gradual deterioration in administrative practice, that makes the last two centuries of the Middle Ages less interesting for the student of government. Although Edward II's reign has been characterized as marking the final great administrative changes before Tudor times, what it achieved was essentially yet another reorganization and redeployment of existing offices. The real struggle was still that between king and intimate advisers on the one hand and great lords on the other for control of the whole administrative apparatus, rather than for any fundamental revision of that apparatus. But it cannot be stressed too much that it was the struggle for control and the use or misuse of the administrative machine, rather than the machine itself, that had now become the prime question in English politics. The executive skills of Chancellor Robert Baldock and Chamberlain Hugh Despenser, Jr., could not save a king whose domestic and foreign policies were unpopular and ill-conceived.

The last two centuries of the Middle Ages were dominated by the struggle between king and barons for control, the mounting debts occasioned by the Hundred Years' War and by the prodigality of kings, the rise of constitutional government (or "mixed dominion"), especially the lawmaking and tax penalty powers of Parliament and the partial disintegration of the system of what A. B. White called "self-government at the king's command." In administration there were many tortuous developments, including changes in the hierarchy of control, shifts between departments, and the corruption of the system of assignments and loans—all of which took place within the structure evolved by 1327. The process has been well studied for the fourteenth century,[1] but a serious analysis of the "fifteenth-century breakdown," if such it was, remains to be done.

One of the major developments in administration during this period was the institutionalization of the privy seal as the prime mover in government,[2] chiefly by warrant but also by direct orders and summons on subjects and on outsiders (a fact that, because its documents, unlike those of the great seal, were not kept on annual rolls, makes the study of late medieval government more difficult).

The appointment of a separate keeper of the privy seal, one of the baronial demands in 1311, was a regular feature of government from the time of the reforms of Edward II's closing years. Now, as in the early history of the justiciars and chancellors, the influence of great men, notably the great pre-Renaissance scholar Richard Bury, the dynamic keeper William Kilsby, and the political bishop William of Wykeham, can be seen molding the structure and work of the keepership. The Ordinances of Walton of 1338 (a great act of administrative reorganization, perhaps occasioned by the involvement of Edward III in the Hundred Years' War), though they were probably abortive, stated the primacy of the privy seal in government with the most uncompromising clarity; however, the measures proposed to achieve that primacy, whether over so-called household or state departments, particularly the duty of enrolling warrants for payments, were not implemented. And, indeed, the whole notion of a "concentric" system of government, with circles of activity spreading outward from the king and his intimates, was hard to enforce when the king was a busy field commander far from home. But it was finance and military service, not administration, that lay behind the great constitutional advances of this time, as well as of the rest of the fourteenth century. In only one matter did the lords and commons in Parliament oppose the privy seal—from 1300 on they sought to stop its use as a means of interfering with the due process of common law.

---

[1] T. F. Tout, *op. cit.*, vol. V.

[2] A factor leasing the far greater importance of its keepership. See A. Slavin, *The Precarious Balance,* Volume III in this series.

The rise of a new, or series of new, royal seals to authorize administrative action—to give direct expression to the royal will or whim—was perhaps necessitated by the institutionalization and location in a fixed place, and consequent separation from the king, of the privy seal and its office. The privy seal office was probably located in London from the early fourteenth century. The story is rather complex, because it is one of experiment and change, not easily unraveled.

The first of the intimate royal seals, the "secret seal," emerged in the early reign of Edward II. As a new royal instrument it was associated with, though not confined to, the Chamber, where it was lodged. Under Edward III it was supplemented by the "griffin seal," through which Chamber manors were administered.

Replacing the secret seal as the personal instrument of the king was the "signet," which appeared in the middle years of Edward's reign. The official who kept this seal was the secretary, whose office was traceable to the early years of Henry III but who was not to emerge as the senior servant of the king until Tudor times. But already, from mid-fourteenth century, the signet, in addition to the sign manual (or royal signature) and the oral orders of the king, was the most personal of royal instruments. It could move the privy seal as well as the great seals and could be used for direct communication with subjects and foreigners. Its preeminence was enhanced under Richard II, and as a threat to their political influence, was the special object of attack by the "appellants." Its symbolic role as the sign of majesty was dramatically expressed in the story of Richard II's abdication in favor of the Lancastrians, in which his handing over of the signet to Henry symbolized his acknowledged defeat. In the fifteenth century Bishop Thomas Bekynton's secretaryship under Henry VI represented a big step toward the era of the all-powerful secretary Cecil in the reign of Elizabeth, and both Yorkist kings greatly increased the use of the signet. As noted above, the sign manual rose in importance at the same time, at first as a supplement, but in the fifteenth century as an alternative, to the signet and the privy seal. This undoubtedly reflected the new literacy of the pre-Renaissance.

Among the household organs the chief feature of the fourteenth century was the revival of the Chamber and the decline of the Wardrobe. The Chamber, as stated in the Ordinances of Walton, was to have had a key role in checking expenditures, and in the Hundred Years' War it came to share with the Wardrobe the functions of war office. Besides special assignments, it had the revenues of specific escheated manors and overseas rents, administered by the griffin seal. This source of revenue was terminated in 1336 but was revived late in the fifteenth century under Edward IV. In any case, though Exchequer rivalry checked its independent growth until the Yorkist and Tudor periods, its possession of the secret seal made the Chamber a useful channel of royal expenditure; and when Richard II sought to evade the limitations on his power by the opposition, his "chamberlain knights" played a key role as military leaders, as councillors, and as manipulators of the commons in Parliament.

The Wardrobe, overgrown offspring of the Chamber in the thirteenth century, suffered under Edward III from the separation of the privy seal office, the rise of the signet, and the growth of the Chamber. In addition, the subsidiary wardrobes, Great and Privy, emerged as full-fledged organs of the household. The Wardrobe continued to be a major source of war administration in the first decades of the Hundred Years' War, drawing huge sums from the Exchequer, raising loans, issuing its own "bills" against the sources of revenue at home, and paying troops. But its primacy was gone, and it went into slow decline in the later stages of the war. In the fifteenth century it reverted to its pristine role of a domestic office without national importance.[3]

The Exchequer, shorn of its nonfinancial judicial activities since the reign of Edward II, was able in its reorganized form to pursue its stately way as the chief accounting office of the king and realm. Without its Receipt Rolls, in fact, and the bundles of warrants that authorized its expenditures, the financial history of the later Middle Ages could not have been written. In the fourteenth and fifteenth centuries the chronic indebtedness of the crown, exhibited by a multiplication of "assignments" and "fictitious loans" that resulted in a complete falsification of royal accounts, the same sum being recorded several times over,[4] led to attempts at drawing up general accounts and even rudimentary budgets. But the absence of a clear-cut hierarchy of financial authority, the ignorance of what budgeting really involved, the overextended ambitions of the crown, notably in the French wars, and the stubborn notion of the barons and of Parliament that the king should "live of his own" meant a descent into that fiscal chaos that reached its depth in the days of the carelessly generous and ineffectual Henry VI.

The other great state arm, Chancery, also continued fairly smoothly on its charted course in the later Middle Ages. With its system of writs and enrollments and its variety of warrants for use of the great seal, it was able to provide the nation with good government, insofar as an administrative machine could do that. Its importance grew, if possible, with two new developments: the decline of the household departments as administrative organs and the rise of its own jurisdiction, especially in cases outside the purview of the common land court, such as "uses," or grants of land transferred to evade power of forfeiture. Moreover, the chancellor—as president of a rising court, as chief

---

[3] However, in 1542–4 the master of the Great Wardrobe was in charge of war finances in Scotland.

[4] For an explanation of "assignments" and "fictitious loans," see E. F. Jacob, *The Fifteenth Century* (Oxford: Oxford University Press, 1961), pp. 440ff.

royal spokesman in Parliament, and as key figure in the Council—gave luster and importance to the department of which he was head. The organization of its secretarial activities and its maintenance of official archives can be studied in its numerous rolls (at least ten series exist for this period) and in the Ordinances of 1389, which set forth the numbers, grades, and duties of Chancery clerks. The master of the rolls emerged as second to the chancellor. Since Edward I's reign Chancery had been established at Westminster, whence clerks and messengers could scour the land and be seconded to Parliament, to the Exchequer, and to the household, as well as perform the manifold internal duties of the Chancery itself. It is not too much to say that even without the surviving records of the offices that moved or were moved by Chancery, the records of Chancery would still supply historians with a good idea of the way England was governed in the fourteenth and fifteenth centuries.

Justice

Whereas the military responsibility of the king remained largely personal, his much more sophisticated and complex judicial obligation led to widespread delegation, and to the fusion of institutions dependent on local custom with courts and procedures deliberately instituted by the king, justiciar, chancellor, or chief justices of the highest courts. A review of the major developments after 1154 is made possible by the magnificent work of a series of antiquarians, editors, and legal historians from Elizabethan times on. The prince of legal historians was, of course, the great Maitland, but all owe an incalculable further debt to other scholars.[5]

One particular error that needs to be scotched at the outset is the view of many scholars that the sole aim of medieval justice was profit. No doubt this was a factor. But the church, the traditions of the people, and the ideas of the king and his advisers all conditioned men to believe that justice was the principal goal of political life. The cynics have a point, as do most muckrakers, but it is not a particularly important one.

The royal and the local courts were still far from integrated in 1154. At the center, the Curia Regis, as yet not divided into such functions as the Council, Common Pleas, and so forth, and no doubt already meeting *ad scaccariam*, continued to adjudicate both civil and royal pleas. In the counties and honors

[5] Notably G. O. Sayles in *The Court of King's Bench: The Laws and History* (London: 1959); T. F. T. Plucknett on statute and criminal law in *Edward I and Criminal Law* (Cambridge: Cambridge University Press, 1960) and *The Legislation of Edward I* (Oxford: Oxford University Press, 1949); Bertha Putnam on the justices of the peace in *Proceedings Before the Justices of the Peace* (London: 1938); and Margaret Hastings in *The Court of Common Pleas in Fifteenth Century England: A Study of Legal Administration and Procedure* (New York: Shoestring, 1947).

(the great estates of leading barons), local courts dealt with the mass of lesser business, usually based on the "appeal" (accusation) of the plaintiff. The courts of the hundred (a subdivision of the county), occasionally enlarged for the sheriff's tourn (the biannual visit of the sheriff to see that the tithings, or police groups, were in order), had entered the process of appropriation by, or sale to, the holders of private courts. While the honor court of the baron had an indeterminate jurisdiction over the knights and freemen of the fief, the chief private courts were those of the manors, with their principal concern for un-free tenants. From the Curia Regis *ad scaccariam* to the manor court, administrative, financial, and judicial business remained thoroughly intermingled. The system of local justices of the peace and of itinerant justices detached from the royal court to deal with important local cases continued from the days of Henry I. It is widely recognized today that Henry II's "innovations" were in fact elaborations of experiments made by Henry I at least thirty years earlier. For example, it has been shown that both the judicial writ and the jury system, once thought to be an "invention" of Henry II, had a long, if obscure, history in both Frankish and Anglo-Saxon times.[6]

One problem that constantly recurs in a study of medieval justice and administration—it is a version of the fundamental problem of freedom versus order—is that of royal (or central) initiative as against slow growth from below. It has already been stated (in connection with kingship) that the role of the monarchy has been ever increasingly recognized as central to the development of England. Yet when all the facts are considered—the fact that government officials were not highly trained specialists, the very smallness of the royal bureaucracy, the appalling state of communications (hampered not only by bad roads but by great tracts of forest and marsh)—it is clear that local courts must have had a flourishing life of their own, and that the famous "self-government at the king's command"[7] is no modern romantic shibboleth but a true reflection of the way things were.

Yet Henry II's lawyers—especially the great justiciars whose lives have recently been unraveled[8]—were undoubtedly the major catalyst in transferring "age-old custom" into a more or less effective system of national justice. By borrowing from Roman law, inventing new processes, and instituting new offices, they built a superstructure of royal justice—the common law—on the regional and local courts and rules inherited from an earlier age.

The growth and differentiation of the justice administered at the center may occupy first attention. From early on there must have been special judicial

---

[6] R. C. Van Caeneghem, ed., *Royal Writs in England from the Conquest to the Great Charter* (London: Seldon Society, 1958–9).

[7] A. B. White, *Self-Government at the King's Command* (Minneapolis, 1933).

[8] F. J. West, *The Justiciarship in England* (Cambridge, 1966).

sessions of the Curia Regis. But we do not hear of a specifically judicial body until 1178, in an ordinance reducing the number of justices from eighteen to five. This "specialization" of the royal courts, indissolubly linked with the replacement of local justices by itinerant justices (whose functions were set forth in a quasi-official way by the Assize [forerunner of the Statutes] of Clarendon in 1166 and more definitely by the Assize of Northampton in 1176) led—by a process now lost—to the establishment of the Court of Common Pleas and the King's Bench, in which there was, broadly speaking, a division of function between pleas involving the king and those between subjects. The latter did not clearly emerge until late in the thirteenth century, by which time new actions like trespass, a law action designed to redress a wide variety of damages to another person or his property, had vastly increased royal business. This development must have helped the emergence of the Council as a separate body that could be appealed to as a last resort and wherein "equity," an expression of royal prerogative, could be exercised. At the same time, the Exchequer was able to gradually shed its load of judicial business.

Simultaneous with the development of specialized courts at the center, and fostering them, there arose the twin pillars of common law: the writ and the jury. The judicial writ, like the judicial court, was a development from a much more generalized administrative instrument. Basically, and originally, it was a royal order that justice be done. Thus through writs addressed to local officers the royal obligation to do justice was to transform local custom into common law. From the first, such writs were especially concerned with seizin (possession), and this was to be the greatest preoccupation not only of writs but also of assizes until the end of the thirteenth century. From Glanvill's *De Legibus* we learn how Henry II "instituted" the three basic writs of seizin—novel disseisin, mort d'ancestor, and darrein presentment, processes by which recent disseizins could be remedied by the investigation of local juries.

The way in which writs multiplied and the distinction between writs starting an action ("original") and writs obtained in the course of action can be traced through the books of the law writers Glanvill, Bracton, Fleta, and in the *Register of Writs.*[9] The creation of these writs was largely a function of the new professional judicial class that emerged in the thirteenth century. The effect of the statute *in consimili casu* of 1285 was to give Parliament the lion's share in the creation of new writs. A litigant seeking a writ had to pay for it.

---

[9] Glanvill and Bracton, the two earliest and most important law writers, can be studied in translation. H. de Bracton, *On the Laws and Customs of England*, trans. and ed. S. E. Thorne (Harvard, 1968), and R. de Glanvill, *The Treatise on the Laws and Customs of the Realm of England*, trans. and ed. G. D. G. Hall (London, 1965). Fleta and the early Registers of Writs have been published by the Selden Society, 72 (1955) and 87 (1970), respectively.

Hence, as mentioned earlier, a special office of Chancery—Hanaper—was created to handle the portion of writs by clients. The pattern of courts and processes was fully established by the end of the thirteenth century. After Edward I there was slow growth and supplementation but little innovation.

One aspect of justice that remained especially close to the king was that of procedure by "plaint," at first by oral and later by written petition. This process could lead either to formal trial in an established court or to the exercise of royal prerogative. Much of the "common plea" justice was of this nature. Complaints against royal officials would of course go to the King's Bench or to special commissioners. The special sessions of Council that were known as "parliaments" also attracted a steadily increasing volume of petitions, so that ordinances had to be issued in 1280 and 1290 leading to the preliminary sifting of such actions and to their frequent diversion to other bodies. Finally, in the fourteenth century Council and Chancery began to specialize in equitable jurisdiction—that is, when the common law provided no remedy. The distinction between these two bodies was not at first clear-cut, as even in the fifteenth century the Court of Chancery might be identical with the Council. Perhaps the largest volume of litigation of this kind arose from the rapid evolution of the "use," an old and complex device separating legal from de facto ownership, now much used to evade the penalties of treason.

At this point it may be useful to attempt a distinction—not essentially a medieval one—between different kinds of legal action: criminal and civil, real and personal. The main differentiation in the Middle Ages was not between criminal and civil pleas, but between king's and subject's cases.[1] It should be noted that the king could always intervene in a case between subjects and claim an interest, even on the flimsiest of pretexts. This does not mean that the modern student is obliged to jettison such divisions as they arise naturally in his mind; he merely has to recognize the extent to which he is imposing rather than recognizing categories.

Pleas between subjects fall into two categories: personal and real. Anglo-Saxon law codes and their Norman continuations had been largely made up of the penalties attendant upon infringement of personal rights; a large amount of what would later be called criminal law was either not recognized at all (i.e., subsumed under private grievance and dependent for redress on private initiative) or given a certain public quality by the addition in certain cases of a royal fine (wite) to the prescribed private compensations (wer and bot). The distinctions between theft and personal injury, or between theft of an object and seizure of land, were not clearly made. It was simply that if a person

[1] For an introductory discussion, see G. O. Sayles, *op. cit.*

suffered harm (and this might include the king), he had to seek redress in the local courts, where by oath and ordeal the matter was settled.

In the twelfth and thirteenth centuries there was a slow assertion of royal influence in the exaction of penalties for criminal actions, rapid erosion of private responsibility (in the form of trial by battle, a form of legislative deal for the settlement of important cases between clients), and the establishment of the concept of "felony" (i.e., capital crimes). The notions of felony and of crown prosecution were intimately linked.[2] Henry II's reign, it can be stated without question, marked a great step forward in the legal remedy for criminal acts. The monarchy continued to increase its powers and its wealth in the service of society.

With the introduction of feudalism and its elaborate system of rights and obligations, and with the concept that all land is the king's, the need and opportunity to draw a distinction between personal and real actions became apparent. Probably for a while the "landlord," from the king in his Curia Regis to the baron in his honor court, was the judge of real pleas—of questions of landed right and possession (the two were not yet distinguished). The "community's" interest was expressed as early as the *Leges Henrici Primi*, one of the first English lawbooks, written about 1118, which stated that cases between tenants of different lords should be adjudicated in the sheriff's court. The interest of the king was expressed in the "writ of right," concerning title to property, which was available from an early time and brought royal injunction to bear on the settlement of cases. According to *De Legibus*, the great lawbook of Henry II's reign, the writ of right had become mandatory for all cases involving title to land. This, the earliest of common law writs, of course, applied to freemen only; the vast majority of those concerned were knights or greater barons, and while there was the threat of transfer to the communal courts most cases were commenced in private courts, until such courts began to wither during the thirteenth century.

A vast new impulse was given both to real actions and to royal law, with the introduction of "possessory writs" in the reign of Henry II. These writs were confined at first to recent dispossession (of land or some right involving land); but in the thirteenth century the writs multiplied and the period they covered was lengthened, so that in fact they came to decide title as well as possession—notably in the important "writs of entry."[3] Through these writs the plaintiff was able to delay a defeat in the tenant's title. The ensuing confusion had to be tackled in the great Edwardian statutes.

The transformation of local custom into common law proceeded in personal

---

[2] For an introduction see T. F. T. Plucknett, *Edward I and Criminal Law*, esp. chap. 2.

[3] The best introduction to the origin and development of seizing as a legal concept is found in the works of T. F. T. Plucknett, most accessibly in his *Concise History of the Common Law*.

actions *pari passu* with those in real actions. Here again royal intervention was the decisive factor. The year 1166 (the Assize of Clarendon) is the accepted date for the emergence of the process of indictment before circuit justices into the light of history. The earlier origin of this process was probably Danish. Certainly by 1176 (the Assize of Northampton) the indicting juries of hundred, county, and vill were in full operation. Yet it is not to be thought that they superseded the ancient process of appeal. Nor, of course, was "trial by jury" introduced.

The jury, canonized by a number of legal writers on the common law,[4] had a joint Scandinavian and Frankish origin. Of the origins of the jury it may suffice to give two quotations from Van Caeneghem: "Indeed, the recognition [declaration of facts under oath], as we find it in *novel disseisin,* was clearly at the confluence of two old streams of recognitions: those imposed from above in the famous inquest of Carolingian origin and those less famous but equally important recognitions by a body of sworn neighbours, which, since Anglo-Saxon times, were . . . freely employed to settle disputes. . . ." And "the recognition in the form of an authoritative royal inquest is indeed one-half of the history of the jury; the free local recognition between litigants is the other, and as far as England is concerned the older half."[5] The original idea was the testimony of the local community, predominantly in administrative inquiries. But the *Domesday Book* (1086), the greatest compilation of information traceable to the jury process, was both an administrative and a judicial document. And this dual function was never abandoned, though the two streams of development gradually diverged. Even the possessory juries of Henry II's time were fact-finding, not judgment-making bodies. Yet given the feudal notion of "judgment by peers," the idea of the trial jury was bound to emerge. Presumably the Grand Assize, by which a jury could be invoked by the defendant in a land case in place of trial by battle, was the first known use of such a use. It was made mandatory by the Statute of Westminster I (1285). It was ubiquitous in the high and late Middle Ages and no doubt contributed to those "law's delays" that encouraged the rise of swifter, if more arbitrary, processes in the fifteenth and sixteenth centuries. The jury, needless to say, was inseparable from the royal writs that authorized its empaneling.

The system of writs governing cases of seizin and title, with additions such as trespass, was deeply modified by the legislation of Edward I. The impact of that legislation on real and personal law, and on criminal law, has been brilliantly expounded by T. F. T. Plucknett.[6] Read in conjunction with the

---

[4] Such as Fortescue and Coke.

[5] R. C. Van Caenegham, ed., *Royal Writs in England from the Conquest to Glanville* (London: Seldon Society, 1958–9), pp. 55, 60.

[6] T. F. T. Plucknett, *The Legislation of Edward I.*

"classical" studies previously mentioned, and with the work of G. O. Sayles on the King's Bench, the state of law—in truth, the full-grown common law "system" of 1300—can be unraveled by the attentive reader.

One of the main developments in the fourteenth and fifteenth centuries was the adjustment of statute to common law; the rise of the Inns of Court (i.e., the professionalization of the judiciary); the vexed question of the putative breakdown of the criminal side, offset by the rise of the justice of the peace; and the emergence of "equity" in Chancery and Council to remedy the defects of the land law.

The adjustment of statute to common law was a complex process controlled by the justices of the royal courts. By mid-fourteenth century the primacy of statutes was established. The fifteenth century remains the neglected child of historical study in this as in other areas. Margaret Hastings' study of the Court of Common Pleas has certainly shed some light on this issue.[7] But it is in the arguments recorded in the year books, official compilations of arguments used in the courts, that the full answer may lie.

The professionalization of the judiciary has its roots in the twelfth century and is still not complete (nor probably should it be). Its growth in the fourteenth century is associated with the introduction of Roman law from Italy; the absorption of much of the method and some of the substance of that law into English practice (most profitably studied in the great lawbooks; and the divergence of the theoretical training in the universities from the practical instruction in the Inns of Court.

The origins of the Inns of Court, the London schools for the training of common lawyers, are surrounded in mystery. The physical displacement of the Knights Templar as a result of the dissolution of that order, which had long outlived its consenting functions, clearly made room for a place where apprentice lawyers could have rooms and facilities for instruction. Their origins probably lay in the thirteenth century. But their mode of instruction, their student composition, and their general way of life do not become clear until the fifteenth century, with the survival of records and descriptions. Clearly the students, with their coveted goal of sergeantry, which gave them the powers of pleading and even judging, and, if successful, probably a justice-ship, had to be versed not only in the writs of common law (their first task), the statutes (learned through "readings"), and the canon law of the church courts, with which they might clash or cooperate, but also in the arts of pleading and argument. The earliest records of the laws are "mootings." By the fifteenth century aristocrats were studying at the Inns of Court without any intention of a professional career, but simply to equip themselves for survival

---

[7] *Court of Common Pleas*, pp. 170, 241.

in a litigious era. It may be added that the laws also provided an education in literacy and other pursuits suited to gentlemen.

Criminal courts were much modified in the later years of Edward I. The unwieldy and terrifying "general eyres," with their omnipotent powers of inquiry into crime and administrative failings, gave way increasingly to special judicial commissions, such as those of oyer and terminer, which tried specific listings of common pleas, and those of trailbaston, which tried disturbers of the peace (complementing the justices of assize, who dealt mainly with civil motions). Even so, the decline and on occasion disappearance of old local courts left a vacuum. To remedy this it became common to appoint (or have elected) "keepers of the peace" from about 1200; in the fourteenth century these "keepers" acquired judicial powers, and the "J.P.s," or justices of the peace, the cornerstone of local justice, emerged. New powers were constantly added to these prominent men of the shire; the sheriffs dwindled in their shade. The scope of their work has been described by a number of scholars.[8] Apart from combating crime, they often had to impose laws on prices and wages, and to decide how to apply the growing body of fifteenth-century social legislation. Unfortunately, the bulk of the fifteenth-century records are lost.

The J.P.s' role in combating crime was not to be fully realized until the Tudor Star Chamber emerged to enforce their powers and rulings. In the meantime, the criminal side of the King's Bench and the development of Chancery and Council as judicial bodies did something to combat crime and to meet the inadequacies of the Edwardian land laws to regulate titles and tenures. Unfortunately, the judicial work of these bodies still awaits its historian. Yet there is sufficient evidence of pleadings before the King's Bench and Chancery to confirm that they were diligent in prosecuting criminals even in the fifteenth century; how successful they were is another question.

The remedy of "defects" in the land laws, especially the evolution of the law governing uses, has been vastly illuminated by the researches of J. M. Bean. The perennial land hunger of the medieval gentry is now generally accepted; whether this was exercised through violent disseizin or subtle legal devices is a good question. What Mr. Bean has shown is that by uses the aristocracy of the later Middle Ages and even Tudor times was able to counter the erosion of feudal revenues, to circumvent some of the legislation of Edward I, and to evade the penalties of forfeiture; and that by the middle of the fifteenth century at the latest Chancery was the regular court for enforcing respect for the use.

---

[8] Notably B. Putnam, *op. cit.*, and T. F. T. Plucknett's accompanying comments. See also C. Beard, *The Office of the Justices of the Peace in England* (New York, 1904).

The Community of the Realm

From this survey of administration and justice we turn to the question of royal control and initiative. It must be stressed first how economical the administrative machine was: at every point the work of the paid officials of the crown, or curiales, was supplemented by the unpaid services of bishops, magnates, and gentry. Hence there developed a body of men at the center of national affairs who felt themselves specifically the trustees of national interests: they were "the community of the realm." This economy was achieved only at the price of leaving considerable power in the hands of the subjects. But it was only when this latent power was channeled to the center in the form of conciliar and parliamentary government that it became a real challenge to royal sovereignty—indeed, that the question of sovereignty arose in men's minds. The initiative, both in drawing subjects into the central organs and in using them in the localities (e.g., as J.P.s and coroners), usually came from the king. But he was as a result the captive of his own creation. Among law writers, from Bracton and his interpolators to Fortescue, this fact of constitutional or mixed government was recognized as a characteristically English discovery.[9] It is unwise to see the result—as seventeenth-century polemicists naturally did—as a struggle between despotism and democracy. Cooperation was stronger than conflict, especially under a king who was militarily successful and in harmony with the spirit of his greater subjects. Yet it is permissible for the twentieth-century as for the seventeenth-century observer to see with hindsight the looming and occasionally overt clash between two notions— "descending" and "ascending" theories of government, as Walter Ullmann has called them.[1]

Council

From early in the thirteenth century the restive barons had realized that control of the center, even more than local immunities, was the key to their power. Against Henry III, with his rather authoritarian notions of government, they waged a twofold attack, resisting taxation in Parliament and insisting on a share in the newly emergent Council. Following unofficial

[9] Fortescue was especially forthright. See his *The Governance of England,* ed. C. Plummer (Oxford, 1895), chaps. 1–3.

[1] See especially the chapter entitled "Conservation and Tradition" in his *History of Political Thought: The Middle Ages* (London, 1965). "Descending" means autocratic, from God down through the hierarchy; "ascending" means democratic, arises from the feudal order, and was especially notable in England.

usage, we may refer to this as the "parliamentary" and "conciliar" way to power. The follies of Henry's foreign policy, notably his Sicilian commitment, and the emergence of a powerful leader gave the barons success in both goals for a brief while with the Provisions of Oxford (1258–9) and the regime of Simon de Montfort. At one and the same time, Parliament and Council were brought under Simon's control and local barons were utilized; and thus the ambitions of Montfort and his allies advanced. It is useless to discuss how "popular" the reforms of Oxford were, though it has been shown that they were grounded in serious thought and supported by many of the middling classes (knights and merchants), as well as by the "dark force" of de Montfort's ambitions.[2] The chief lesson, prophetic of the depositions of 1327, 1399, 1461, and 1483, was that the only safety for an individual or group who wished to dominate the king lay in the latter's death or exile or, ultimately, in the emergence of a theoretical safeguard against royal despotism. The "regality" of the royal person was too sacred, the administration too fully geared to royal direction, for a hostile subject to challenge his master without actually getting rid of the king. The council of domestics and officials was probably enlarged frequently enough after the traumatic experience of the "barons' wars" of 1264–5 to keep the principal subjects happy. But it was two other factors that, until 1295, made Edward I's reign the greatest cooperative venture yet undertaken. The first was the king's fulfillment of the ideal of a chivalrous, militarily successful leader. The second was the establishment of regular parliaments that could share in policy and legislation as well as in justice.

The distinction between "king and Council" (concerned with the "business of the king") and "king and Parliament" (concerned with the "business of the king and kingdom") can be discerned in the records of the time; but it was only one of the notions that affected the evolution of a constitution. Canon law maxims and modern interpretations of Roman jurisprudence—in such matters as *quod omnes tangit* (what touches all should be approved by all), *plena potestas* (full power, a condition of true representative government), and *lex regia* (the law of royalty)—were also influential. These ideas gave scope for the king, barons, and middling groups to work out a modus vivendi, if not a smoothly functioning constitution. The initiative came from the king and his advisers, but the direction that initiative took was conditioned by the mentality and the physical resources of the subjects. Hence in Edward I's statutes, the greatest body of legislation enacted in the Middle Ages, there is a nice balance between the requirements of strong and efficient government and the interests of the wealthier subjects. Parliament did not play a large part in this lawmaking.

[2] R. F. Treharne, *The Baronial Plan of Reform* (Manchester, 1932), and his subsequent articles, notably "The Significance of the Baronial Reform Movement, 1258–67," *Transactions of the Royal Historical Society*, fourth series, vol. XXV (London, 1943).

Like the Great Council of the past centuries, it was not a legislature but a place where the king could deliberate with his subjects on major issues. Its judicial business, supplementary to the common law and in the hands of the curialist element, required fixed terms and greater definition. By the same token, the torrent of petitions from private persons and groups that inundated it at these sessions had to be curbed by special ordinances in order to leave the king free to treat of the great business of the realm. It is the legal, petitionary side of Parliament that has left the main record; its consultative functions are demonstrated in the preambles and addresses of parliamentary writs of summons, in the preambles of executive orders, such as military summonses, and in some legislation.

The drawing of the middling classes into the life at the center followed naturally from their dominant role in county, borough, and manor. Their cooperation was obviously essential to the operations of government, whether it be tax collecting, military command, or judicial decision making. Their role at the center was sometimes demanded by the lords (as in 1254 and 1264–5) or, more frequently, by the king. It was never regular, and only marginal when it did occur, until the reign of Edward II. But the precedents were established, and the now discredited notion of a Model Parliament of 1295, on which the subsequent Parliament was modeled, still has its usefulness in that for the first time the "full" assembly appeared in broad daylight. About actual proceedings at these assemblies we know very little.

In Edward II's reign the struggle for the control of the executive became fiercer. At first, in the ordinances and certain prior concessions of 1309, the baronial group tended to rely on the banishment of Edward's favorite, Piers Gaveston, and the consent of Parliament to administrative changes. The royal household, inasmuch as it figured separately in the Ordinance of 1311 and the Ordinance of 1318, meant the domestic officers of the king: the aim was retrenchment, not control of the administrative function. After the great defeat at the hands of the Scots at Bannockburn (1314) the struggle centered in the Council. The weakness of Thomas of Lancaster, Edward's cousin and by far his most powerful subject, meant that conciliar control eluded the ordainers, but for a brief period under Pembroke, the brilliant leader of the putative "middle party," the baronial opposition secured effective control of the king and nation (1316–19). After that, it was king and intimates against the opposition, the battle swinging first to the king (1322, Battle of Boroughbridge) and then decisively and mortally against him (deposition and death of Edward II, 1326–7).

Under Edward III the centrality of the Council to the whole question of control, even sovereignty, became apparent. Success in war and a promise of cooperation with the great lords saw Edward safe in the saddle from the time of the destruction of the regents (Isabella and Mortimer, 1330) until the crisis of 1340–41. The settlement of that crisis, occasioned by Edward's failure to wring sufficient funds for his continental plans from the home government, dominated by Archbishop Stratford (Chancellor, 1335–7, 1340 April–June), was in the form of a series of statutes that confirmed the dominance of Council in executive matters and of Parliament in the taxation field. Edward, his eyes ever more firmly fixed on the crown of France, probably paid little heed to domestic affairs. Hence the decades after 1341 saw a permanent Council of lords ensconced in the seat of English government and the establishment of Parliament as the supreme legislative body. In the latter process the rise of requests for legislation of a public nature, in the form of the "common petition" of the commons (knights and burgesses), was a decisive factor. When after the Black Death (1348–9) Edward sought to curb the papal direction of English church affairs and to regulate the soaring wages of the depleted work force, it was largely on the initiative and through the instrumentality of the Parliament of lords and commons that he did so. And in 1362 he conceded parliamentary control of customs, which he had agreed to in the matter of taxes on movables twenty-two years previously.

Thus far—until about 1360—the cause of cooperation, with king, lords, and commons sharing in the joyous enterprise of despoiling France, had held England together as never before in history. The establishment of the Order of the Garter symbolizes the high achievement of those years. The Council was no longer "officials," and the parliaments were a joint enterprise of king, lords, and commons. After that there was a renewal of conflicts and a loss of high purpose, only briefly regained in the heady days of Henry V.

The struggle, as it emerged in the last decades of the reign of Edward III, particularly in his years of senility, was over the composition of the Council. This body, now unquestionably the supreme advisory body—with considerable administrative powers, and with a growing judicial function scarcely curbed by parliamentary resistance based on Magna Carta—became the plaything of contending individuals and groups. The evidence for the Council's emergence in the fourteenth century as a sort of "cosovereign" is to be seen both in the administration, where the Council could move the seals of Chancery and Exchequer without royal intervention, and in the theory of "king and crown," whereby the latter achieved a sort of suprapersonal quality.

From 1340 the Council shared in the executive role of the crown. Whether it exercised this role independently turned in the main on the king's situation. If he was senile (Edward III, 1371–7) or a minor (Richard II, 1377–81, Henry VI, 1422–37) or ill (Henry IV, 1410–13), the Council became de facto sovereign. Yet it lacked stability. The "clerical" element, exemplified in men like Bishops Wykeham and Beaufort, was liable to attack at the hands of military giants like the royal princes Gaunt and Gloucester. Military fortunes could affect the supremacy of one or another individual or group, as did the military reverses of 1370–77, and the loss of France in 1449–51. Wykeham and Gaunt, Suffolk and Somerset, even Henry VI himself, were in turn victims of such defeats. Dynastic and territorial factors also entered in, notably in the successive usurpations of the throne by Lancaster and York. New instruments were forged to express these hostilities. Impeachment, that is, trying a minister before the lords on the accusation of the commons, which can be studied as a legal device, represented in political terms at once the use of the Commons by ambitious councillors and the emergence of Parliament as a contender for sovereign authority. Appeal by the lords or a group of lords, mainly obviating the use of the Commons had a similar significance. No wonder that a great scholar like William Stubbs tended to see in such developments the advent of constitutional monarchy and parliamentary sovereignty (though he was aware of the rise of faction). The abiding fact was the emergence of conciliar government, backed by Parliament, as a necessary adjunct to personal monarchy.

To match this new importance, the Council began to use a seal (the privy seal) and to keep records, while administrative organs recorded their authorization *per concilium* (by the Council) without reference to the king. No continuous records of Council meetings exist, but those that do survive make it clear that that body really had a corporate identity by the late fourteenth century, that its competence was as wide as the king's condition allowed, and that it contributed much to the stability of the nation. Even for Edward IV's reign, when its own records peter out, the Council continued in an honorable, if curtailed and less aristocratic, role.

Two periods of Council are particularly noteworthy: the minorities of Richard II (including the last years of his enfeebled grandfather) and of Henry VI. They deserve a closer scrutiny, for they pose an important question: Had the great lords and the remnant of officials who attended Council achieved enough collective wisdom to manage affairs effectively, or was the "capture" of the center by the lords a disaster for national progress?

In the minority of Richard II the establishment of a Continual Council representative of the main factions was a great stabilizing force after the political turbulence of 1376, during which the commons had attacked leading royal advisers. But this body seems to have lasted only until 1380, when Parliament was instrumental in securing its dismissal. The full implications of this act became clear only after John of Gaunt's dominant personality was absent (i.e., after July 1386). It then became evident that in the intervening years interest and opinion had crystalized around the maturing young king and his intimates on the one hand (the "court party") and around great "appellant" lords—notably Gloucester and Arundel—on the other. The result was the mighty confrontations between king and appellants from 1386 to 1388, so important in constitutional history.[3] Control of officials—including their trial and death, as well as their appointment and dismissal in Parliament—took precedence over the Council, though the old idea of a special council to reform the realm was included in the appellants' program, and this council did for a while intervene decisively in the operations of the administration (without introducing any important reforms). With the total triumph of the appellants in 1388, the Continual Council was restored and actually directed the government for a year, until Richard II regrouped his forces. When he recaptured the control at the center, he was nevertheless constrained to share executive power with the Council. Then the rather makeshift solution of 1377 was consolidated, and its rules of conduct were laid down (in the Council ordinance of March 1390) under the direction of the resurgent king. Parliamentary control, asserted at intervals between 1376 and 1388, was lessened, but inevitably a "court party" within the Council was mustered by the king to counter the ambitions of "mighty subjects"; if he had not driven Henry of Lancaster to revolt by confiscating his lands, a revival of central authority might conceivably have emerged. As it was, a glittering renaissance in art and manners was promoted by the ambitious young king.

In the interval between Richard II and the premature death of Henry V in 1422, Council continued to exercise vital influence. Henry IV's Council, especially in its relation to the commons, has recently received close scrutiny;[4] perhaps the main conclusion is that despite the commons' pronounced and explicit interest in the composition and powers of the Council, an interest that reached its height in 1406, the former body effected few changes. An aristocratic Council seemed to suit the commons very well. Knowledge, not direction, was their objective. Henry IV's declining health, and the desires of Prince Henry to rule, gave force to this new situation. When Prince Henry succeeded as Henry V in 1413, he was able to use this instrument, along with a revitalized household, to give England stability and victory.

The real test came in 1422, when Henry VI, then a year-old babe, inherited the throne. Two views expressed by the same authority reveal the difficulty of evaluating the ensuing period. S. B. Chrimes writes on the one hand that Council "was able to maintain its coherence and collective responsibility"; on the other hand he states that "its lack . . . of administrative efficiency and the difficulty of repressing the personal ambitions and interests of individual councillors and lords contributed much to the ultimate ruin of the dynasty."[5] The tension between Humphrey of Gloucester, a "Renaissance type" prince

---

[3] See p. 64.

[4] A. L. Brown, "The Commons and the Council in the Reign of Henry IV," *E.H.R.*, LXXXIX.

[5] S. B. Chrimes, *op. cit.*, pp. 252, 253.

who sought a regent's powers with much legal justification, and Bishop (later Cardinal) Beaufort, who usually had the backing of the majority of the Council, provides the most dramatic episodes of the fifteen years of conciliar government.

The question of the relations between Council and Parliament in this period is as yet inadequately explored; perhaps we may say that, as under Henry IV, Parliament was the forum wherein conciliar tensions could be resolved or at least patched over, but not a directing body. Another unresolved question concerns the relation between the "lords of the Council" and ordinary "official" councillors, if the distinction is valid. But whatever the failings of the Council of Henry's minority, the story of really critical indebtedness, of war-weariness, of defeat, and of the rise of aristocratic rivalry to calamitous proportions begins with Henry VI's assumption of majority in 1437. The minority Council, for all its frailties, avarice, and contentions, served the nation well; that it did so was in no small degree due to the statesmanlike and militarily proficient figure of the duke of Bedford, who not only defended with brilliance the fragile English hold on a resurgent France but found time to return on occasion to heal the breaches in the Council when they got out of hand. The historian cannot sever institutions from the personalities who led, or served, them.

Henry VI resurrected certain aspects of royal authority that were to be the hallmark of Yorkist and Tudor government: the king's "prerogative" in grants and appointments, royal control of the administration through personal seals or the sign manual, and notably the advance, for a while, of the secretary and his office under Bekynton. But Henry's intentions were to fail. The Council ceased to be a place where great subjects could thrash out their policies and reconcile their enmities; the king got hold of the levers of power, but he misused his authority by taking poor counsel and was by character unable to use his power either to fight for or to finance his realm; finally, abler men began to turn to the rival dynasty of York as a solution for defeats and debts of staggering proportions. A "system" that depended so fully on the character of the king had produced its nemesis: a personal ruler who indulged his private piety and personal favoritism to the loss of the nation.

The Yorkists built on Henry VI's abortive experiment of a return to personal government, making extensive use of the sign manual and the signet and its secretaryship, of a revived Chamber which received the issues of extensive lands, largely from forfeitures, and of the privy seal. We now know that the apparent lapse of the Council is illusory, and that a body of less aristocratic composition had an important role in advising the king and administering his will. The loss of conciliar and secretarial records makes the investigation of Yorkist government a perilous venture, but it is probably a true generalization that the Middle Ages concluded with the historically successful combination of personal executive instruments, an effective but more subservient Council, and a shrewd financial policy that had long been lacking. The transition to Tudor government was simple and unrevolutionary.

Parliament

It has been noted above how the "parliaments," or special sessions of Council, had emerged by the fourteenth century as fairly regular meetings of twofold function: (1) the tending of advice and consent by the important men of the realm, usually by church and lay magnates, but occasionally and briefly supplemented by elected representatives of counties and boroughs; and (2) the hearing of petitions from individuals and communities for remedies not provided by the common law or for the granting of favors, a function requiring regular dates or terms and performed by king and advisers. A plenum, or "full," parliament probably meant at first an assembly of king, councillors, and magnates, though it is still possible to argue that "plenum" meant open rather than full. The magnates were basically the greater tenants in chief. Hence there is a close, but not absolute, correspondence between those summoned personally for military service and those summoned to Parliament. Yet from the first the king exercised discretion about whom he would summon.

The standard form of summons of the "commons," or *communitates,* was by writ to the sheriff; ordinarily two representatives were chosen from the county and two from each borough. Attempts to ensure that the county representatives were "dubbed" or "belted" knights, though not without effect, eventually failed. Too few of the knightly class were actually getting knighted (i.e., by dubbing and/or belting).[6] The interpretation of "borough" was left to the sheriff, and at first burghal elections were held in the shire court. Eventually the borough court or council secured the right to elect its representatives, though in a variety of ways. County representation remained fairly stable; boroughs seemed to do a lot of bargaining to be included in the list or otherwise summoned. The extent of the actual wish for representation on the part of local communities, as against compliance with royal demands, has never been agreed upon. We can see with hindsight that representation, not only parliamentary but legal, was one of the greatest of medieval discoveries. It resulted from a combination of royal needs, of customary practices, and of legal (mainly canonical) maxims and devices.

The functions of representatives varied. Primarily they were called to give consent to taxation. This purpose remained the most persistent one. Royal

---

[6] On these conventions, see R. Baber, *The Knights of Chivalry* (London, 1970), pp. 27–8. Dubbing refers to the light blow with a sword that created a knight. Belting was the act of putting on the sword-belt.

THE PARLIAMENT OF EDWARD I.
Courtesy The Bettmann Archive.

convenience as well as the people's preference was the driving force and dictated the introduction into the writs of summons a clause granting "full power" to the representatives to commit their constituencies. Besides giving consent to taxation, the representatives brought up petitions from local groups and individuals, as well as from their electors. Consent to legislation was also sought, but this was not at first a major factor. The duration of their stay in Parliament was initially very brief—say two or three days. It should be noted that the knights and burgesses did not form a "house" in the first seventy-five years of their attendance; at first knights were more closely associated with the magnate element. A feeling of corporate identity grew as a result not only of common interest but of frequent reelection of the same persons. Thus a primarily administrative device of thirteenth-century monarchs paved the way for a new, extended notion of the community of England.

At the end of Edward I's reign a series of dramatic confrontations between king and "popular" leaders occurred as a result of Edward's urgent need for funds for his war in France and Wales; the climax was in the autumn of 1297, when Edward, then in Flanders, had to ratify the "confirmation of the charters" granted by his regent son. The essence of this concession was that the king agreed not to levy "aids, tasks, or prises," without the "common consent of all the realm." The arbitrary levy of taxes on movables and on supplies was thereby averted. As Parliament was the natural (though not the only) place where such consent could be obtained, this concession was of importance in the development of parliamentary powers in taxation.

With the accession of Edward II Parliament took on more importance. A clause was added to the coronation oath binding the king to abide by what the "community of the land" should determine. This was probably a political bargain in a time of crisis. What it meant had to be worked out; but it is surely not a coincidence that the Ordinances of 1311 required the consent of the lords in Parliament to a whole range of executive actions, such as leaving the country, granting lands and gifts, and appointing officials in which the king had hitherto been free to act as he wished. The lords, in fact, emerged at this time as a "peerage" with a more defined personnel and a major stake in the government of the realm. Edward's failure to consult them was a partial reason for his defeat at Bannockburn in 1314. The position of the commons also became clearer. The term "community of the realm" was extended from king and lords to include the commons, and their summons to at least a part of the parliamentary sessions was becoming almost regular. At this time too we begin to read of "common petitions." The Statute of York (1322), though annulling the Ordinances of 1311, granted the commons as well as the lords a consenting voice in important business: "The matters which are to be established for the estate of our lord the king, and for the estate of the realm and of the people, shall be treated, accorded, and established in parliaments by our lord the king, and by the assent of prelates, earls, and barons, and community of the realm, according as it hath been heretofore accustomed." This clause, like the clause added to the coronation oath, has been explained away by some historians.[7] But the plain meaning is that the commons were now to share with the lords in a limited role in government. The reference to this participation as being in accordance with past custom was conventional medieval mythology.

A remarkable document of about the same time (probably *c.* 1321), the *Modus Tenendi Parliamentum,* very likely stated one reformer's view of what Parliament was all about and was later in the century to have an influence on Irish parliamentary development; in this document, or program, the commons are already seen as the one essential part of Parliament and as having a predominant role in taxation. Accompanying the rise of Council after 1341 was the establishment of Parliament as a regular institution, with almost annual meetings (that is, on average). The twin forces of royal needs and increasing collectivity of action of the subjects joined to produce startling advances in Parliament's powers, notably for the regulation of all manner of taxation, of military levies, and of church-state relations, advances achieved with a minimum of friction and ill-feeling. In fact, what was said about the Council is also true of Parliament: the collaboration of king and nation in a great enterprise was the decisive feature of its evolution.

Royal need of money to finance the wars with Scotland and France meant constant demands for taxation—the yield of which was often already pre-empted by the royal creditors. The standard tax on movables of one-fifteenth (for rural areas) and one-tenth (for towns) evolved in the previous century, continued to be the main source of revenue, and was always raised with parliamentary consent. Already inadequate, it was frozen in 1334 and (after certain reductions) remained fixed for the remainder of the Middle Ages. The aim of Parliament, on the whole successful, was to prevent the king from raising new revenues without consent. To meet his mounting costs, Edward resorted to massive borrowing and assignments of revenue. The story of his default on these loans, and its effect on Italian banking, is not our concern here. In addition, Edward sought to raise new or "defunct" taxes, which Parliament either banned or sought to control. The revival of demesnial tallages in 1332 was opposed by Parliament and had to be revoked in return for a tax on movables. It was at this time that we first hear of the joining of knights and burgesses in a common assembly and of the discussions between commons and lords known as "intercommuning." But it was in the matter of customs revenue that the real conflict arose. Here Edward sought to interpret the required consent as applying to the

[7] See pp. 28–9.

actual taxees—namely, the merchants in wool. The result was a series of conventions, such as that of 1342, in which the wool merchants granted "maltolts" (customs taxes over and above the "ancient" custom). The commons, asserting themselves in place of the more compliant lords, secured statutes guaranteeing that future grants and aids (1340), tallages (1348), and customs charges (1362–3) would require their consent in Parliament. The idea that the payer was the grantor gave place to the view that the "community of the realm" was the legal consenting body. These statutes were the cornerstone of future parliamentary progress, but they must not be regarded as "constitutional law." Statutes could always be repealed, and they were often ignored, while interpretation was a very wide and loose business by modern standards.

This raises the question of statute making. The deposition of Edward II marks a turning point. For after 1327 the common petition became the normal basis of legislation—that is, the formal initiative passed to the commons in Parliament.[8] The common petition, which did not necessarily originate with the commons as a whole, dealt primarily with common business; but it was the kind of petition most likely to lead to legislation. The substance of that legislation in the fourteenth century—church and state (Provisors and Praemunire, regulating Rome's relations with the English church, 1351, 1353, 1390), wages and prices ("laborers," 1351, 1353), treason (1352), the wool staple (1353 and after), livery and maintenance (1390 and after), and sumptuary laws (1363)—affected every aspect of English life. The origin of the laws might lie in the interests of the commons themselves, in the lords, or in the household and judiciary. But nearly all ultimately (an ordinance of Council tended to be regarded as a temporary measure) came to be "sponsored" by the commons. The power of the commons may not have been *substantially* great, but *formally* the basis of their sovereignty was being laid. However, the notion that the first prerogative of the commons—namely, consent to taxation—was conditional on a favorable hearing of their petitions was already adumbrated as early as 1348: the idea of "redress before supply" was in the air.

The initiative of the commons in legislation continued in the fifteenth century. The tendency to institutionalize this initiative is seen in the famous Petition of 1414 and Henry V's reply, which in effect conceded that petitions would not be changed after being accepted; acceptance in fact was still a matter of royal prerogative. The logical conclusion of this was the inclusion of "the form of the act" (i.e., the actual wording of the ensuing statute) in the petition, first specifically spelled out in the attainder of Henry VI in 1461. The actual,

[8] See H. L. Gray, *The Influence of the Commons on Early Legislation* (Harvard, 1932), partially acceptable modifications by S. B. Chrimes, *English Constitutional Ideas in the Fourteenth Century* (London, 1936).

as against the formal, initiative could thus eventually more easily shift to the crown, owing to its having expert draftsmen, and to its representatives in the commons. Indeed, with the Tudors, the king was never so powerful as in time of Parliament.

These basic taxational and legislative strides of Parliament led naturally to its involvement in government. It must be stated quite categorically that in the Middle Ages neither the commons nor the lords in Parliament achieved a regular share in government, a regular control in the administrative hierarchy. What had been hard for the barons of the Great Council in the thirteenth century was impossible for the representatives in the fourteenth and fifteenth centuries. Nevertheless, they could and did interfere in the executive side of politics in a sporadic way.

The first form of interference was a natural outgrowth of Parliament's legislative power: the turning of the petition to the task of destroying unpopular councillors or curiales. The complexities of the crisis of 1341 over Edward III's charges against Archbishop Stratford are only of interest here in showing the commons and lords working together to demand trial and appointment of ministers in Parliament. The principle of impeachment was foreshadowed. Parliament was again the forum for a change of ministry when John of Gaunt and his supporters attacked the Caesarean clergy, notably Bishop Wykeham of Winchester, who were blamed for military failure. But the actual process of impeachment—accusation (in the form of a petition) by the commons and trial by the lords—was not achieved until the Good Parliament of 1376. In the legal sense it was not a revolutionary step. But the fact that some of the king's right-hand men—Latimer, the king's chamberlain, and Lyons, a London merchant, and several others—were accused of financial misdoings by the commons, found guilty by the lords, and temporarily dismissed and imprisoned was of prime importance as a precedent. Gaunt, whose men they were, soon secured their release. But when in Richard II's youth the opposition sought in Gaunt's absence to overthrow the king's hated ministers, the same procedure (among others) was resorted to. The result was the great trials of 1386 and 1388, seen by some historians as the true emergence of Parliament as a "high court."[9] In 1386, led by Gloucester, Richard's uncle, the commons and lords used a refined form of impeachment in an effort to imprison Richard's chief minister, Michael de la Pole, earl of Suffolk. Richard fought back hard, reinstating Suffolk after Parliament had dissolved and (in 1387) obtaining a judicial opinion on the treasonous nature of his opponents' acts. The issue between king and Parliament was never to be so clear again until the seventeenth century. On the one hand the lords in Parliament (who took

[9] So argued by B. Wilkinson, *op. cit.*, vol. II.

the initiative in 1388 by substituting appeal for impeachment) declared that there was a "law of Parliament" above the common law and established their point by the execution or exile of the chief royal ministers. On the other hand the king secured the verdict of the royal justices in both 1387 and 1388 that the procedures of the estates of Parliament were illegal. The cynic may call the whole series of events a naked struggle for power; but in fact the question of sovereignty, of the law and the king, had reached the highest point of debate in the Middle Ages. That the debaters failed to "engage," that their interests were at stake, is no excuse for ignoring the momentous nature of the confrontation. The issue was kept alive in the fifteenth century by the impeachment of William de la Pole, Earl of Suffolk, in 1450. It is no accident that the king was again deposed within a decade.

The depositions of Edward II, Richard II, Henry VI, and Edward V were as "illegal" as the impeachment of the two Suffolks. But illegality did not rob them of significance; they were similar in that they reflected the confrontation of the mighty of the land in naked force with the desperate attempts of the protagonists to clothe their acts in the garb of law. The expedients resorted to ranged from military power (the "hand of God") through pseudoabdication to the solemn deposition by the "estates of the realm." The notion of parliamentary title—or perhaps one should speak of parliamentary ratification—was invoked by Henry IV, Edward IV, Richard III, and Henry VII to bolster their more solid claims to the crown based on conquest and right. Whatever the legal problems—and they were many and complex—the spectacle of a succession of crowned monarchs going to oblivion in a flurry of proceedings in what looked like parliaments left its mark for all time on English politics.

More mundane but more solid was the development of Parliament's say in fiscal matters of an executive nature—that is, over and above the right to consent to taxation. This authority at first took the form of an indication of where the money voted was to be spent. The wool subsidy of 1353 was specifically appropriated for the war in France. From then on this kind of directive was quite normal. Harmless and unenforceable statements were one thing; but sporadic efforts were made to enforce these directives by means of audit of government spending and eventually parliamentary appointment of treasurers to handle the money itself. In 1340 and 1341 parliamentary commissions were appointed to audit the accounts of the collectors of the aids granted for the war. In 1379 parliamentary audit and survey of revenues were conceded in the special conditions of Richard II's minority. In fact the frequent, if not regular, supervision by audit and appointment of "war treasurers" dates in essence from Richard's reign. The Lancastrians continued this form of "constitutionalism"; in 1404 two treasurers were appointed to receive, and account to Parliament for, a grant for the defense of the realm.

Foreign Policy and War

The direction of war and of foreign policy (in medieval terminology "defense of rights and obligations") was indisputably the "king's business" in the early Middle Ages. A wise king undoubtedly consulted with the "wise men" or his "natural counselors" before starting on a course involving money and bloodshed. As we have seen, the varying fortunes of the Plantagenet kings depended to a great extent on the confidence they could elicit in their leadership in these matters. Edward II, however, was the first monarch to concede explicitly to the magnates in Parliament a say in war and peace. The subject awaits serious study for the years 1327–1485. Pending that, a few salient points may be made.

Edward III constantly consulted Parliament on his dealings with Scotland and France. In 1331 the lords in Parliament advised peace with France, and in 1333 the knights in Parliament advised on Scottish relations. Ten years later both lords and commons recommended an honorable peace with France, but when it became clear that an honorable peace was not possible, they went on to urge vigorous warfare. Then, in 1348, the commons made their famous reply abdicating their role as advisers on war and peace in favor of the great lords (now dominant in the Council), because they (the commons) were "so ignorant and simple." This was an ill omen for the future; the failure to involve the commons in foreign policy decisions, in view of the prevalent notions of consent, though not a serious matter when things were going well, would make it easier for them to deprive king and Council of both troops and supplies in the following century.

The lords, either in Council or in Parliament, continued to be constant advisers to the king in decisions about war and peace, and the commons were consulted for the purpose of approving those solemn treaties designed to bring peace (e.g., Treaty of Paris, 1360; Treaty of Troyes, 1420; proposals at Arras, 1435). Occasionally Parliament sanctioned the appointment of commissioners to conduct diplomatic relations, and of course foreign affairs were included in articles of deposition or impeachment of unpopular kings and ministers. The Yorkist period saw a decline in parliamentary consultation on these matters; but the line between matters exclusively the concern of king and advisers and those requiring advice, and even consent, from Parliament remained blurred. Resolution of this question was to be effected only after stormy confrontations in the postmedieval centuries.

To what extent can we say that a "parliamentary constitution" had been established by the Middle Ages? The opinions of older historians like Stubbs and even Maitland[1] have been rather unceremoniously discarded by most

[1] W. Stubbs, *op. cit.*; F. W. Maitland, *Constitutional History of England* (Cambridge, 1919).

modern writers. However, B. Wilkinson sees the fifteenth century as the culmination of a long evolution, in which king and councillors, lords and commons, struggled to reach a proper balance between liberty and order.[2] Fortescue proudly compared England's "mixed regality" with the despotism of France. Should he be dismissed as a visionary or propagandist, along with the other writers of his age? He wrote nothing on the many so-called privileges of Parliament tabulated by Stubbs.[3] Perhaps these privileges were indeed wayward instances rather than constitutional advances. But it can be argued that there were certain solid achievements that may be labeled "constitutional" and certain isolated gains that were necessary ammunition for later founders of modern liberal politics.

The two major questions on medieval government that have attracted the attention of all constitutional historians are freedom of speech and freedom from arrest. The latter was actually the first to arise. For the M.P.s were, after all, suitors at the royal court. As such, their freedom from arrest had precedents going back to Anglo-Saxon times. There are examples of both lords and commons being protected in this way in the thirteenth and fourteenth centuries. The real question—freedom from arrest, not by creditors or plaintiffs, but by the king himself—hardly arose in the Middle Ages. In Thomas Thorpe's case (1453–4) both king and chief subject (duke of York) had an interest in his imprisonment on a relatively trivial charge, though he was speaker of the commons. The judges refused to adjudicate on the privileges of this high court of Parliament; nevertheless, they conceded a limited, though large, freedom to the members. Thorpe remained in prison, and a new speaker had to be elected. Under the Yorkist kings members of Parliament were released from trial or imprisonment by royal authority. Neither the commons nor the lords secured the right to override the common law courts in the Middle Ages: a defaulting member had to rely on royal (usually the chancellor's) intervention.

The question of freedom of speech raises some very interesting problems. Presumably the early meetings of the commons were entirely unofficial—they were not part of Parliament. We know nothing of those early meetings, most of which lasted only a day or two. Inasmuch as they were "private," no special immunity, but also no special royal interest, was involved. With the incorporation of the commons meetings into Parliament in the fourteenth and fifteenth centuries the situation changed. The only extensive report of a commons debate is the unofficial account of the Good Parliament (1376).[4] Extraordinary latitude prevailed; but then the circumstances were extraordinary too. We can judge from the commons' attitudes on such matters as taxation, equitable

[2] B. Wilkinson, *Constitutional History of England in the Fifteenth Century* (London, 1964).

[3] W. Stubbs, *op. cit.*, vol. III.

[4] *Anonimalle Chronicle*, ed. V. H. Galbraith (Manchester, 1927).

jurisdiction, church lands, and papal privileges that debate was free and fierce in the fourteenth century. The case of Haxey (1397), a clerk of Parliament who was found guilty of treason for moving the commons to protest against certain royal practices (including intimate matters of the royal household), was and is a cause célèbre in the area of free speech. While the question of Haxey's membership in the commons remains open, the fact is that the reversal of the judgment against Haxey in 1399 was in terms of the commons' privilege. That is its importance. Under Henry IV the commons secured some protection for their debates by getting royal acknowledgment that the speaker alone had the right to report on their conclusions. The case of Thomas Yonge (1455), an M.P. who was imprisoned for urging the right of the Yorkists to succeed Henry VI on the throne, shows how dependent the commons were on the favor of the monarchy, or its most powerful servants, for the exercise of their privileges. Power and law were not always in accord. In spite of much recent careful investigation we can still conclude, with Bishop Stubbs, that parliamentary freedom of speech cannot be documented to any large degree in the Middle Ages.[5]

A further, also somewhat intractable, question is the extent to which Parliament became an "institution" (like the Exchequer, Wardrobe, and so on) as against a "meeting" in the later Middle Ages. Of course, its rolls continued to develop—from a record of private petitions to documents that typically included such public business as the chancellor's address and some record of policy discussions. The speakership added formal sanction to the discussions, or rather conclusions, of commons' debates. Regular appointment of "receivers" and "triers" of petitions and the regulation of their procedures and powers gave form to that aspect of Parliament's work. Although they did not acquire a seal (for Parliament never became an administrative organ), the clerks of Parliament—first of the lords and from 1363 of the commons—established a secretariat. Very briefly, the first stage of the American constitutional pattern —the division of executive and legislature—can be discerned in its primitive form.

There remains one very broad question: To what extent were king and Parliament representative of the "nation"? Writers as far apart as Stubbs and A. F. Pollard have thought that they were so.[6] It is perhaps an anachronistic question, for "nationalism" is generally considered to be a very modern phenomenon; certainly perusal of the evidence lends little credence to the view that it had much significance in the Middle Ages. Yet with hindsight we can perhaps perceive a nation and a "national forum" in the making.

---

[5] W. Stubbs, *op. cit.,* vol. III.

[6] A. F. Pollard, *The Evolution of Parliament* (London, 1926), esp. chap. 7.

The first point to note is that the concept of the "community of the realm," or the "community of the land," with the concomitant notions of "utility of the realm" and "necessity," was emerging into both theoretical and practical usage from Edward I's reign on, and that the first of these terms apparently came to be used more especially for "the king, lords, and commons in Parliament" during Edward II's reign. A study of its use would suggest the presence in the later Middle Ages of the idea of a group of varying size and authority that "embodied" the realm, that legally speaking was a "corporation." In this sense the community of the realm was just another of the units that proliferated in the Middle Ages—along with Christendom, empire, realms, counties, boroughs, vills, chapters, monasteries, and so on. It was a useful, semi-idealistic concept that helped avaricious and aggressive individuals to fulfill themselves in a constructive way.

The lords, the original community of the realm, never fully abdicated this role. Wise kings incorporated them in their Councils; the doctrine of the majority committing the whole was already present in 1215 and prevailed under Henry III; the notion of "peerage" reinforced their privileges and exclusiveness in the fourteenth century. The lords wrestled with the king, and among themselves, for influence over the commons—through the granting of liveries and the enticement of service, through pressure on the sheriff and other electoral officers ("laboring"), and through "joint committees." Moreover, through the rise of notions of chivalrous "caste" in the fourteenth century the growing self-confidence of the gentry and burgesses was set back, so that they came to look to the peers as natural leaders, in the way that the lords had looked to themselves in the thirteenth century. The movement in this direction has to be linked to the social and literary history of chivalry, to royal initiative in the creation of new ranks like duke and marquis, and to the emergence of "royal appanages" or grants of land and office to younger sons. The decline of the peerage came not, as was once thought, with decimation in the Wars of the Roses, but with the natural dying out of many key lineages. Yet though the Tudors effected new direct links with the commons, the English peerage had seemingly limitless powers of adaptation and recuperation and was to rise again in later centuries.

It was noted earlier that the commons were representatives of local communities—those of the county and of the borough. But just who composed these local communities? Needless to say, local privilege, tenurial or hereditary, was rampant. It is also true that there is no generally applicable rule. Yet there are clues in returned writs, in statutes, and in local material that make total agnosticism unnecessary.

The student must first accept the fact that a great number of elections were made by the sheriff without any real "election" at all; in this the sheriff was often guided by some local magnate of influence—though the very efforts made by lords to influence elections of M.P.s in the fifteenth century is evidence that it was by no means a simple matter of unchallenged control. In fact, elections of M.P.s as a result of pressure on sheriffs were frequently, and sometimes successfully, challenged in the fifteenth century. The formal electoral bodies of the shire representatives were the "full" county courts (i.e., all the freemen of the shire). Attendance at shire courts tended in the twelfth and thirteenth centuries to be restricted by tenurial and other limitations, but by the fifteenth century, with the rapid decline of villeinage, some of these courts were very large bodies indeed. Just how large their constituency could be is illustrated by the Huntingdonshire evidence of 1450, to the effect that though 494 freeholders voted in the election, only five sealed the indenture (sealed certificate) of return required by statute in 1406. This evidence confirms the tenor of the 1429 and 1432 statutes limiting the numbers of electors to the forty-shilling freeholders resident in the shire; according to the preamble of the statute of 1429, too many "poor and valueless" persons had been taking part in elections. The difficulty is that the indentures of election, the only really firm evidence, indicate very small electoral bodies; on this we have to be rather skeptical. We may envisage, within a highly variable situation, a core of influential knights and squires with the dominant voice and a large, scarcely controllable, crowd of less substantial people who often played an important role. Basically, in any case, the electorate was confined to "men of property"— that is, substantial yeomen, gentlemen, squires, and knights.

The borough representation presents an even more varied picture, though borough records have survived in sufficient quantity to give us a fair idea of the main elements in the variety.[7] The number of boroughs sending representatives, after declining fairly rapidly in the fourteenth century, leveled off at about eighty in the fifteenth century. The pattern whereby the southwest sent a disproportionately large number was already established. Elections took place in either county or borough court, usually the latter (sometimes by a borough delegation to the county). Behind the "community" of formal electors was a small group of wealthy and established citizens who actually made the choice, and from among whom the M.P.s were chosen. This group, it would appear, was not as small as the indentures required by statute after 1406 would lead the incautious student to believe. Nevertheless, it is to be counted in tens rather than hundreds. Normally it was self-selecting; occasionally, as at King's Lynn in Norfolk, it was a jury nominated by a rather elaborate procedure. The consent or ratification of a larger body was frequently specified

---

[7] See M. McKisack, *The Parliamentary Representation of English Boroughs in the Later Middle Ages* (London, 1932).

(e.g., "others of the community" at Norwich). Reelection was sufficiently common for the borough M.P.s to develop a corporate character corresponding to that of the knights of Parliament.

More serious than the existence of such narrow oligarchies to the representativeness of the commons was the flagrant and increasing flouting of the statute that required borough M.P.s to be resident burgesses. The rapid "invasion" of the borough representation by gentry and (to a much smaller degree) officials occurred at the fastest rate in the opening decades of Henry VI's reign. This lack of interest, or false economy, of the English merchant and craft class in influencing the affairs of the realm must have seriously weakened the commons as a whole.

From this review of the question we may conclude that the community of England did indeed find expression in Parliament by the end of the Middle Ages in the form of a loosely organized association of flexible bodies, peers, and representatives of county and borough oligarchies, knit together under the king. It was not an "institution," with all that term implies today; it was summoned and dismissed by the king. But its members, by rallying to royal opponents and helping in the destruction of kings, had shown that they were proud and self-confident men.

Chapter Three
LOCAL COMMUNITIES

Introduction

England was throughout the Middle Ages overwhelmingly rural. A history of England can be either an account of the "national matter," confined of necessity to the activities of a few very great men, or an attempt to describe the evolving life of the countless communities—vill and manor, borough and town, guild and parish, priory and minster—on which were focused the essentially local interests of the vast majority of the inhabitants. It is on the nature of these communities that a serious study of English civilization must turn. In fact, if we recall that the king and his court were yet another community—"the community of England"—we can argue that the study of "groups" is the clue to medieval England.

It is useful to keep in mind some of the polarities that lend significance to the study of English local communities. These include freedom and slavery, individual and group, community and lordship, custom and contract. The tension between these polarities, undetected for the most part by the people themselves, has been illuminated by a number of general studies, especially in the area of vill and manor.[1] In fact, the challenge of the community-lordship question has been the starting point of most scholarship in this field. Alongside the attempts at generalization and analysis must be set the growing volume of studies of individual towns, manors, and honors.[2] The day is yet far ahead when the general and particular can be successfully combined.

The origin of fief and manor has been the most sedulously cultivated of the general areas of interest. The problem of "German" or "Roman" priority is

---

[1] See the section on "Local Communities" in the Bibliography of this volume.

[2] For example, F. R. H. Du Boulay, *The Lordship of Canterbury* (London, 1966); F. M. Page, *The Estates of Crowland Abbey* (Cambridge, 1934); J. A. Raftis, *The Estates of Ramsey Abbey* (Toronto, 1957); J. W. F. Hill, *Medieval Lincoln* (Cambridge, 1948).

actually a cover for an interest in the question of freedom and authority, German being equated with "free" and Roman with "unfree." Briefly, did the manor descend from the slave-run villas of the Romans, or did it evolve from the partial subjection of the German freemen? On balance, a modified Germanism is the "dominant orthodoxy" today. The persistence of the primitive Germanic community under the growing power of lordship is to be acknowledged. On the other hand, the ancient nature of lordship and the strong Roman contributions to the manor have also had their advocates.[3] So we cannot write of the evolution of a free peasantry into servitude, or of the triumph of Roman over Germanic social ideas. Let us therefore plunge into the situation as it was in the middle of the twelfth century.

The diverse and evolving Anglo-Saxon social arrangements had by 1154 received and absorbed the imposition of feudal military obligations from above, at the hands of the Norman nobility. Some manors have yielded extensive information about the issues we have sought to isolate. The structure of society as it affected the lowest and the middle classes can thus be illuminated.

A few basic facts about the manor demand attention. First, the division into demesne and tenements was crucial to full manorial development. The demesne, the immediate source of the lord's sustenance, was normally worked by the servile tenants (*villani*, or villeins). The various services they performed were at the heart of manorialism and seignorialism. The relation of these services to the size of estates and to the lay or ecclesiastical character of the lord has been explored with important results by E. A. Kosminsky.[4] In brief, from an examination of the Hundred Rolls Kosminsky has found that in the late thirteenth century unfree services tended to vary directly with the size of the estates. But this general pattern, it should be emphasized, covered a wide variety of exceptions in individual estates.

The conversion of labor services into direct payments to the lord was one of the most important developments for the medieval peasant. In general, it reflected and fostered contract instead of status, fluidity instead of stability. Bargaining and mobility grew at the expense of subjection and immobility. The process was already under way in 1154; it developed in the thirteenth century (though offset by the capitalist notions of some lords who saw services as a means of cutting costs) and swept all before it in the fourteenth century.

To replace services the lord could do two things. He could manage his demesne with household and wage labor (*famuli*) or he could rent it out. The former solution, characteristic of what has been named "high farming," especially widespread in the early fourteenth century, meant elaborate super-

---

[3] F. Seebohm, *The English Village Community*, 4th ed. (London, 1890), is the seminal work for this school.

[4] E. A. Kosminsky, *Studies in the Agrarian History of England* (Oxford, 1936).

vision. The latter, and in the end dominant, method saw the rise of "lease-hold" and is especially characteristic of the fourteenth and fifteenth centuries. Leasing the demesne turned the lords into *rentiers* and made way for the rise of franklin and yeoman farmers to positions of wealth and importance. The role of such matters as population trends, international trade, currency reform, war, and revolution has been debated without effective consensus. The thesis that population changes were the crucial factor in the rise of the yeoman classes is the most widely accepted of a great variety of interpretations.[5]

Household and Family

The households of great lords were modeled on that of the king. From the few records that have survived, it would appear that in the thirteenth century the baronial household included, besides the nucleus of family and guests, a corps of major officials and their subordinates. Usually there were two stewards (one domestic, one for the overseeing of lands and manors) and a chancellor, wardrober, marshal, and secretary. The household of the Lord Edward, so highly developed that he took it with him as the royal household on his succession, also had treasurers and auditors. Beneath these officials was a vast array of minor officers or servants, such as buyers, butlers, ushers, porters, and bakers. The giving of livery to the household became a normal practice, and of course the whole honor court was continuously on the move.[6]

This baronial council of knights and officials was modeled on the Curia Regis. Auditors traveled around the lord's estates, examining and checking manorial accounts. Income and expenditures were in the hands of two treasurers, wardrobers, or receivers-general. A greater steward presided over the council, made local appointments, supervised the estates, and acted for the lord in most matters. Usually he was a knight or a lesser baron. A lesser steward managed the household and was head of all the domestic officers. The annual accounts of the greater stewards have survived as "ministers' accounts," rendering down to the tiniest detail the produce of individual manors. For the life of the baron's household, one turns to the daily accounts, drawn up every night under the steward's direction. Here too the detail was meticulous. Close members of the family—wife, sons, and so on—often, as in the case of the Lord Edward, had their own daily accounts. In fact, one of the principal

[5] M. Postan has written voluminously on this and related subjects. Probably the best summary of his views is to be found in the *Cambridge English History*, vol. I, 2nd ed. (Cambridge, 1966), pp. 549ff.

[6] The following account is largely based on M. W. Labarge's lively and enlightening study of a baronial household: *A Baronial Household of the Thirteenth Century* (London, 1965).

sources of evidence on the operations of the baron's household is the daily account of the Lady Eleanor de Montfort for 1265.

Chaplains and clerks also had an honorable place in the household. One chaplain, the almoner, distributed food scraps and clothing to the poor, visited the sick and imprisoned, and supervised the occasional poor men's feasts. Daily mass was said by another chaplain, and a clerk was responsible for the upkeep and transportation of church vestments and vessels. Other clerks wrote up the accounts and maintained the often elaborate correspondence with king, relatives, and allies, besides sometimes acting as buyers of household supplies. A lower hierarchy was in charge of the various offices—chamberlain of the chamber, butler of the buttery and the drink, marshal of the Marshalsea (with disciplinary powers), and so on.[7] In a knightly age the marshal, who was in charge of the stables and horses, could be a very important person. Finally, there was the mass of launderers, maids, and grooms who carried out the menial tasks.

The personal family of the lord was at the center of this vast estate. The lady of the household—wife or widow—was a person of great authority. With full legal powers, she would frequently be in sole charge of at least the domestic household and often, if the lord was away at war or in council, of the whole complex barony. Kinship was deeply felt; not only the immediate family but distant relatives kept in close touch. Close ties could on occasion lead to violent jealousies. Respect for ancestors was intense; it included both title (the right to one's land) and care for their souls and was expressed in the erection of tombs and in the founding of chantries, chapels where prayers were said for the dead in the later Middle Ages.

Title became an increasingly intricate business—it was probably the least worthy achievement of England's law system. By the thirteenth century land could be held in seven different ways: in fee, in dower, by courtesy, for life, for years, at will, and from year to year. Tenure in fee descended through the eldest son or was divided among the daughters. The donor could impose conditions on the lands he alienated—for example, descent only in the male line (by "tail male") or assignment to certain others on the death of the recipient. Tenure by courtesy was the life holding by a widower of his wife's inheritance. A widow, on the other hand, received only one-third of her late husband's estate—this was tenure in dower. Tenure for life was frequently extended almost indefinitely by grants "in survivorship." The last three categories of tenure became important in the later Middle Ages, as did the "use," a device by which a trustee or group of trustees held the land on behalf of another who either legally or practically was unable to secure his title. This practice, which

[7] *Ibid.*, p. 67ff.

evaded the common law, meant that the common law courts lost a fair amount of business to Chancery, which had jurisdiction over uses from the middle of the fourteenth century. We may conclude that family and affinity were ties that, even if occasionally begetting bitter warfare, generally contributed to the stability of medieval society.

The Manor

The services of the villeins, at the root of manorial life, were supplemented by other important elements in estate management. There were dues in kind owed by all manner of tenants; the monopolies—of mill and oven in particular; the specific duties and dues with regard to pasture, meadow, and woodland (wards and herds); and the judicial and military rights of the lord, which bore most heavily on the tenant in the form of financial exactions (scutage and fines).

Our knowledge of the manor is drawn from extents, surveys, account rolls, and court rolls. A study of representative samples of these sources in each century in which they are available has yet to be undertaken. At the present time there are several brilliant studies of individual manors or manorial complexes,[8] and much use of manorial sources for special purposes, but no carefully selected sampling and analysis.

The economic management of the various types of manors and the jurisdiction of the manorial court have left enough records for a reasonably clear picture to be constructed. The corporate existence of the vill has been carefully examined.[9] Life for the peasant in the high Middle Ages was nasty, brutish, and short. However, it was relieved a little by the ministrations of priest and vicar, solaced by the lore of the local "wise woman" with her herbs and "low magic," and enlivened by coarse sports and the occasional strolling storyteller and group of players. As the relatively fixed round of duties and work of the seignorial period gave way first to high farming and then to an increasingly "open" market economy, this routine existence gave place during the fourteenth century to a more fluid, less secure state of affairs in which the enterprising might make a small fortune. War too, through wages and booty and ransom, offered an avenue of adventure and improvement. T. Rogers is probably right in his assertion that the later Middle Ages, with its declining prices and rising wages, was indeed a golden age for the adaptable and enterprising among

---

[8] See note 2 above. Also F. G. Davenport, *The Economic Development of a Norfolk Manor* (Cambridge, 1906).

[9] Notably W. O. Ault and H. M. Cam. See, for example, W. O. Ault, *The Self-Directing Activities of Village Communities in Medieval England* (Boston, 1952) and H. M. Cam, *Liberties and Communities in Medieval England* (Cambridge, 1944).

the peasantry.[1] Nor is there reason to doubt that the prowess in archery of the better class of peasant imbued him with a sense of value and hence, through his victorious service in the royal armies, with a rudimentary patriotism that began to transcend the fixed and local loyalties of the thirteenth century.

The complex of land in a typical midland village has been usefully divided into five categories: the individual plots, the common fields, the meadows, the common, and the waste.[2] The individual plot, or "close," of a peasant approximates most nearly to modern property holding: it involved no services or dues. But it was insufficient to maintain a family, and most peasants had to rely for their main sustenance, and of course for any commercial farming, on their holdings in the common fields; the minority served as artisans or wage laborers.

The common fields represent by far the most intriguing feature of the manorial economy, and the part most requiring cooperation. The two-field system of rotation was in general use from an early time to the end of the Middle Ages. But the three-field system, adopted over a long period in many places since the ninth century, had the advantage of yielding more produce. In the two-field system it was simply a matter of alternating, from year to year, between fallow and crop. In the three-field system one field was planted in the fall with wheat, the second was planted in the spring with oats, barley, or vetches, and the third was left fallow. In this way medieval man was a successful conservationist.

Beyond the arable on which the grain was grown lay the meadows. Here too for the hay-growing period the peasants and lords had their own lots, and a manorial official, the hayward (or hayhedge), supervised the fences that kept out the livestock and (presumably) divided the individual lots. Here was grown the fodder indispensable for winter feed.

The common was distinguished from the arable and the meadow in that it was open to the livestock of the whole community during the "off season" when it was not being exploited by individual peasants. In this period it was indistinguishable from the first two parts of the village. The number of livestock each peasant could graze on the common was, of course, related in at least a rough way to the size of the basic arable holding.

The common was similar to the final category of land, the waste, in that it was subject to continual encroachment on the part of both lord and tenants. The waste formed an indeterminate area beyond the closes, fields, and common. Here the peasant had certain rights; the keeping of pigs (pannage), the

[1] J. E. Thorold Rogers, *Six Centuries of Work and Wages* (London, 1884).
[2] H. S. Bennett, *Life on the English Manor* (Cambridge, 1960 ed.), is the principal source for this and the discussion that follows.

gathering of wood (usually restricted to fallen or loose timber), the picking of wild fruits, and the cutting of turves or reeds for fuel and shelter.

The relative roles of individual, whether lord or peasant, and community have aroused a good deal of speculation. The ploughed fields of the manor were divided into furlongs and these were subdivided into strips. Both the lord's demesne and the tenants' holdings consisted of a given number of strips scattered among the various furlongs. Hence the nature and timing of ploughing, sowing, and reaping had to be fixed by common agreement. This communal decision probably rested on ancient custom, and at a time lost to history it was determined by trial and error. Sowing by hand (scattering) and reaping by hook or scythe were individual activities, but ploughing, which involved draft animals (mostly oxen, but occasionally horses), required a pooling of resources. In the late fourteenth century there is evidence both of contracts, "marrows," between individual peasants to achieve this and of encroachments by unscrupulous neighbors ("false husbandmen who falsely plough away men's lands").[3] The individual enterprise involved in these contracts and encroachments indicated here may have been a development of the previous century; indeed, it is probable that most of the ploughing in the twelfth century was done on a cooperative basis. The same principle applied to the carting of the grain from the fields to the stacks and barns.

The basic service on the lord's demesne was also concerned with agriculture. The amount of this service varied greatly from manor to manor and from peasant to peasant. Broadly speaking, the larger the peasant's own holding, the greater the service he owed; and the freer a peasant, the less arbitrary the amount and times of such services. The regular due, varying from three to five days a week, was, as the nature of the service suggests, "week" work. Additional or "boon" work, theoretically voluntary, was owed usually at harvest time; a meal and perhaps ale ("wet boons") were sometimes provided by the lord. In addition to week and boon work, the peasants owed a host of other services, varying with place and person—for example, harrowing, manuring, hedging, and carting.

An example of the heavy weight of services lying on the twelfth-century villein is given in a survey in Henry II's reign[4] made by the monks of Ramsey Abbey of the manor of Elton, Huntingdonshire. Each virgater, a holder of approximately thirty acres, owed these services on or in connection with his lord's land: from Michaelmas (September 30) to August, two days of work per week, with a third day of ploughing during Christmas, Easter, and Pentecost; from the beginning of August to September 8, three days of work per

[3] Robert Mannyng of Bourne's *Handlyngge Symme*, quoted in H. S. Bennett, *ibid.*, p. 45.
[4] Provided in translation in *English Historical Documents*, vol. II, ed. D. Douglas and Grant Greenaway (London, 1953).

week; and from September 8 to Michaelmas, work every day except Saturday
In winter the virgater ploughed half an acre and sowed it with his own seed
which he reaped along with another half-acre in August. He owed carrying
services, or payments for rights to the common—a sum called "heusire." He
paid fourpence at Michaelmas, a usual day for dues, and a halfpenny for wool
He had to run errands, carry timber, make fences, and cart grain at harvest
Each five virgaters paid fourpence for fish and each two virgaters owed one
cart of thatch; presumably on an annual basis. When required, the peasant and
his family performed boon work, at which time they would be fed by the
farmer.

Some peasants had particular jobs, rather than sharing in a general obligation
Such were the overseers (messors) in charge of sowing and harvest and the
various herds, which included the sheep-herd (shepherd) in charge of live
stock. At first doing this service in return for holdings, they later became
wage earners. Such tenancies shade off into the status of artisan and represen
a curious mixture of servility and privilege.

Besides services, the peasant owed certain judicial and military obligations
miscellaneous payments, and observance of monopolies. Attendance at the
manorial court was obligatory "from three week to three weeks." The tri-
weekly court was part of the thirteenth-century kings' and lawyers' efforts to
reduce the variety of actual practice to some kind of uniformity. Another such
effort was the 1267 rule that a freeman owed no suit unless it was imposed in
his charter or was of long standing. The Tudor distinction between court
for the "free" and "unfree" had no medieval basis. It rose from the fact that
the royal and communal (county and hundred) courts were the proper place
for minor cases among freemen, leaving the administration of court custom a
the basic business of manorial courts. But though the higher jurisdiction of
lords (e.g., over felonies) was wiped out by thirteenth-century kings in th
few cases where it had been assumed, the "leet" jurisdiction and view of
frankpledge in which the policing occurred remained attached in many case
to manorial courts. So suit of court remained a burden on freemen for thi
reason alone, quite apart from the fact that they too were involved in th
routine of the manor and might have unfree holdings.

Military obligation was not a manorial due: it went by county, hundred
and vill. However, it deserves mention here, along with suit of court at th
hundred and county levels, as one of the few direct royal burdens on th
peasantry.

There remain the miscellaneous dues of peasants to be considered. They ma
be classified as dues in kind, monopolies, and personal servitudes. A peasan
might owe a dozen eggs, a chicken, or a larger due at certain seasons or o
certain occasions. These dues were a continual drain on the peasant's resource

and a brake on progress. The "heriot," often consisting of payment of the best beast, was owed on the death of a tenant; it was the most onerous of the manorial dues, especially since it was accompanied by other payments like mortuary; the payment of the second best beast to the priest. Tithes were the tenths of all gains (the greater tithe) and of all livestock and all growing things owed to the local rector. By the thirteenth century the right of the lord to tallage the unfree at will had become, in most cases, an annual tax.

Of the monopolies, those of grinding grain at the mill and baking in the oven were the most burdensome, with the monopolist often charging exhorbitant fees and grossly cheating his customers. The former in particular aroused the ire and even sparked the revolt of peasants. In Chaucer's Prologue to *The Canterbury Tales* we have a picture of popular conceptions— though we know well enough to distrust Chaucer as a guide to general fact. The lesser monopoly of the oven, perhaps by nature unenforceable and not widespread in England, aroused less antagonism.

All these services and dues became in the thirteenth century the subject of statements of the "custom of the manor." It may be suggested that this custom, because of its great variety, was the outcome of a series of large and prolonged conflicts between the lord and his tenants. Evidence of such struggles certainly exists, but it would be hazardous to suggest any common origin. The question of whether the custom enshrined the oppression of the lord or guaranteed the privileges of the peasant will to a large extent depend on one's presuppositions about economic theory. It is possible to state with some objectivity, however, that the custom was a bulwark in the twelfth and thirteenth centuries against the lawyers' assertion of seignorial ownership of the villein—that is, against the possibility of slavery *tout court*. However, in later centuries, when individual enterprise displaced manorialism, it became a means of oppression. In fact, the very reduction to writing of the customs of the later thirteenth century probably represented a counterattack by the lords on loosening ties in an effort to increase their profits in an expanding market. In the peasant revolts of the later Middle Ages the destruction of records of servitude was one of the first objectives of the rebels.

The process of assarting, or "internal colonization," was still vigorous in the century after 1154. New holdings, though few new villages, were still being created at the expense of the waste. This process, resulting from the pressure of an expanding population, had to be slightly regulated at the national level. Two early statutes (Merton, 1237; Westminster II, 1285) gave limited rights of "enclosure" (that is, rights of lords to consolidate fields previously held in common) but sought to protect the "sufficient pasture" of the tenants. The same process of colonization threatened the forests, parks, and warrens wherein the lords, at the expense of tenants, sought to keep vast tracts of country for the hunting of game. The pressure was so great that these hunting privileges had to be protected by severe penalties.

Vill and Manor Institutions

Alongside and inextricably bound up with the manor was the vill. It has been said that "to all but the lawyers and the lords of the manor, the communal living of the villagers, working, rejoicing and mourning together, was a greater reality than manorial rights and administration."[5] In baldest terms, the lord's complex of rights (the manor) was matched by the local community's own organization (the vill); older historians would say that land-lordism was superimposed through various circumstances (notably war and famine) on the original "free" vill, and such a myth does have its attractions. At any rate, by 1154 vills existed as local communities; they were either divided among various manors, subunits within manors, or "ideally" coterminous with manors. The vill is a shadowy community, though its legal and political aspects have been brought increasingly to light. Like the county and hundred, it was a unit in royal administration and justice (though it may not have had its own court). But it was also a self-regulating community. It could enact bylaws, send jurymen to the county and assize courts, and be amerced (or in modern terms, fined). If it had not existed from ancient times, the subdivision of manors would have made its invention necessary.

The insecurity of the villein in his tenement was one of his distinguishing marks in common law; but the researches of Ambrose Raftis into peasant property and its descent have shown that there was a law of the manor or vill that in fact made the unfree tenant into a "sort of vassal of the lord with his own 'rights' and 'law.'"[6] The independence of the peasant was further manifested in the brisk traffic in small holdings—a vill as against a manor activity. This practice lasted until the fifteenth century, when small holdings were consolidated. Group activity by the vill as a whole was not infrequent; many local laws were laws of the vill rather than of the lord, and as the lord's grip slackened, the appeal to the "ordinances" of the vill increased. It has been noted that "the common laws of the village were set by those implicated."[7]

The vill owed military service in the county levies and local police service and may have collectively elected its representatives when selective service was introduced in the tenth century. It had to keep up roads and bridges. It assessed the principal tax—that on movables. It could be amerced by the king for failure in frankpledge or for failure to turn in criminals. The lord could make levies

[5] J. Bagley, *Life in Medieval England* (London, 1960), p. 25.
[6] A. Raftis, *Tenure and Mobility* (Toronto, 1964).
[7] *Ibid.*

on it as a unit. But above all it regulated its own life: it made bylaws governing communal activity, negotiated with neighboring vills on common rights, resisted incursions by aggressive lords, set up committees to work out problems with manorial lords, and leased itself from lord and king for a farm. It could endow and repair churches. In economic matters the vill might own or farm out a mill. It sent delegates to plead before royal courts and commissions. To do many of these things it often had a common seal. Unwalled, the vill occasionally had to take sides in civil wars, as in the famous case of Peatling Magna, Leicestershire, recorded in 1266. The villagers of Peatling demonstrated their loyalty to the baronial rebels at great cost to themselves.[8] In short, the vill was to peasants what the county was to knights and freemen.

At the head of the manor was the lord; but between lord and individual manor stood the bailiff and the reeve. A basic problem in medieval history is that of the authority of the reeve. Was he an authoritarian ruler, enforcing services, hearing pleas, and imposing fines much like an Angevin despot? Or was he essentially "head of the court," working with those who owed suit of court in his control of the estate? This question—of the primacy of individual or group—is after all more important than the closely related question of manor and vill, and the study of the latter should be subordinated to it.

To enforce his rights and to administer his manor the lord had an echelon of officials whose duties, particularly at the higher levels, frequently overlapped. Some lords, of course, ruled their manors in person: they were local squires to whom national or even county obligations were an irksome diversion from the business of the agricultural year. But most lords of any substance had a steward, perhaps a man of high rank himself, who presided over manorial courts, supervised the annual accounting, and directed the economy of the manor. The steward could be expected to descend on the manor like a thunderbolt, arresting the obdurate and fining the recalcitrant. Each year at Michaelmas the steward (or, in more highly organized estates, special auditors) examined the income and expenditures of the manor in meticulous detail. This precise accounting gradually replaced the levy of a farm from each manor late in the twelfth century.

In more constant daily contact with the tenants were the bailiff and reeve. Normally the bailiff was free and appointed by the lord or steward, whereas the reeve was a serf and elected by the tenants. This "normal" practice admitted of a high degree of variation. The good bailiff was responsible in every particular for the conduct of the manor at the annual accounting. The reeve might work with him, or in his place. Less mobile, he was in closer contact with the serfs, of whom he was a wealthier representative. Though frequently freely chosen by the vill, or "community of the manor," he might be appointed

[8] For the story see F. M. Powicke, *King Henry III and the Lord Edward* (Oxford, 1947), II, 509–10.

either arbitrarily or from a short list prepared by the local peasants. At least on occasion the peasants were willing to pay for the right of election. As time went on, many serfs obtained an exemption from this onerous and sometimes dangerous position, so that the practice of attaching the obligation of reeve service to a particular tenancy grew. Every aspect of the manorial round—ploughing, carting, reaping, sowing, building, and riding on errands—came under the bailiff's or reeve's supervision. The reeve, while owing primary allegiance to the lord of the manor, also enforced the rights of tenants both against each other (e.g., in the collection of debts) and not infrequently against the lord: "They were servants of the whole village as well as the lord's officials."[9]

Similar in duties and status was the hayward, while the beadle was particularly concerned with discipline—for example, enforcing attendance at court. The recompense of these officers was highly varied; the steward, as has been noted, was often of knightly or squirely rank, with appropriate endowment; the typical bailiff was a wealthy freeman with residence and robes at the manor; the unfree reeve was exempt from services, or at least the more onerous ones, and probably had numerous perquisites, such as free grazing rights.

The manorial court, in which so much of the business of the manor was conducted and whose rolls are so valuable a guide to many aspects of rural life, was a microcosm of the relationships between lord, community of vill, and individual tenants. The lord himself occasionally presided, but usually he was represented by his steward; and to the lord accrued the "profits" of justice. But the judgments, or "dooms," were made by the whole body of the court, sometimes referred to as the "community of the whole manor." Indeed, a case might be adjourned if there was not a full enough attendance. Nevertheless, a certain group of villagers often came to make up the court. Frequently, the tasks of presenting and inquiry were delegated to juries. Here the distinction between free and unfree was more common; two juries, one from each category, were often empaneled. Juries, apart from those whose composition was laid down by royal law (i.e., leet juries), could be of various sizes, and their activities covered a multitude of judicial and administrative functions.

In the manorial court the complex of services and rights that made up the community was regulated, often in the form of fines for breaches of law. These might range from strictly farming matters (e.g., straying cattle or encroaching of the arable) to the petty crimes covered by leet jurisdiction. The "articles of view," that is, their frame of reference, as well as the lists of fines spelled out this multifarious business. Although the activities of manorial courts tailed off in the later Middle Ages as the custom of the manor and the leet jurisdictions themselves weakened, they continued to regulate a remarkable amount of the peasants' daily lives.

[9] On the reeve, see H. S. Bennett, *op. cit.*, pp. 169ff.

By the second half of the thirteenth century many manors had begun to shift from services to wage labor; there followed a period of about fifty years when high farming was at its peak. This system involved the great expansion in numbers of the *famuli*—ploughmen, herds, carters, and so on—who cultivated the demesne in return for wages. Sometimes, as at Forncett, in Norfolk these wage laborers were housed and fed as well as paid by the lord. This phase was a response to the expanding market for produce. Another feature of high farming was the development of seignorial organization. At the top was a group of highly skilled officials, accountants, and lawyers, often assembled in a baronial council. The supervision of the local manor was improved by the creation of regional units, like the custodianships of Christ Church, Canterbury, or the bailiwicks of Ely, the abbey-bishopric in Cambridge. There is some evidence of increased productivity through wider adoption of three-field rotation, more extensive use of manure and marl, and more intense sowing.

By the middle of the fourteenth century the era of high farming was over (though of course there was a continuous overlap of different schemes) and the age of leasehold had begun. The dissolution of unfree services, begun by wage labor, was now carried to completion. The disruption of the old custom of the manor was not smooth; flights of peasants, confederacies, and revolts occurred on a wide scale. Usually the movement was gradual, but occasionally, as at the priory of Christ Church, Canterbury, a sweeping revolution was carried out by one determined lord, in this case Prior Chillenden (1391–1411).

The disintegration of the manor in the fourteenth and fifteenth centuries was manifested in many ways. The disappearance of services and the attenuation of servile dues were the most notable changes. This was accompanied by a steady rise in the process of manumission; as the demand for land lessened, the lords could no longer hold their mass of tenants in servitude. The final step, which also had the paradoxical effect of staying the process of disintegration, was the evolution of copyhold, that is, tenure by "copy" of a contract between lord and peasant. This form of tenure became widespread by the middle of the fifteenth century; and with the gradual omission of all reference to servile dues, the right of alienation, and subletting, copyhold became in point of fact a form of "fee simple." What happened in the fourteenth and fifteenth centuries was the partial triumph of the individual peasant at the expense of both lord of the manor and community of the vill. This was shown in the free movement of peasants from manor to manor, traced with detailed accuracy in the studies that have been made of Ramsey Abbey. In one year alone, for example, over twenty-six peasants migrated from the manor of Warboys, a village appurtenant to Ramsey.[1]

[1] A. Raftis, *op. cit.,* Chaps. 6 and 7, where a full analysis of mobility in this important East Midland complex of villages is conducted.

The county court was the focal point of the "community of the shire." Here knights met with representatives of vill, hundred, and borough under the presidency of the sheriff, J.P., or visiting justices. The knights elected coroners, and especially in 1258 and 1339, sheriffs. While normal business tended to fall into the hands of a few privileged men, on such occasions as a general eyre or an election to Parliament the court became a truly representative body. The knights of the shire were busy in such well-known capacities as sheriffs, under-sheriffs, coroners, M.P.s, commissioners of array (that is, supervisors of the military), and J.P.s, as well as in a great number of other judicial and administrative functions. They were the (usually) unpaid county offices of the kings. Hence it was a largely unpaid officialdom that kept the nation's business in good shape. They must have come to know one another very well, since they were brought together not only by official duties but by a great deal of intermarriage, by hunting, by the education of one another's children, and so on. The judicial and administrative aspects of this activity in the early Middle Ages have been admirably described by A. B. White as self-government by command of the king.[2] One example, out of hundreds given, is the sending of four knights to the king's court (Curia Regis) to verify a claim of default of justice.

Between the county and the vill and manor stood an intermediate organization under its bailiff, the hundred. Probably the majority of legal cases, besides the organization of men in tithings (frankpledge), took place here in the twelfth century. From then on occurred a steady erosion. A great number of legal cases —by 1272 a considerable majority (358 out of 628)—were granted to private lords, usually for a fee farm, or annual rent. The rise of common law courts deprived the hundred of all but minor cases in trespass and debt. Nevertheless, a considerable number of free tenants (an average of between thirty and forty) continued to meet every three weeks for these actions, and often larger numbers for the biannual sheriff's tourn. Hence, although the hundred court was not notably an elective community (the bailiff usually contracted for the job with sheriff or lord), it was an important, if steadily declining, body, not small enough to be an economic unity but sufficiently close to be a community in which ties were forged, men got to know one another, and the justice that keeps a society healthy could be done.

Towns

Outside king and Parliament, the community that probably obtained the greatest degree of self-government and freedom for its members was the community of the borough and the city: *Stadt Luft macht frei* ("town

[2] A. B. White, *Self-Government by the King's Command* (Minneapolis, 1933).

air makes free") is the old German saying. While this general rule has many exceptions, with special privilege continually rearing its ugly head, it is still a valuable clue to medieval urban society.

By 1154 the Anglo-Saxon boroughs, many of them rural fortresses, had been strengthened in their trading and industrial interests by the increased continental connections of the Norman dynasty. In the period after 1066 the growth of urban communities accelerated. They may be studied in relation to four developments: the borough farm, the commune, the free borough, and the merchant guild.

The acquisition by citizens of the right to pay the farm of their borough directly to the king, instead of as part of the shire account, represented an important step toward autonomy. It is to be found as early as the reign of Henry I and was probably in part a royal concession designed, successfully, to stave off municipal revolutions. In constitutional terms this right involved in many cases the election by the burgesses, the leading members of the town, of their officials, the borough reeve or bailiff—a classic example of "self-government at the king's command." The only instance of the adoption of a "sworn commune" (association of burgesses) in England was London, and that was short-lived. The English way of gradualism began early. In Henry II's reign nine boroughs received the right to pay their own farm, though Henry was more cautious than his grandfather in that he never granted such privileges in perpetuity. Of these nine, four were new to the privilege. Royal revocations left only five boroughs farming their own revenues at the end of the reign. Two towns—Gloucester and York—made attempts to set up communes in Henry II's time.

The great period of the acquisition of borough liberties was that of the reigns of Richard I and John. It seems improbable that either monarch was solicitous of municipal freedom; in John's case, however, weakness at home was not a conspicuous characteristic, and one cannot rule out a new awareness of the value of popular support. The main motive was almost certainly financial. Richard and John granted the borough farm in perpetuity to eighteen boroughs. The high point, according to J. Tait, was the grant by Count John (the king's brother) of the commune to London in 1191, quite distinct from the restoration of the farm a year previously.[3] The commune played a large part in French municipal growth; the London episode of 1191 was almost an isolated event in English history. Gradual evolution was the keynote of English developments.

The grant of "free borough" and the earlier grant of "free burgage" were

[3] J. Tait, *The Medieval English Borough* (Manchester, 1936). Most of this discussion is based on Tait's study. See also C. Stephenson, *Borough and Town* (Cambridge, 1933), and C. Gross, *The Gild Merchant* (Oxford, 1890).

two of the most significant ways of conferring liberties on a town. The grant seems to have had, on the basis of burgage tenure, a highly variable content. Burgesses of free borough were certainly free of servile dues, such as heriot and merchet (fines for marrying). They had their own courts. Often a town modeled its liberties on another town that had earlier achieved this status. In the thirteenth century the title "borough" (which is not a category separate from "free borough") was withdrawn from less substantially privileged towns, and the new category of "market town" was invented to fill the gap. For towns certainly did not revert to servile status. In brief, while burgage tenure anticipated and was incorporated in the free borough, the other features—a court, freedom of toll outside the borough, and so on—were added in a variety of combinations to different towns.

Very often the liberties enjoyed by a borough were not spelled out in its charter; they were covered by some omnibus terms. Thus all the more valuable are the charters that do spell out the particular freedoms of a free borough, such as those of certain Welsh towns, which refer to "gild merchant, general exemption from tolls, a free borough prison." In the case of Hull, a major port in Yorkshire, liberties included "right of devise, return of writs, freedom from external pleading, an elective coroner, a royal prison and gallows, . . . freedom from tolls throughout the king's dominions, lot and scot in tallages by all enjoying the liberties, and two markets and a fair."

The grant of "merchant guild" was a frequent element in early borough charters. The aldermen of the guild were a parallel force to the mayor and bailiffs of the borough. But they were more than this. In the twelfth century, when borough government was rudimentary, the merchant guild acted as a pioneer of later burghal self-government through the activities of the guild and its officers. Until the development of borough government, the merchant guild acted for the burgers in their relations with the king and other outside bodies. Hence the guild, however much it must be distinguished from the borough,[4] provided the setting within which many (not all: London was the most outstanding exception) town governments took their form. It is significant that the guild hall was often the seat of town government in the later Middle Ages.

The merchant guild, of course, has a history of its own quite apart from its contribution to town government. The guild was a trading monopoly: exclusion of foreign traders was the basis of its power. It has been suggested that at least a third of the thirteenth-century parliamentary boroughs had merchant guilds.[5] Their basic privileges, as stated in their charters, were remarkably uniform. Some such phrase as that in the charter of Beaumaris, Wales (1296),

[4] C. Gross, ibid.
[5] Ibid.

was almost universal: "They can freely merchandise in the aforesaid town without paying toll . . . and . . . no one who is not sworn and admitted into the aforesaid gild can merchandise in the said town." In some towns industrial as well as commercial monopolies were granted (e.g., the processing of cloth and victuals at Newcastle-under-Lyme). But it was trading, both wholesale and retail, that gave the merchant guild its unique stamp; to escape guild restrictions, when they could be escaped, it was necessary to make heavy payments to the "brotherhood."

The share of the merchant guild in borough government remains a matter of debate. Certainly by "scot and lot" or aids guild members supported the borough's financial obligations (largely payments to the crown); such payments were self-assessed at "drinkings." This duty of payment was primary. But in addition, as at Ipswich, in Suffolk, the merchant guild had its own officers—an alderman and four associates—distinct from the portmen (bailiff, coroner, and others) of the borough. In some towns guilds maintained separate treasuries and rolls. The guild's court was more a tribunal of commercial arbitration than a court of pleas, and the guild had no police or military duties. Finally, in matters of residence and tenure the rules of guild membership were much looser; foreign merchants or even lady residents in an adjacent county might join the guild, though they were excluded from the borough. These distinctions between borough and guild must be firmly maintained; nevertheless, it is true to say that they were aspects of one and the same body, and that during the period of weakness of borough autonomy (prior to Richard I) the handsome grants of privileges to guilds paved the way for fuller town self-government.

Although the formation of boroughs and town communities certainly produced assemblies at an early date (notably the "morning speech" of the merchant guild and the less vigorous portmanmoots, or town assemblies), it was not until the quasi-incorporation of the critical decades 1190–1215 that conciliar bodies appeared to express the common will. These usually elective "councils," frequently with twenty-four members but also with as few as six (as at Oxford), had the widest variety of powers. They would normally be made up of leading merchants. Broadly speaking, they were either advisory, legislative, or administrative. Thus the twelve portmen of Ipswich were "to govern and maintain the borough, to render its judgements, and to ordain and execute all things." The *jurés* (councillors) of Leicester had similar powers. The Northampton council had a vaguer commission to help the mayor in the execution of his business, while the twenty-four at Winchester were to "aid and advise."

Beyond these *jurés* or *echevins* one can sometimes discern a larger body of citizens acting as a group. This larger—perhaps one can say extended—body could and did arrogate to itself the title of "community" (*communitas*), as against the ruling corporation of mayor, reeves, and council. The powers of this larger community were never spelled out in concrete terms; it may be assumed that they were largely advisory. This rather negative view of the town government naturally prevailed at times of civic unrest, from the time of the great rebel Simon de Montfort onward. It is perplexing, since the ruling group was naturally the community that had legal responsibility; perhaps the contrast of "king, lords, and community" or of prelate and officials against the chapters of abbey and cathedral offers an enlightening analogy. However, in most cases the "community" seems to have included both the ruling corporation and the freemen of the borough or city excluded from actual government.

Craft guilds were a mere handful in the twelfth century. Their rapid multiplication in the thirteenth and fourteenth centuries represented an additional and rich element of group life in the boroughs. From the late fourteenth century these guilds were created by the municipal corporation itself, and their main task was to retain the monopoly of manufacture and sale previously exercised by the merchant guild. In fact, the merchant guild, when it did not disappear, simply became a name for the collectivity of crafts. The way to "freedom of the borough" was generally through admittance to a craft; but only in rare cases, and for short intervals, did the craft guilds as such obtain a share in the municipal government. For example, at Beverley, in Yorkshire, they obtained a veto power over alterations in bylaws, and at York a share in the election of the mayor. Generally speaking, the craft guilds were among the most creative forces in the later Middle Ages; spontaneous in origin, they provided good fellowship (in their morning speeches), training, maintenance of standards, security in illness and unemployment, corporate devotion, and theatrical entertainment. In many cases a royal or municipal charter confirmed, if it did not originate, their authority. Conflict hindered any aspirations the guilds might have had to challenge the small groups ruling the towns. Indeed, craft guilds developed their own oligarchies of masters, a development that led to fiercely contentious attempts at creating journeymen guilds (consisting of men who had not achieved the status of "master") at the end of the era.

The nature of internal guild regulations may be illuminated by the ordinance of the London cordwainers of 1271, one of the earliest extant evidences of craft organization. The guild was divided into two groups—the cordwainers proper (*alutarii*) and the workers in "bazen" (*basanarii*)—and each craftsman had to remain in his own group. Cofferers, who worked in cowhide, were excluded from the guild. Apprentices had to be admitted before the mayor and show proof of their good character; each apprentice was required, as in conditions of censorship, to pay two shillings to the city, two shillings to the poor box, and premiums of forty shillings (for cordwainers) and twenty shillings (for workers in bazen). Later ordinances prohibited servants from having apprentices and masters from giving out work to servants in their homes. Cordwainers often had to combine to obtain credit.

Although the craft guilds succeeded only for brief periods and in a limited number of towns in securing control of the town governments, they played a large part in the lives of the inhabitants. Many originated as religious fraternities, and all kept, or developed, some religious activity—from keeping a candle burning before a patron saint to endowing and rebuilding churches and hospitals. Some crafts were primarily commercial and multiple in their wares, such as the grocers; others were primarily industrial, such as the tailors. The former crafts, of course, were the wealthier, as evidenced by the Subsidy Rolls (records of local tax assessments) of 1319.

By the middle of the fourteenth century the distinction between "great" and "lesser" crafts was established; in London the domination of the twelve great livery companies began.[6] These companies, whose masters wore the uniform or "livery" of the guild, were unlike the lesser crafts because they derived their power directly from king and Parliament rather than from the city government. In times of national conflict between kings and their "great" subjects, notably under kings Edward II and Richard II, the companies ranged themselves on one or the other side of the contestants according to internal interest—as in the odd alliance of John of Northampton and John of Gaunt. Moreover, by restricting livery to the most prosperous members, the great crafts facilitated the development in the fifteenth century of subordinate journeymen or yeoman guilds, whose function was approximately that of the modern labor unions. The great crafts of course sought to regulate and control the guilds in their own interests.

The "common council" or "assembly" of the years after 1350 began, no doubt, as an attempt to accommodate the demands of the increasingly organized middling and lesser tradesmen in the "closed circle" of conciliar government as it had grown up in the years of urban enfranchisement. It may also have owed something other than detail (e.g., the use of "speakers" and the *plena potestas*—full power—of representatives to speak for the communities) to the inspiration of the commons in Parliament. The constitutional story is complex and incomplete, owing in part to the faulty preservation of town records. In London, where the records and chronicles are most complete, one can trace the emergence of special assemblies, probably derived ultimately from the ancient folkmoot, or common assembly, in the course of the thirteenth

---

[6] To understand this complex process, see G. Unwin, *The Guilds and Companies of London,* 4th ed. (London, 1963), p. 76ff.

century. Such assemblies, called together by individual summons, afforced the hustings for business of common welfare and selected the chief officers of the city. The police (or watch) system of ward obligation seems to have been the basis of selection, as established in the quotas of 1346. This system was preceded by various experimental forms of assembly in which the ward was almost always the constituency unit. During the reign of Edward II the commoners won a say in the custody of the common seal and also the right of election. An ordinance passed by an "immense" commonalty in 1346 fixed the ward representation (at twelve, eight, or six).

The period 1322–85 was one of increasing tension, occasioned by the pressing claims of the greater guilds to control the electoral machinery. Guild pressures are discernible in the thirteenth century, but it was not until 1312 that temporary guild control of the common council was achieved. After one or two further experiments in this direction, guild control was achieved for the last time in 1376 (with six, four, or two delegates from each guild represented in the assembly, after which control reverted to the wards). From this year too dates the councillors' oath of loyalty. The guild system was, however, associated with the radical wing of aldermen, notably John of Northampton, and when this group was overthrown the wards once again became the electoral units—finally so in 1385. At the same time the common council was brought into greater subjection to the triumphant aldermen. However, the guilds, and by the end of the fifteenth century the liverymen, retained control of the annual elections of officers. The *congregatio* (common council) of London, limited as it was, nevertheless went as far toward democracy as any town government in England. The highest number of members recorded was 528, in a special meeting of 1340; such a number was clearly unwieldy, and after 1346 a figure of 100 to 200 was more usual.

These fourteenth-century developments in London were closely intertwined with national politics, for after 1300 at the latest London was truly the national capital. Hence it was in association with the baronial reform movements of 1311–18 and 1376–88[7] that the main civic upheavals took place. In 1312 it was in the presence of the Lords Ordainer that the representatives of the wards sought to establish responsibility of the aldermen to their constituents. In the same context the crafts asserted their authority in 1313. This authority in limited form, annual election of aldermen, and participation of commoners in aldermanic control were granted in a charter of 1319. This "popular" movement, so closely associated with opposition to the king and his favorites, was abortive. In the 1370s and 1380s the "popular" party tried again. From 1376 to 1383 John of Northampton, a draper, worked with the guilds to over-

[7] See pp. 61 and 65–6.

throw the dominant oligarchy and especially the power of the victuallers. Cheap fish was the key platform. Curiously, this movement was in reaction to the peasants' revolt of 1381, the chief charge against the fishmonger alderman Walter Sibill being his complicity with the rebels. When another victualer, Nicolas Brembre, was elected mayor in 1383, Northampton's national allies deserted him. Although Brembre was to fall victim to the king's enemies in 1388, the flamboyance of Northampton had lost the cause of London reform. Thus municipal and national politics were curiously interwoven.

The establishment of common councils or assemblies to supplement the ordinary council of twelve or twenty-four was characteristic of most English towns in the fourteenth and fifteenth centuries. Judging from such records as survive, most were merely extensions of the oligarchy. At Norwich thirty to fifty *meliores et discrecciores* ("better" and "more discreet" men) were summoned from the four leets (the equivalent of wards), in addition to the twenty-four elected councillors; this larger council was reduced in the fourteenth century to twenty-four, and the guilds, as in London, won a share in their composition. In the fifteenth century Norwich was given a constitution specifying twenty-four aldermen and a common council of sixty, both elected by wards; further, the general body of freemen won a share in the election of officials. Lynn likewise emerged in the fifteenth century with two councils—the twenty-four and also the common council elected by the nine constabularies, or town divisions. The widespread adoption of this "two tier" system reflected the growing unrest of the community; the councils represented attempts to accommodate, at worst stifle, the interests of the guildsmen. So important was this development that when local agreement did not produce results, royal charter or parliamentary grant was invoked to effect the change. The system was never universal, and the extent of "popular" participation varied enormously. Yet its evolution shows that local communities were thinking along the same lines as the king and his advisers at the center.

It is a widely held view that the continental medieval town was a "collective fief." In the sense that the city and borough, and to a lesser extent the merchant town, had immunities and obligations vis-à-vis king and county, this is true of the English town too. Moreover, the gradual shift in some towns from royal or baronial reeves to mayor and council as chief court and governing body is an apt illustration of this fact. One might say that the reeves or mayor of the full-fledged medieval town constituted an elected, often repeatedly reelected, lord of the collective manor. Because of the richness of its records, London provides the best study of the relations among the leading citizens, mayor and aldermen. It was in times of crisis—notably the reign of Richard II—that the full implication of these relations was manifested.

Underpinning the constitutional fact of city, borough, and town was the economic activity of merchant, tradesman, craftsman, and laborer. The merchant traders were the most important single group in the town, and as we have seen, the merchant guild played a key role in the evolution of most urban constitutions. The commerce of the guild was usually local, for international trade was channeled through the great fairs (loosely controlled by the nearby town or city), rather than through the town markets. However, the variety of local products grew steadily, and their manufacture and sale in shop and market reflected a growing wealth in the nation as a whole. Even in the case of national and international trade, the merchants normally belonged to some guild—as evidenced by the connection between the guild mercers (cloth dealers) and the Merchant Adventurers, who handled the international trade in cloth.

The craftsmen and laborers followed fast on the heels of the merchant traders. But they were a much less specifically urban group than the traders. In many respects crafts could be better conducted in rural areas—in villages, by rivers, or at the site of raw materials. The miners of coal, tin, iron, and lead, for instance, were of necessity nonurban, and many towns saw to it that noxious secondary crafts were kept outside their walls. The most highly organized and independent of these miners, the tin workers, were a predominantly rural group located in Devon and Cornwall, though because of administrative requirements the towns of those counties were part of the tin-mining districts.

Apart from the extractive industries, however, there was a tension between county and town in English manufacturing. The towns offered markets and freedom; but they also meant more intense regulation of prices, wages, hours, standards, and qualifications. Hence there was always a tendency for manufacture to escape to the villages, where regulation was less severe. This struggle between town and countryside was particularly notable in the case of the cloth industry the greatest of England's, as of most other medieval nations', economic enterprises.

Early English clothmaking seems to have been largely urban. From records of payments to the king we learn of weavers guilds in such centers as London, Winchester, and Oxford. Local "laws of weavers" show that they were excluded from the governing bodies of the towns and had indeed to give up their craft to become freemen. The standards of cloth production were the first to be nationally regulated, as Magna Carta clause 35 (1215 version) and the Assize of Cloth (1197) bear witness. While the bulk of the cloth produced for the home market was of a coarse variety, high-quality cloth from such centers as Stamford ("scarlets" and "blues") and Lincoln ("scarlets" and "greens") won fame in Europe as well as supplying royal and magnate households. The first peak of the urban cloth industry seems to have been reached shortly after 1250. The records leave no doubt of a rapid decline and actual depopulation in the cloth-manufacturing towns in the following century. The probability is that by restrictions and regulations the English clothmasters had priced themselves out of the market, but there is evidence that a rural industry, at least partially offsetting the decline, took their place.

The urban cloth trade revived in the early years of Edward III's reign. In fact, Edward helped its revival by a series of measures supporting the settlement of foreign clothworkers in England. With the multiplication of guilds and the growth of Parliament in the fifteenth century, there was a fresh wave of regulation on both a local and a national scale. Both kinds of regulation were partly designed to fulfill the purpose of the earliest controls: protection of the government's financial interest and of the consumer or middleman. Such rules forbade the excessive stretching of cloth (a process known as "tentering") and attempted to establish national units of measurement. Statutes and local ordinances battled against a thousand ruses on the part of dishonest merchants and craftsmen: *caveat emptor* was not a medieval slogan. Other laws of injunction sought to settle the rivalries of interest and prejudice that arose among merchants, craftsmen, and journeymen and between different towns or between foreign and native industries. Both social and economic considerations led to sumptuary laws prescribing different qualities of cloth for different income groups. National interest led to the prohibition of cloth imports in the fourteenth century and to the banning of a great variety of imported goods in the fifteenth century. Only rarely, as in the case of the Yarmouth monopoly of the herring industry, did Parliament step in to defy a local interest.

The control of the economy by those with the largest stake in it—the merchants and wealthy craftsmen—was assured doubly by their representation in town councils and in Parliament. The merchant guilds exercised this control to keep the crafts in subjection and to outlaw the association of journeymen and apprentices. In times of scarcity, as after the Black Death (1348–9), the prices of both labor and commodities were regulated. The success of these controls must not be overestimated. All forms of medieval regulation were liable to widespread evasion. Hence craft guilds were able to develop their own courts, and journeymen were able to form their own fraternities. The rudiments of national regulation, which occupied much of Parliament's time in the last century of the Middle Ages, never did more than modify the essentially local, autonomous nature of English industrial life.

The effect of guild regulation of industry and trade on the economy was undoubtedly restrictive. Yet the view of eighteenth-century laissez-faire economists—that all restriction on free competition was basically retrograde—needs qualification. Moreover, in a society organized into highly defensive groups, it was essential that merchants and craftsmen band together to protect their interests. Central government encouraged this development for its own purposes. Further, some of the industries, such as the booming late medieval cloth industry and the stannaries (the organizations of tin miners in southwestern England), escaped overzealous local regulation. This intensively regulated trade served medieval England well. Even the notion of a late medieval decline has not stood up to modern investigation, though it still has its champions. Perhaps the most telling evidence of growing prosperity was the threefold increase in taxable wealth between 1334 and the early sixteenth century.[8] This must count against individual cases of declining town population (e.g., York and Winchester) and deserted villages. In this process London and the south were the principal gainers. In city, town, and guild, in fairs and national bodies like the staplers, the men who sold raw wool overseas and the merchant adventurers, a viable and generally thriving commercial life took root and contributed to the richness of English life. So powerful were these staplers, who were located at cities from the late fourteenth century, that they were a force that had to be reckoned with in national politics.

The relation of local and national economic entities to royal finance, and indeed to royal policy in general, has been illuminated by many writers.[9] In the years 1272–1345 English financial activity was dominated by Italian creditors, whose enormous loans were secured by special privileges and liens on the customs revenue and subsidies of laymen and churchmen. Despite their enormous reserves, these Italian firms—the Frescobaldi, the Bardi, and the Peruzzi—were eventually bankrupted by a combination of Italian and European (especially English) ventures. They had been essential to the early years of the Hundred Years' War. Thereafter Edward III had to rely on English syndicates, who based their credit primarily on London but also on northern and East Anglian enterprise. These English syndicates drew on the whole gamut of European fiscal activity. They relied heavily on the rate of discount at which they could acquire royal obligations. This meant that for a lesser sum than that of the original guarantee, they could gain the right to collect taxes, customs, and debts. Leading figures among these royal creditors were Walter Cheriton and William de la Pole, the founder of one of the greatest late medieval aristocratic dynasties. But these English creditors in turn got their fingers burned. The later stages of the Hundred Years' War had to be financed by war profits, London merchants, and wealthy lords. The wool staplers entered the scene after 1407 and became regular creditors after 1430. In fact,

[8] R. S. Schofield, "The Geographical Distribution of Wealth in England, 1334–1649," *Economic History Review,* 2nd series, vol. XVIII (1965).
[9] See the articles of E. Miller and E. B. Frydte in *The Cambridge Economic History of England,* vol. III (Cambridge, 1966), and bibliographies.

the whole staple system was to a large degree the product of royal financial needs. But great magnates, of whom Cardinal Beaufort is the best known, rivaled the staplers as royal creditors in the fifteenth century. Individuals and towns were also pressed into the service of royal needs; excessive pressure of this type contributed to the opposition to Richard II and thus to his downfall. It should be stressed, however, that belief in the king's ability to rule and to make gains for his subjects was fundamental to royal credit. Hence it was that Henry VI was unable to maintain the flow of supplies that had helped his father to become the last great hero of the Hundred Years' War.

Chapter Four
CHURCH STRUCTURES

The popular, and not entirely inaccurate, conception of the medieval church is one of an elaborate, wealthy, and rigid hierarchy ranging from the ever more magnificent curia at Rome to the humblest parish and hermitage. It is also a conception of an all-embracing complex of law and custom directing the lives of clergy and laity alike. This picture is to a certain extent the product of the experience of the post-Tridentine church (i.e., the highly centralized church that emerged from the sixteenth century Council of Trent) and vague recollections of the Spain of the Inquisition. The facts are somewhat different and conform more closely to the lay society depicted in Chapters Two and Three. True, there was more hierarchy and more system in the ecclesiastical than in the lay order. But this "descending" structure was tempered by the existence of a multiplicity of individuals and groups busily involved in protecting their privileges and fulfilling their purposes. Moreover, any idea of a rigid conformity is quickly dispelled by an acquaintance with the medieval satires on church practices, which reached the level of high art in the works of Chaucer and Boccaccio. The monolith of Catholic Christendom dissolves on closer scrutiny.

The medieval church was very much in the world. From pope to prior, consciousness of the value of land and of rights in land was universal. In fact, the history of a church or monastery can be written, much as that of a lay community, largely in terms of land holding, of leases, and of exactions; indeed, the story of the papacy has of late been most fully explored in terms of taxes and administration.[1]

Yet in spite of the accumulation of such evidence, the student should perhaps give priority to the ideals and teachings of the church. For it was in these, and

---

[1] W. E. Lunt, *Financial Relations of the Papacy with England*, 2 vols. (Cambridge, Mass., 1939, 1962); G. Mollat, *The Popes at Avignon, 1305–78* (London, 1949); G. Barraclough, *The Medieval Papacy* (London, 1968).

not in the temporal preoccupations shared in common with king, baron, and peasant, that the church contributed most profoundly to the evolution of mankind. A brief account of these ideas is presented in the next chapter in the context of medieval cultural history.

Rome

The fact that the English church was both de jure and de facto a province of the Catholic church centered in Rome appears in a number of ways. Papal confirmation of episcopal appointments, conferring of privileges and dispensations, provisions, translations, taxation, judicial settlements, and so forth, were a regular part of English life. Pilgrimages to Rome were of daily occurrence and took precedence over all others. Canon law, an ever growing body of biblical, patristic, conciliar, and papal decisions, first compiled authoritatively by the canon lawyer Gratian (early twelfth century) and taught with elaborate commentaries and glosses, was as binding in England as in any other part of Christendom. English church legislation represented but the local implementation of universal rules. As will be noted below, such local regulations varied by commission or omission from those of other countries—as in the matter of lay responsibility for naves of churches—and there were local rites and traditions. This was English "custom." It is not an adequate reason for regarding the medieval English church as "Anglican" in any post-Reformation sense.[2]

The extent of centralization of power in Rome has been the subject of general works in such areas as law and finance; but general surveys of papal jurisdiction, the operations of legates *a latere* (cardinals dispatched by the pope), English attendance at general church councils, and many other related topics are badly needed.

Papal legates, English cardinals, and even an English pope bound the church in England ever closer to Rome in the middle of the twelfth century. Moreover, papal judges delegate adjudicated English legal cases, and English canonists contributed to the corpus of church law. Papal overseeing of the English episcopacy took many forms. The archbishops usually went to Rome to receive the pallium (a vestment symbolizing papal plenitude). Through this and through papal confirmation of the election of bishops, the English church of the twelfth century was closely supervised. There was resentment at the sending of papal legates, but this was resolved to a large degree by the conferring of legatine powers on English prelates. The knotty question of Canterbury's

---

[2] Maitland laid that ghost to rest in his critique of Stubbs' brilliant but biased researches. F. W. Maitland, *Canon Law in the Church of England* (London, 1898); W. Stubbs, "Law Administered in the English Church" (London, Ecclesiastical Courts Commission, 1883).

claim to precedence in status over York was solved by giving York equal rights; St. David's of Wales was made dependent on Canterbury, but St. Andrew's of Scotland was freed from York. Papal overseeing was notable in relations with religious houses; for example, ninety-six letters from the papacy were directed to St. Albans alone in the years 1122–98.

Not only did England receive the full force of Roman legislation and Bolognese studies in the twelfth century; in return Englishmen contributed to the international code of law out of all proportion to their numbers: over two-fifths of the papal letters in decretal collections were of English provenance. Nevertheless, the existence of an *Ecclesia Anglicana* with its own identity and practices was generally accepted. The autonomy of this local church may perhaps be compared with the position of palatine, semiautonomous earldoms, such as Chester, in the secular order. Its independence was largely due to two institutions: the monarchy and the archbishopric of Canterbury.

The Norman and Angevin kings set definite limits on the extent to which popes could directly intervene in the affairs of their subjects, lay and ecclesiastical; in this they combined Anglo-Saxon insularity of tradition with a fierce Norman sense of possession. Z. N. Brooke has shown how English kings exercised these rights and surmounted the crises brought on by conscientious bishops.[3] The king's consent was required at every step of the exercise of papal authority. Dedicated archbishops could and did challenge royal authority, or traditional insularity, or laymen's arrogance in their appeals to Rome. But throughout the Middle Ages Roman pontiffs usually were sufficiently aware of the realities of power to prefer accommodation with the monarch to direct confrontation in alliance with idealistic clerics.

The conflict between Henry II and Thomas à Becket, Archbishop of Canterbury (1162–70), was the most dramatic of all these crises, the more so since the principal participants, Henry and Becket, had been close friends and since the twelfth-century biographers have left a personal record unmatched by any medieval successor for its individual interest and vitality.

The issue in the 1160s was, in personal terms, whether Archbishop Thomas could defend from Henry's wrath the liberties of the church as he conceived them, or, in less personal terms, whether clerical privilege such as appeals to Rome, the right of the church to try its own members in criminal cases, and the right to excommunicate subjects of the English king could stand up to Angevin despotism. In wider terms still, it was a conflict between Christendom and the political community of England. Only Thomas himself, it would appear, wanted a fight to the finish—even the papacy urged caution and compromise. The finish toward which Thomas struggled was inevitably his own.

[3] Z. N. Brooke, *The English Church and the Papacy* (Cambridge, England, 1931).

The issues for which he fought were principally the rights of clerical courts, particularly in the trial of criminal clergy, the free election of bishops, and freedom of appeals to Rome. It was Henry II's insistence on the formulation of the royal "customs" governing church–state relations of his grandfather in the Constitution of Clarendon (1164) that, in view of Becket's character, made a conflict *à outrance* inevitable. As so frequently happened in such cases, Henry used base means to bring Becket to his knees: he tried to "frame" Becket on charges of misconduct during that chancellorship (1154–62) in which he had actually served Henry vigorously in restoring royal power in a strife-rent realm. Becket had to flee in 1164. His exile ended in 1170 on a note of reconciliation so vague as to be attributable only to the survival of the two protagonists' mutual respect. The murder of Becket forced Henry to yield on many points, notably the right of the clergy to be tried in church courts (known later as "benefit of clergy"). But both Henry and his successors retained a large stake in the governance of the English church. For example, while canon law required the election of bishops by the free vote of their respective cathedral communities, in point of fact the English monarchs controlled such elections, with occasional papal initiatives, by including the names of their own candidates in the writs licensing elections. And while the royal courts ostensibly gave up the right to try criminal clergy, such devices as the "writ of prohibition," which stopped trials in church courts if the case involved property, brought many clergy before the common law courts. Nevertheless, ties with Rome were strengthened, notably in the reception of canon law, in papal jurisdiction and legations, and in the trial of criminal clergy by churchmen alone.

The story of papal-English relations from Becket to the Reformation is, reduced to simple terms, one of ever growing legal power on the pope's side but of actual lay intervention on an increasing scale. Papal control was expressed in direct orders (through letters or legates), taxation, and provisions (nomination to church offices). These initiatives were closely interwoven. Thus the summit of theoretical control, the making of England into a papal fief in 1213, also involved new payments to Rome. Moreover, papal nuncios, with or without full (plenary) powers, who participated in the government of the country or the advising of the king in times of minority and crisis, were also usually concerned with taxation and legislation.

The reign of Henry III was the heyday of the plenary papal nuncio. The conditions following John's submission to Pope Innocent III, the long minority of the king, and then Henry's deep piety and loyalty to Rome coincided with the rule of masterful and brilliant popes. The story is complex. Otho's legation as papal nuncio in the 1240s, in which he at times presided over the English church, led to considerable legislation and taxation; but there was no question of authoritarian imposition. All manner of means, such as provincial councils, diocesan synods, ad hoc assemblies of bishops and other clergy, and above all negotiation with individual diocesans and heads of houses, were employed. The question of consent to papal taxes was raised in acute form, and the agreement to a tax by English delegates at the Council of Lyons (1245) was a small step toward parliamentary church government. King and Council were drawn into the negotiations as interested parties, so much so that papal demands for money in the 1240s proved a precedent for those of the king in the 1250s. Per contra, opposition to the former provided precedents for resistance to the latter. The visits of Otho and his successors led to a testing, hardening, and evolution of English church institutions, notably the introduction of an elective element in convocations (the assemblies of the clergy of Canterbury and York provinces). The first *systematic* use of representation on a national scale was in the church rather than in the kingdom.

The legations of Otho and, later, of Ottobuono (1266–8) constituted a high tide of papal direction. The latter, during his visit, helped the king's claims to tax the English church. Representing both pope and College of Cardinals, these men exercised a generally beneficient influence on English church life.

Papal influence was great not only in laws and taxes; it also extended to appointments and provisions. Bishops, usually superior in quality to those chosen by chapter or king, were "appointed"; an outstanding example was Edmund Rich, Archbishop of Canterbury, 1233–40, one of the most saintly, learned, and universally respected of English archbishops. In a period of learned and able archbishops, six out of seven were in effect papal appointees. Provisions to cathedral prebends (valuable cathedral offices with appurtenant land holdings) and to other benefices by Rome also became a major practice for the first time, exciting a minimum of opposition. The acceptance of papal direction was largely due to the beneficient form it took and to the care with which lay patrons' rights were respected.

Papal legislation and jurisdiction were strongly felt in the thirteenth century, for it was then that the Decretals were codified, commented on, and extended. The full organization of the papal chancery and camera furthered their vigorous execution. Apart from the aforementioned legates *a latere,* the most effective application of canon law was by way of papal judges delegate. A monastery claiming an advowson (the right to appoint the rector of a church), a bishop seeking to enforce visitation rights (that is, to visit and reform churches in his diocese), or a rector deprived of his tithe,[4] might seek a judicial tribunal appointed in Rome, which promised speedy and final settlement. As in secular

---

[4] The tenth of all produce of the parishioners, which formed the basic stipend of the rector.

law, delays were in fact costly and aggravating, so that a settlement by way of compromise between litigants was of extremely frequent occurrence.

Edward I was far less complaisant than his father, and at the same time the caliber of the popes during his reign was poorer. He conducted strenuous quarrels with archbishops and popes, curtailed church endowments (by his statute *de religiosis*), and only at the end of his reign turned to Rome for help against domestic and foreign enemies. Against this, he was a crusader and a formally devout son of the church, with many splendid benefactions to his name.

In the fourteenth century, when the popes fled first into France and then into the adjacent city of Avignon (not a remote exile, but at the hub of Europe), partly as a result of French royal pressures, and partly to escape turbulent Roman politics, and when hostilities between England and France deepened, the question of papal power became more acute. The papal curia constantly extended its claims in matters of jurisdiction, taxation, and appointments over the churches of Christendom, largely in an effort to finance the recovery of papal control of the papal states. On the other hand, English kings, although impeccably orthodox, were leading an embattled "community of the realm" in costly and lengthy warfare. Hence the growing papal claims were countered by legislation and evasion on the part of king and Parliament.

The advantages of papal direction are to be seen in the working of the constitution *cum ex eo*, whereby papal initiative worked to increase the education of the English clergy. Other papal interventions were of less certain value or effectiveness. Examples were the defense of the friars against such enemies of their privileges as Richard FitzRalph, Archbishop of Armagh (1348–60), and the university authorities, the insistence on the right of Franciscan monks to hold property, the unification and strengthening of the general chapter of the Benedictine monks, and the encouragement of the latter's university affiliations. Decrees against pluralism in the cure of souls (i.e., a single cleric having more than one benefice—the basic clerical holding—without instituting an ordained vicar) had but a partial success. Though it could not be rooted out, pluralism was reduced considerably and was kept under loose control.

The system of papal provisions was greatly extended by the Avignon popes. The yield of annates (the first year's revenue of a benefice), "services" (payments of a wide variety to the officials of the papal court for privileges and appointments), and allied taxes helped replenish the ever empty papal coffers, but these and other measures provoked a growing opposition, which can be measured in the complaints of both individual critics and the commons. These led eventually to the parliamentary legislation of 1351, 1353, 1390, and 1393, directed against papal appointments and jurisdiction, more a reflection of rising nationalism than of real hurt. Lay domination of episcopal and lower clerical appointments actually increased; moreover, aliens figured largely only in lucrative prebendal appointments. The king tended to use the new legislation as a lever in negotiations with Rome, rather than in a consistent way. In spite of royal opportunism, the quantity of alien provisors dwindled and all but disappeared in the last medieval century. National autonomy, whether hurtful or beneficial, was the most notable feature of the pre-Reformation church.

The English influence on the papal curia and on canon law also declined markedly. For a brief while, at the councils of Pisa (1409) and Constance (1414–17), English bishops—notably Bishop Robert Hallum of Salisbury—played an important role in the task of reform and reunification of the universal church. Moreover, as part of the settlement of 1417–18, whereby he emerged as the head of a united church, Pope Martin V agreed to greater English autonomy and greater English participation in curial government. In its inbred Italian character the reunified papacy after 1417 was almost as "alien" as had been the French papacy of the Avignon period. And the Italian popes used their relations with England to promote prince bishops like Henry Beaufort, Bishop of Winchester, and John Kemp, Archbishop of Canterbury, to the cardinalate, not to mention humiliating Henry Chichele, Archbishop of Canterbury (1415–43), by forcing him to go against his better judgment in pressing for the repeal of the Statute of Praemunire (the law limiting appeals to Rome). Hence a mood of stubborn nationalism prevailed in England. When the later fifteenth-century popes sought to tax the English clergy for the defense of Christendom against the Turks, the English church leaders—notably Archbishop Thomas Bourgchier of Canterbury (1454–86), in 1464—responded with appreciation of the need but a clear indication that English clerical taxation must be through the medium of the monarchy, if at all. As one writer has put it, the English attitude was one of "passive recognition of the pope's leadership . . . faint acknowledgement of his right to obedience . . . dislike of taxation and . . . effective dominion of the king. . . ."[5]

It should not be thought that the English nationalism, xenophobia, and antipapalism cut off all traffic with Rome. Englishmen went to Rome as ambassadors and proctors (i.e., legal representatives of clients); petitions and appeals flowed into the papal courts; and legates (though none of the caliber of the thirteenth-century giants) and papal tax collectors came to England in considerable numbers. Judgments and dispensations streamed from Rome to English clients. An English proctor at Rome could count on a steady and lucrative business from both clergy and laity. The ordinary, common intercourse between Englishmen and the Roman curia has always to be kept in

[5] F. R. H. Du Boulay, "The Fifteenth Century," in C. H. Lawrence, *The English Church and the Papacy in the Middle Ages* (New York, 1965), p. 219.

mind as a contrast to insular legislation and dislike of "foreign" taxation. Simple devotion to the Chair of St. Peter existed alongside a temper in which a seemingly harmless papal order restricting the length of shoes could elicit the comment of a contemporary orthodox observer that "the pope's curse would not kill a fly." The fact that the English clergy paid over twice as much to the king as to Rome perhaps serves as a measure of the actual situation in the fifteenth century.

The Episcopate

The archbishop of Canterbury was primate of England. Yet York, the head of the second province, exercised an independence, beneath pope and king, that reduced Canterbury's claim to one of mere precedence— that is, of superiority in rank rather than authority. After the twelfth century Canterbury's supremacy over York depended on legatine commission rather than on any institutional authority, and with the conferment of legatine authority on York in the fourteenth century, even this power was lost. Canterbury's control of Wales (St. David's) was firm, but in Scotland papal intervention prevented York from dominating St. Andrew's. In general, apart from the legatine authority, the pope successfully opposed Canterbury's efforts to establish a British hegemony. The archbishops usually consecrated their bishops, carried out visitations, enjoyed custody of spiritualities in time of vacancies (i.e., had partial control of a diocese's wealth during a vacancy), and heard appeals from episcopal courts. In addition, they often played a major role in England's political life as chancellors, diplomats, and members of the royal Council.

The bishops were primarily administrators, in spite of constant exhortations by popes and moralists to preach. Though canon law required the election of bishops by cathedral chapters, in point of fact royal nomination or papal provision was usually the decisive factor. Papal influence in the choice of bishops, which reached a high point in the first half of the thirteenth century, gradually declined as rising royal and conciliar influence smoothed the way for the Reformation. This is not to say that the bishops grew markedly worse in quality. There was a lack of great spiritual leadership in the final century of the Middle Ages; but this perhaps reflected more a general decline in clerical spirituality than the method of election. In any case, if less active in reform, less learned, and less saintly than their predecessors, these later bishops were usually efficient and educated.

The bishops were key figures in both church and state. Of course, some of their state duties (e.g., military service as tenants in chief) were with few exceptions discharged by deputies, but attendance at court, Council, and Parliament, diplomatic activity on the king's behalf, and service in the various law courts must have occupied much of their time. As London emerged as the national capital, it was convenient to have a town house or palace there; many of these were situated among the houses of lay magnates on the road between the "City of London" and Westminster Palace. The bishops' cathedral duties were largely performed by such officials as chancellor and dean, while diocesan government was often in the hands of leading administrators and judges called "officials," archdeacons, and a host of supporting officers. Nevertheless, whether as royal advisers and officers or as ultimate directors of the national church, the bishops were key figures in the life of the nation.

The thirteenth-century episcopacy was probably the most distinguished of all periods for the learning, piety, and ability of its leaders: it was also a period of vigorous legislation and organization of subsidiary organs of the church. After 1327 the curialist bishops began to predominate: never absent even in earlier centuries, these royal servants for whom promotion in the church hierarchy was reward were rivaled only by the protégés of the powerful aristocracy. The legal formality of papal provision hid the actual fact of royal, or later conciliar, choice. The worldliness and absenteeism of bishops grew increasingly in the years immediately preceding the Reformation. Yet even at their worst, bishops were usually intelligent and active men, and in the gray days of the fifteenth century they were busy founding schools and colleges. The English bishops were overwhelmingly "secular" (i.e., not monks or friars) after the middle of the twelfth century, though regular clergy were often appointed to outlying sees like those in Wales, or to northern sees, such as Durham and Carlisle.

The contrasting types of English bishops may be illustrated by a brief account of the saintly Hugh of Lincoln (twelfth century), the learned Robert Grosseteste, also of Lincoln (thirteenth century), and the administrator Thomas Langley of Durham (fifteenth century). Hugh (c.1140–1200) came to England first as prior of Henry II's Carthusian foundation of Witham, one of the few English monasteries following the extremely rigorous rules of the Charterhouse in southern France. He was of noble Burgundian family, educated by a community of canons regular, where he made his first profession, and was already noted for his severe self-discipline and his diplomatic talent when summoned to England by Henry II. As prior of Witham and subsequently as bishop of Lincoln, he handled the turbulent king and his family with firmness and tact. Hugh's virile personality, which made his austerities all the more remarkable, lent him a fierce energy in all the manifold activities— directing a priory, ruling a diocese, and acting as diplomat or counselor to the king—to which he was called. He made constant war on the typical abuses of the medieval church—laicization, pluralism, absenteeism, ignorance, and immorality. He did much of this in person rather than by letter or legislation. At times he ignored royal commands in order to carry out his obligations to the sick and the poor, but usually he smoothed things over by his diplomatic eloquence. As a judge (often with jurisdiction delegated by the pope), he was in great demand. His fulminations against corrupt officials, whether clerical or lay, often led to reform or removal. Yet it was his ascetic life, with its rigid adherence to the rules of the strictest of orders and frequent scourgings, together with his numerous alleged miracles, that led to his canonization in 1219.

Robert Grosseteste (c.1168–1253) was the greatest of the scholar bishops who adorned the thirteenth-century church. He was of humble origin. One of the first, and certainly one of the most brilliant, of Oxford University students and teachers, he produced scholastic studies in biblical and scientific matters that were seminal and profound. As teacher and bishop, he welcomed and helped the often unpopular mendicant orders that had recently arrived in England, the Dominicans in 1221, and the Franciscans in 1224. As bishop of Lincoln (1235–53) he had oversight of Oxford's affairs, and his sympathetic attitude did much to ensure that university's remarkable independence. He ran a well-ordered diocese and fought hard for church rights against the king and court, yet he was willing to defy the pope on a matter of principle. Through constitutions (laws for his diocese) and visitations he promoted education and uprightness in his clergy and warred against pluralism and absenteeism. He was a great fighter and a devoted friend, influencing church and state through his contacts with men of power and his utter lack of subservience.

Thomas Langley (died 1437) is an outstanding example of the educated, hard-working, late medieval curialist bishop. He rose to high political office through the channels of baronial and Lancastrian patronage. The accession of Henry VI in 1399 led to his swift promotion: from secretary to keeper of the privy seal and from keeper to chancellor, a position that he relinquished in 1407, until his reappointment in 1417. As the royal "first minister" he served the Lancastrian kings ably and was a strong supporter of the government during Henry VI's minority. Between 1418 and 1420 he enjoyed a near viceregal position, but in later years he was overshadowed by great magnates such as Cardinal Beaufort and Duke Humphrey of Gloucester, the king's uncle and Protector of the Realm during his minority. As bishop of Durham (1406–37) he was also head of a semiautonomous palatinate; he ruled his patrimony vigorously and well, defending its privileges from severe assaults both within (from, for example, William Ewer, a tenant who sought to enlist royal power against the bishop's authority) and without (from the Scots). His diocesan duties, in view of his high political rank, were largely deputed to the usual officials. However, he not only made good appointments; he also kept a watchful eye on diocesan affairs, making frequent visits and at least one full-scale visitation. Hence, while he must be classified with those curialists who were the favorite targets of late medieval reformers, he actually kept his bishopric in a thriving, if not spiritually lively, condition.

The bishop's household was much like that of the king or lay magnate. Despite large annual incomes—ranging, from land alone, from Winchester's £3,000 per annum to Rochester's £183 per annum (1291 evaluation)—the bishops were continually in debt. The reason was simple: their revenues were far from being fully realized, a fact that led to often repeated legislation against nonpayment of rents and tithes. Expenses were high. Payments had to be made to pope and king. Vast feasts and lavish hospitality were expected. A hierarchy of clerical and lay officials had to be paid—chaplains, clerks, auditors, bailiffs, squires, and sergeants, to name but a few. Then there was the upkeep of manors and payments for immense trains of carts and horses (for bishops had to perambulate like kings and magnates). It is no wonder that many bishops were deeply in debt to Italian, and later native, moneylenders. Men like Beaufort, who was able to pile up a fortune and even finance (at interest) whole military campaigns, were rare indeed. In fact, Beaufort is an extraordinary figure in other respects, unequaled in wealth, magnificence, and political power by any other medieval bishop.

Convocations and Synods

The convocations of Canterbury and York, perhaps best considered as two branches of one institution, were the supreme lawgiving bodies in the English church. The only times the two assemblies met together was during the visits of papal nuncios from Rome. The more usual and by the thirteenth century regular meetings of separate provincial convocations were associated with the rise of Parliament, which they encouraged and drew encouragement from. The king's writ to the archbishops usually set the summons of such assemblies in motion, and from the fourteenth century this seemed to be the rule.

Representatives of chapters and diocesan clergy came to the convocations to reinforce the bishops and abbots. Chapters were first represented in 1225, and diocesan clergy in 1256. This practice, spurred by the refusal of taxation by a nonrepresentative convocation in 1283, became normal after 1300. Parliamentary influence—especially as the *praemunientes* clause, which ordered the summoning of representative clergy to Parliament, became a dead letter—is obvious, for from then on, representation had to be in convocation rather than in Parliament. True, the convocation did not acquire the initiating power of the lay commons; but in certain features, such as corporate deliberation, a speakership (the "prolocutor"), and a system of subcommittees, it rivaled or excelled the latter body. From the king's point of view taxation was clearly the main motive for the summoning of convocation; but in the minds of the archbishops legislation was probably uppermost. In neither sphere was the assembly noteworthy for originality; it tended to follow tamely in the footsteps of the curia at Rome in the one matter, and of Parliament in the other.

The representation of dioceses in convocation was as dependent on the "community of the diocese," reflected in the age-old diocesan synods, as the lay representation in Parliament was dependent on the "community of shire and borough." According to the Durham constitution of 1312, diocesan synods included all beneficeholders, archdeacons, priests, vicars, and chaplains. Yet such full representation was far from the rule. These diocesan synods often considered taxation demands from the crown as well as dealing with "internal" business. The latter included a wide variety of homiletic, educational, and moral legislation,[6] which reflected on the whole the monolithic character of the church, as reorganized by the Lateran councils of the twelfth and thirteenth centuries, rather than the enterprise of local bodies.

Diocesan Officers

The convocations and diocesan synods represented the element of collaboration in the church, however limited by hierarchical notions. But the main body of government and jurisdiction belonged to the bishops, their officers, and the staff and courts of those officers.

Strictly episcopal powers (e.g., ordination of clergy and consecration of churches) could be delegated only to clergy of episcopal status. This posed a difficult question, since the large body of curialist bishops spent most, or even all, of their time in the royal court. Two kinds of bishops were appointed from at least the early thirteenth century to carry out these functions: suffragan bishops and bishops *in partibus infidelium* (that is, bishops appointed to areas that were not Christianized). The duty of preaching was only too often neglected, a sin duly castigated by critics like Thomas Gascoigne, the combative fifteenth-century chancellor of Oxford University.

The most important agent of the bishop (though without specifically episcopal powers) was the archdeacon. His office dates back to Anglo-Saxon times, but he does not emerge as an official with distinct powers and often a definite area of authority (hence the need for more than one archdeacon in a diocese) until after the Norman Conquest. In fact, widespread territorial subdivision dates only from Henry II's reign. The archdeaconries often coincided with the secular counties. The archdeacons were accorded judicial powers, including

[6] C. R. Cheney, *English Synodalia of the Thirteenth Century* (Oxford, 1941).

the right to conduct visitations, though this practice declined in the fourteenth century and then essentially disappeared. They often supplemented rural deans (see below) as heads of rural chapters. There was considerable variety in their terms of appointment and in their relation to cathedral chapters. But one thing is certain: in the absence of the bishop they gathered, or had delegated, to themselves an immense number of administrative and judicial functions. In certain large archdeaconries, like Richmond in the province of York, they had vast powers, being quasibishops who held courts and appointed commissions. Some aspects of the archdeacons' jurisdiction were specifically theirs; other parts were arrogated in the later thirteenth century from the rural deaneries and chapters. But it is a sad fact that the archdeacons of the later Middle Ages were known as grasping extortioners, and that many of them were more involved in royal or capitular business than in diocesan administration.

The vicar-general, appointed temporarily in the fourteenth century and as a regular officer in the fifteenth century, had all the powers of the bishop except those requiring episcopal orders. In Hamilton Thompson's words, the vicar-general

was empowered to receive the oaths of obedience from the incumbents of benefices whom he instituted, to issue dispensations for non-residence and letters dismissory for orders, to summon and hold diocesan synods, to collect and receive Peter's Pence [a payment to Rome dating from Anglo-Saxon times] and all sums of money due to the bishop in virtue of his church, to absolve and reconcile persons excommunicated in cases reserved to the bishop, to examine, discuss, and terminate elections of heads of religious houses, and to confirm such elections and provide for the installation of persons elected, or if necessary to annul them; to collect and receive fruits of recent benefices, to arrange for ordinations and commit their celebration to suitable bishops, to examine presentation to benefices and institute presentees, to deprive incumbents or usurpers of benefices, to admit the purgation of the bishop's prisoners and deliver them from jail, and to execute and return royal writs.[7]

The "official," sometimes identified with the vicar-general, was the principal delegate of the bishop in all "nonequitable" judicial matters. His court (the "consistory court") was a prominent part of the administrative machinery. The official's or vicar-general's jurisdiction was, of course, subordinate to the bishop's own court, though no appeal lay from the former to the latter.

Another very important officer of the diocese was the sequestrator-general, first mentioned in 1265. His duties closely paralleled those of the royal escheator, the officer who took charge of estates that through lack of heirs or forfeiture came into the king's hands. The custody of incumbents too old or

---

[7] A. H. Thompson, *The English Clergy* (Oxford, 1947), pp. 47–8.

incompetent to perform their duties and the inquiry into dilapidations (the decay or neglect of church buildings and furnishings) came within his purview. He also had oversight of testamentary matters and occasionally audited accounts of executors. He has been called the " chief collector of the archbishop's spiritual revenues." In 1311 William of Kelloe was appointed sequestrator-general in Durham, with powers to impose and relax sequestrations (suspension of income), grant probate of wills, and so on. Bishop Thomas Langley had sequestrators in each archdeanery in Durham, with special powers in testamentary cases. Sometimes these officials had the title of "commissaries-general." In some degree they superseded the archdeacons in the later Middle Ages.

The rural dean was to a certain extent in competition with the archdeacon, especially when the latter had a specific district, though the deanery was usually a smaller area. As agents of the bishop, rural deans were responsible for the general supervision of the clergy in the deaneries, which were widely created in the twelfth century. Like the archdeacons, they had powers of visitation, but in general their activities were intimately connected with the daily life of the parish: inducting priests, administering vacant benefices, punishing minor offenses of clergy and laity alike, presiding over rural chapters, and helping archdeacons in their judicial functions. They were more likely to be resident and "native" than the archdeacons. In the fourteenth and fifteenth centuries their subordination to these officers rendered them almost redundant.

In summing up the diocesan hierarchy, we may conclude that "self-government" in church affairs was very insignificant compared with the corresponding situation in lay matters. Authority descended from above, even in the case of synods and convocations, so that what there was of grassroots initiative had to exist at the parish level; and there too it was an exotic plant.

Parish Clergy

The parish clergy, with whom (along with itinerant friars) the bulk of the population came into most constant contact, were the backbone of the whole church complex. Apart from the occasional literary reference (notably Chaucer's "poor parson" in *The Canterbury Tales*), there is little record of them as human beings. The majority were vicars, living on small stipends or on the little tithe (a levy on products other than grain), while the bulk of the revenues of the parish went to the appropriating rector, who might be a monastery, university or college, royal official, or even a landed layman. The rector had to pay for rebuilding and repairs (unless a new endowment was made), and in England the parish vicars, as a result of ecclesiastical legislation from the thirteenth century on, enjoyed a security of tenure and of income rarely found elsewhere.

Appropriation, while widely condemned as an evil, and certainly a constantly growing practice, has often been grossly overestimated by critics. It has been calculated that between 1447 and 1492 only 413 members of religious orders were papally dispensed to hold secular benefices, and of these nearly half were Austin canons or friars with strong pastoral and preaching orientation. It could be argued that a "regular" priest contributed more than could a barely educated secular parson; and the *Festial,* one of the most popular of clerical handbooks, was written by an Austin canon in the fourteenth century.

The value of the parishes varied considerably; over half were worth less than £10 per annum, and only a third over £15. According to the 1291 valuation, the parishes ranged in value from £230 per annum (Lindisfarne), the equivalent of a baronial income, to a mere 3 shillings 4 pence (Tenerton, County Devon), less than a living wage. In addition to the tithe the parishes received innumerable payments for services, such as burial, baptismal, and wedding fees, and further income at times of festival; expenditures included synodals (payments to bishops at times of synod) and procurations (payments in lieu of hospitality). In general, while some clergy lived like knights, the majority were from and of the peasant class.

It has been estimated that in the thirteenth century, when the parish system was fully established, there were 9,000 rural and 500 urban parishes. Legislation to improve the education and morals of the parish clergy figured large in the provincial, synodal, and capitular decrees. Letters and much more effectively visitations sought to enforce these laws. The result was a considerable growth in the number of clergy with degrees and ability. Such growth was "spotty," however; obviously a man like Robert Grosseteste was far more interested in promoting the clergy than a curialist absentee. While the gloomy picture of Protestant apologists has undoubtedly been too dark, it is nevertheless a shock to read the tale of neglect, ignorance, and concubinage (on a grand scale) in the late-thirteenth-century visitations of Canterbury, a diocese long governed by vigorous, able, and even brilliant bishops. We should not be too surprised, however, for a considerable number of these clergy were not even ordained.

Pluralism was a natural product of poverty. It was endemic in the Middle Ages, despite persistent legislation against it. The best that could be achieved in the great majority of cases where cure of souls was involved was a requirement that the pluralist appoint a suitable vicar (it was, of course, completely contrary to church law for a man to hold more than one benefice with cure of souls). In this way, the parish would have at least a partially qualified cleric to look after its affairs. Of minor sins, such as dice playing, hunting, and haunting taverns, little need be said. Laws were passed and penalties imposed, but such solaces for a celibate and rather isolated life happily continued to flourish.

One difficult question is whether the clergy declined in quality in the later Middle Ages. Mr. Heath's study of the fifteenth-century parish clergy has enabled us to gain a more balanced view of this problem.[8] One yardstick he applies is the ownership of books as revealed in wills. On this point it appears that a fourth of the local resident clergy owned one book or more. The majority of these were service books; next followed the sermon collections, among which *Festial* was third in popularity. A close rival was *The Golden Legends,* a very popular collection of pious and miraculous tales. Bibles, or parts of Bibles, were fairly common among book owners. Dictionaries and encyclopedias, such as Bartholomew's *De Proprietatibus* and the *Catholicon,* were occasionally found. We may conclude with Mr. Heath that the parish clergy of the pre-Reformation period were on the whole "neither illiterate nor incompetent," but their tastes and learning were narrow and inadequate for their task. If this was true, it was not so much the fault of the clergy as a result of the fact that no one, from papal curia to university, had given serious thought to just what a parson should be and how he should be trained and equipped for his role.

The teaching of John Wycliffe (c.1330–84) and his followers, the Lollards, if they had triumphed, would have provided the parish clergy with such direction; as it was, the fear of heresy put the authorities on the defensive and led them to root out such initiatives as were made. After all, as we have seen, parish clergy had perhaps improved in matters of morals and literacy. Why rock the boat? But if things had improved, it was in part because of firm action by the bishops against laggard or rascally lay patrons. Only a much less politically minded episcopate could have really fought off the lethargy, the iniquitous effect of dispensations, and the indiscipline of the lower clergy. As for royal or secular control, it was hampered by that very "benefit of clergy" that since the twelfth century had protected all members of clerical orders from trial in secular courts. That this privilege was not foolproof is evidenced by a number of convictions in secular courts. Unfortunately, the main beneficiaries of exemptions were doubtful characters in minor orders. Another problem faced by reformers was the growing body of educated laity, which played havoc with the traditional test of clerical status, the ability to read a sentence or so of Latin.

The local parson was aided in a number of ways by the development of supporting lay parish organizations. One such association, headed by the church warden, took a large burden off the parson's shoulders by assuming, from the thirteenth century on, the upkeep of nave, the provision of vestments,

---

[8] P. Heath, *The English Parish Clergy on the Eve of the Reformation* (London, 1969).

and other activities; for this purpose it raised taxes and received endowments. Another lay association was the parish guild, which not only gave support to the parson but often had a role in the evolution of local government. Some parish guilds were very elaborate and ambitious, like the Guild of St. Nicholas in Bury, founded in 1282, which paid for the Corpus Christi festival, maintained prayers for both the living and the dead, helped the poor, and provided for special services. The vast majority of English parishes had supporting lay associations by the end of the Middle Ages.

Cathedral Chapters

Cathedral chapters, composed of cathedral dignitaries and officers, operated as separate communities, almost entirely divorced from the life of bishop and diocese. According to Kathleen Edwards, their history is "one of constant adaptation to meet the changing needs of church and society."[9] Dean, precentor, chancellor, and treasurer emerged as the four "heads of departments" in the chapters, and increasingly in the twelfth and thirteenth centuries they had their own endowments.

Miss Edwards describes these four areas of power as follows:

The dean was president of the chapter and had cure of souls of all cathedral clergy. The precentor or cantor was in charge of the music and liturgy, and of the song school. The chancellor kept the chapter's seals; acted as its secretary; supervised the schools of grammar and theology; was frequently cathedral librarian and keeper of the archives; arranged the reading of the lessons in choir, and the sermons. The treasurer guarded the church's treasures, and provided the lights and the material necessaries of the service.

The medieval dean had less authority than the post-Reformation dean; as more and more canons became nonresident, the internal life of the cathedral took on a new quality. Resident canons were expected to assume specific duties, and they gained control of the government of the close (the buildings and adjacent lands of a cathedral); they could legislate in the chapter with little or no episcopal oversight. Their powers extended over a wide area of responsibility, but did not often interfere in the work of their colleagues. The vicars-choral became more important, while the grammar school remained the chief educational institution in a cathedral city. Many prebends were "siphoned off" for the support of clergy engaged in royal or papal administration. As the Middle Ages wore on the connection between chapter and diocese became

[9] K. Edwards, *The English Secular Cathedrals in the Middle Ages* (Oxford, 1949) for this and the extract that follows.

increasingly weak; the members of the chapter were engaged in cathedral, national, and papal affairs.

Of the great officers—all priests—who ruled the cathedral's life the dean was the greatest, but by no means all-powerful. His office as head of the cathedral clergy was barely established in 1154 (though, of course, incidental references go back many centuries). The dean's powers were still undefined in the fifteenth century. The greatness of the office is witnessed by the inscription in the cathedral of Exeter: "Present by day and night, rule thou everything, O Dean." But in general the dean was strictly limited from above by the bishop, and from below by his fellow officers and by the chapter. In his relations with the chapter it may be said that the dean had the right to consent, but not to direct. He also had the right and duty to execute the chapter's decisions and to administer its property. In the execution of his duties the dean had the aid of important chapter members like the subdean, the official (a largely judicial post), and proctors. The minor officials could also obstruct his will.

The precentor was an established official by the middle of the twelfth century and was usually second to the dean. His direction of the cathedral's music kept him, with his deputy and assistant, the succentor, fully occupied; only occasionally did his office overlap with that of the chancellor or treasurer.

Though only third in dignity, the chancellor had such wide and varied duties that the members of his department came to outnumber those of the three other great offices. The title is late, widely established by 1154 but not universal for another century; it was a replacement of the earlier title *magister scholarum* (master of the scholars). The institution reflects the burgeoning of both educational and secretarial work in the twelfth century. In the educational field the chancellor continued to direct the grammar schools at the secular cathedrals, often appointing a deputy master; here and there the growth of legal and theological studies led to the establishment of embryo universities under the chancellor (notably at Salisbury). It was from his second office, that of secretary, that the chancellor received his title. As the keeper of the chapter's seals and writer of its correspondence, he had a heavy task, often delegated in part to a clerk and shared with notaries. He was sometimes assisted by a vice-chancellor.

The treasurer, the last of the four great officers, had in his charge the maintenance of the cathedral treasures and the supply of materials for the services. At Wells, he had to provide 350 pounds of wax (for candles) in the course of a year. The materialism of the medieval church is well attested by the expansion of the treasurer's staff, which came to include sacristans and wardens.

The finances of the chapter were subject to the strict control of the whole body. They fell into two clearly marked departments. The first was concerned with the fabric and was administered, under the dean, by "masters of the fabric," with the frequent aid of vicars-choral and chantry priests. The second was the "common fund" of the clergy (as opposed to the main cathedral treasury), a financial department that attained elaborate organization at such cathedrals as Hereford.

Regular Clergy

In contrast to the bishops, with their large-scale involvement in secular affairs, the heads of religious houses tended to remain attached to their proper duties. They rarely acted as public officials or ambassadors, though they were not entirely withdrawn from the outside world. As heads of franchises, they had extensive judicial rights; the abbot of St. Albans, for example, had spiritual power over twenty-four parishes, with no appeal save to the pope. Another outside tie was their growing dependence on the laity. Founders and benefactors shared in their fortunes, though not on such a scale as the great continental "advocates," the men who protected European churches in war or at law. If a layman held these houses *in commendam,* a holding that gave him untitled lordship, he could draw extensively on their revenues. Laymen served as advisers on abbatial councils, and in the fifteenth century it was wise to have a powerful court figure as steward.

Through appropriations, monasteries drew on—some would say, battened on—the secular church. This growing practice, fostered by the papacy, delivered the main revenues of a third of England's parishes into monastic hands by the fifteenth century. In addition, religious houses frequently "farmed out" rectorial rights to laymen, that is to say, they granted the revenues of rectories in return for a fixed fee.

Suit of court, which led to representation in the House of Lords, sat less heavily on abbots than on bishops. Originally imposed on the great Benedictine houses along with other tenants in chief, it was extended to Cistercian houses holding in free alms (that is, free of the usual military service), probably to forward, by securing their attendance at parliaments, the king's intention of taxing wool. The number of heads of houses so summoned in 1215 was eighty-seven. By the middle of the fourteenth century the number had dropped to twenty-eight (of which twenty-three were Benedictine), and attendance grew ever more lax. The parallel duty of military service fell, of course, on the Benedictine abbeys. Although the number summoned by the king was doubled between the twelfth and thirteenth centuries (from twenty-four to fifty), the royal aim was clearly scutage, not military service.

The abbeys' real contribution to English life was at the local level. They were, in St. Benedict's language, schools for the service of God. At the heart of their teaching was the *opus Dei,* the cycle of prayer. The danger was always that this learning would become either overelaborate or a mechanical formula inviting mockery. It was to arrest these tendencies that great reforms were initiated from time to time. The tragedy was that the constant "purgings" necessary to cut back the weeds of self-indulgence and apathy grew less and less frequent after the thirteenth century. Besides their manifest intention of glorifying God and saving souls, the abbeys made many contributions to the outside world: we may note here the great tradition of historical writing in the Benedictine scriptoria (writing departments), which after reaching a peak in the thirteenth century gradually died out. The Carthusians, smallest of the orders, nurtured a piety infused by the new fourteenth-century English mysticism, which enabled them alone to grow in the late Middle Ages and fortified them to resist the Reformation. However, most of the scholarship and vitality in the thirteenth century arose among the friars and continued in a weakened condition in the fourteenth and fifteenth centuries. In terms of organization and wealth, the keynote in the abbeys was centralization and "nationalization" (e.g., in the freedom of Cluniacs, the oldest of the centrally organized monastic groups, from French authority and in the disendowment of "alien" priories). Estate management, which took up a disproportionate amount of the monastic officials' time, was at its best in such bodies as the priory of Christ Church, Canterbury, though in the conversion from direct exploitation of their lands by their own officials to long leases to tenants the abbots tended to lag behind secular lords by several generations.

The truth is that by the end of the Middle Ages the abbeys, like other institutions, had become vastly overendowed, self-perpetuating oligarchies. The fact that they continued to attract endowments, largely in the form of chantries (endowments for prayers for the dead), shows that the combination of superstition and fear of death was not declining in the English mind; it only accentuated the gap between Christian teaching and official practice that orthodox and heretical writers of any stature deplored with increasing vehemence, and that only the brutal action of a lecherous and power-hungry Tudor king could do something to ameliorate.[1]

The main religious development after 1154 was the coming of the friars (see below). This happened in the first half of the thirteenth century. They added preaching and teaching zeal to the contemplative life of the cloistered monks. The Franciscans dominated English learning in the century after 1240 and gave Europe some of its leading teachers and writers. There seems to be no doubt that a summit was reached in the thirteenth century in the healthiness and creativity of the religious life. Some scholars would put it earlier, but certainly to name the thirteenth century is to take into account the new infusion of the mendicants.

---

[1] See Volume III in this series.

Endowments continued to flow in, even if the rather unhealthy bias toward chantries was a feature of the last medieval centuries. The monasteries and friar houses absorbed an immense amount of England's wealth; their "work" of prayer for less perfect men in the rest of the country was their justification and the major incentive to the massive endowments they received. The friars, it is true, were "in the world" in a way that the monks were not. Their claim lay in their contribution to preaching, teaching, and confession. Whatever the justification for their worth, it is arguable that their contribution to society was in the fact that they constituted yet another of the congeries of busy, vigorous communities that made up the national life.

Our knowledge of English monasteries and friaries is comparable to that of constitutional and administrative history, thanks first to their habit of record-keeping and second to the gargantuan labors of David Knowles, through whose writings it is possible to study the subject in every conceivable aspect.[2]

As a guide to the importance of the religious houses in Henry II's reign, we may note that they probably owned a quarter of the nation's wealth and comprised about 15,000 persons. This, it must be remembered, represented a point reached after the unparalleled growth since 1066. This growth had been largely due to the tremendous influence of Clairvaux, and by the end of the twelfth century the Cistercians (formed in eastern France in 1098, and made famous by St. Bernard) almost equaled the dominant and ancient group of Benedictines in wealth, though they outstripped them in dedication. A vast amount of the monks' time and thought was siphoned off from the *opus Dei* to the administration of this wealth. One of the worst effects of these worldly cares was the separation of the abbot from the community he ruled.

The great monasteries of the twelfth century were deeply involved in working out the relationships between abbot and monastic chapter, the role of various "officers," and the relationships with the secular world of bishop, king, and lord. These constitutional matters were closer to the hearts of the monks than the more profound problem of adjusting the rule of St. Benedict, conceived as it was in the later stages of the dissolution of the Roman Empire, to the conditions of affluence and stability. Yet they were related, inasmuch as "constitutions" imposed from above, or deliberations of central bodies, sought to keep in mind the spiritual as well as the material interests of their constituents.

The abbot's domination of his monks was at first qualified only by the advice, tendered by St. Benedict, that he listen to the opinions of his brothers, and by the establishment of more centralized systems within the order by St. Bernard and the other founders of the Cistercians. As the twelfth century progressed, the abbot was variously limited by the privileges of chapters (of

---

[2] D. Knowles, *The Religious Orders in England,* vols. I–III (Cambridge, 1961–2), on which most of the following is based.

governing bodies) and officers. The abbot became very little more to his monks than the bishop to his cathedral chapter. Just where the division of powers came varied from order to order, and among communities. The profession, that is, administration, of the order of new monks remained divided between abbot and chapter; charters, which legalized the acquisition of new lands and rights, had to be authenticated by the chapter as well as the abbot. The chapter was consulted, by law or as a matter of common sense, in the appointment of monastic officials. The power of the abbot is indicated by the strenuous debate about his election recorded by Jocelyn of Brakelond:[3] the whole health and happiness of the community depended on the choice. But Jocelyn also provides evidence, amply confirmed elsewhere, of the limitations the abbot might be confronted with in the *consensus fideorum* (the collective view of the believers). And Pope Innocent III lent the weight of his authority to this capitular sanction.

Henry II had laid down the procedure of election in the Constitution of Clarendon (1164), which specified royal choice from candidates put up by the abbey. Such a procedure was probably fairly universal in the Middle Ages, with the exception of one or two "episcopal" abbeys where officials were also bishops, an occasional free election by the monks, and the fairly frequent custom of the reigning abbot choosing his successor. The election of Samson at Bury in 1182 is told unforgettably by Jocelyn of Brakelond; nowhere else is the reality of the procedure, from the canvassing of candidates to the act of royal approval, so vividly described.

The Cistercians were freer of royal interference than the Black Monks (Benedictines), and their internal arrangements were more specific, since they were the product of law rather than of custom. Their lands, which were held in free alms and usually in unpopulated regions, were far less cumbered than the Benedictines' by elaborate legal problems, duties, and rights. The chapter of a Cistercian abbey was more of a spiritual than a legislative conference. Until the thirteenth century the general chapter of the whole order kept a close eye on the English houses; it was vital to the working of the order as a whole. Yet it can have been but a poor instrument for controlling the monastic houses, given their predisposition to acquiring property and to excessive beer drinking within the limits of the rule.

At first lay brothers were employed by the houses on a large scale, for in England they were not as sharply divided from monks proper as on the Continent. In the early days of Cistercians two-thirds of the members were lay brothers. In later centuries they disappeared as the monks themselves became full-fledged entrepreneurs.

[3] Jocelyn of Brakelond, *Cronica,* ed. H. E. Butler (London, 1949).

From the reign of Henry II English monasteries relinquished their slender hold on "higher" studies like theology and became centers of literary and historical studies alone. The writing of chronicles had, of course, been a high point of the monks' achievement for centuries; after 1154 it became nearly their sole contribution to civilization in England. Local chronicles or annals predominated at the expense of universal or national histories. However, some writers could still transcend, perhaps by a more universal frame of reference or by wit and keenness of observation, the narrow interest of a particular house.

By 1154 the abbot usually lived away from his monks, with his own household staff, rooms, and chapel; conversely, the monks began to formalize their separate existence in their chapters. This autonomy was duly recognized by Innocent III. A whole host of officers grew up from the primitive system of St. Benedict—David Knowles has estimated twenty-five to a monastery[4]— to look after every religious and material aspect of the community's life. As a consequence, revenues were divided between abbot (an estimated average of one-fourth) and chapter, and within the latter, assignations of particular revenues to particular offices were made. A nice balance was maintained between communal and individual activity, with the latter tending, for reasons of efficiency, to gain ground.

It is not really possible to form a clear view of the state of English monasticism in practice until after it had passed its prime; only when the rare insight of individual chroniclers came to be supplemented by the records of official visitations does a reasonably detached picture become possible. These visitations, conducted both by the monks (for the Cistercians by the parent abbeys; for the Benedictines after 1215 by the provincial chapters) and by their diocesan bishops (unless exempt from visitation), undoubtedly had a beneficial effect. The most substantial evidence is from episcopal visitations. The danger with this evidence, however, lies in its misuse: one should no more rely on material that was necessarily concerned with abuses as a guide to the ordinary life of monks than one should refer to criminal records as the basis for one's view of lay society. If bishops thundered against immorality and corruption in monasteries, one must remember that they were concerned primarily with checking such abuse where it occurred. And of course no statistical survey of efficiency and morality is remotely possible; the records are good but far from complete. Another danger with this evidence is that the modern writer will be looking for ideas and actions of a very different kind from those that concerned the episcopal visitor of the Middle Ages; the latter sought to ensure obedience to the rule of St. Benedict and to ecclesiastical law; the former should surely be

---

[4] Knowles, *op. cit.*

concerned with what he considers to be the creative impulse in a civilization.

The two great evils that visitors found rampant in monasticism from the moment the records are available were bad administration and immoral living. Bad administration might mean chronic indebtedness, plain ignorance of the state of one's household affairs, or a failure to enforce one's rights in terms of services, offerings, and dues. The last problem was perhaps the most widespread. It was met occasionally by the removal of incompetent and venal officials (from abbot down), but usually by the insistence by the visitors on the implementation of tried methods of administration, notably the institution of the offices of cellarer, who was in charge of provisions, and bursar, who was in charge of finances and of the system of auditing and bookkeeping. In these ways weaknesses were combated by the vigor of the visitations.

Immorality, or perhaps one should say irregularity, in the lives of the monks was fought with equal tenacity. Here the problem was mainly "good living," a term that applied to behavior ranging from playing chess to eating meat to sexual deviancy—in brief, the escape of natural impulses from the incredible austerities of monastic life. It may be said that the truly outrageous abbot, prior, or monk usually met with punishment, but for the most part the natural tendency of men with good revenue and privileged position to enjoy life overcame the challenging vision of an ascetic life for the greater glory of God. In general, the monks of the first century of visitation (c.1240–1340) showed neither fervor nor widespread decadence; rather they lived at a level of modest and reasonable ordinariness.

Probably the main institutional change in the religious houses of the high Middle Ages was the development of centralized government, with provincial chapters matching the councils and synods of the church. The Black Monks' chapters have been studied by W. A. Pantin.[5] They were instituted by the Fourth Lateran Council (1215) and were undoubtedly a product of both Cistercian and mendicant example. The English chapters went a long way toward producing a body of common law for the individualistic Benedictine monasteries and toward aiding the work of visitors in checking headlong decline. In two sensitive areas, the enforcement of dietary laws and the change from liturgical to educational emphasis, they had but indifferent success. By the end of the thirteenth century, after a series of decrees against laxity in meat eating, the relative indulgence already in practice came to be generally sanctioned. In education the problem of making study an alternative to the manual labor (once an integral task, but now increasingly defunct), at the expense of elaborate liturgical practice, was just as intractable. The trouble was that the majority of monks were scarcely literate. What could theological studies mean to such men? It took a century to get a college established in Oxford, and by

[5] W. A. Pantin, *The Chapters of the Black Monks,* Royal Historical Society, Camden 3rd series, vol. XLV (1931).

about 1340 the moral and intellectual state of the monks had declined even further. Only the existence of important historical schools (at St. Albans), and music and art activities (at St. Albans, Peterborough, and Bury St. Edmunds) offset the general low level of Benedictine achievement.

The religious power of St. Francis of Assisi was undoubtedly the major spiritual event of the thirteenth century; it has appealed to men of all faiths. The luminous joy of the early Franciscans could be but fitfully maintained in the great order to which it gave rise—so, perhaps, it is with all outpourings of the spirit. The period of organization and establishment required laws and involved controversy and litigation. Controversy with the secular clergy and with the established monastic orders drew the Franciscan and Dominican[6] orders closer together in spirit, a closeness that involved a great deal of bitter rivalry but also cooperative opposition to previously established institutions and their privileges. For the communities to which they came the friars brought new preaching, new, more flexible, attitudes to the confessional, and a new glimpse of the holy. They may well have rescued the growing towns from various forms of heresy and disbelief. The story of their litigation concerning preaching, confession, and burial rights against jealous parish clergy is not edifying; yet in this they were part of the stuff of medieval society: the contention between groups and individuals for rights and responsibilities. By the end of the thirteenth century, papal, episcopal, and royal mediation had brought peace in two of the contested areas of friars' rights: preaching and burial. In both cases the mendicants secured certain privileges. They were allowed to meet the laity's demands for their ministry at the expense of parochial clergy. But in both cases too the substantive and allied financial rights of the seculars, including such matters as burial fees, were protected by episcopal licensing and legal limitation. The papal bull *Super Cathedram,* issued in 1300 and confirmed in 1311, stabilized the situation for the rest of the Middle Ages: friars were to be free to preach in their own churches and in public but elsewhere only by invitation; a proportion of friars were to be licensed to confess; and all friars could perform unlimited burials, but a fourth of their dues and legacies was to go to the parish clergy.

The last two centuries of the Middle Ages saw little change, little ferment, and no great movement in the monasteries. The Cistercians, in abandoning the use of *conversi,* became like the Benedictines—in fact, like all great English landlords—rentiers. The monasteries exercised great skill in making the transition from high farming to leasehold, as we know from the records of Christ Church, Canterbury, and of Ramsey Abbey, in the East Midlands; but the adaptation enabled them only to keep pace, not to grow. Their numbers followed fairly proportionately the changes i⸺ ⸺⸺⸺⸺⸺⸺ The en-

[6] The followers of St. Dominic, who from the first champ⸺
the Franciscan emphasis on love and renunciation, arrived

closed orders (that is, those who, at least in law, were confined to their religious houses) reached a peak in the latter part of the twelfth century; the greatest Benedictine house, Christ Church, had 150 members. A tapering off in these communities during the thirteenth century was offset by the meteoric rise of the friars, so that in terms of numbers the year 1300 was the high point of English religious life. The gradual decline in the early fourteenth century, along with catastrophic decimation brought on by the Black Death in 1348 (when 50 percent of the monks and friars, as against 30 percent of the general population, were lost), was followed by a surprising revival in the late fourteenth and early fifteenth centuries. By the end of the Middle Ages the total number was 12,000, compared with 17,500 in 1300. Practical benefits had replaced devotional fervor in maintaining this figure, and the oldest orders fared best. The "religious" way of life, one can assume, continued to rank high in the esteem of Englishmen.

During the fourteenth century the economic affairs of the monasteries showed a twofold development. First, the thirteenth-century high farming was usually placed under the control of obedientiaries, officials, each with his manor or group of manors. But often a committee or an individual (e.g., the monk wardens of Canterbury and the bursar of Durham) had strict control over the obedientiaries, auditing or even supplying the bulk of their revenue. Second, with the transition to leasehold the abbot's or prior's powers increased considerably; in some cases he even combined a great number of subordinate offices in his own person.

A modicum of scholarship flourished at Oxford, and the historical school at St. Albans' monastery had an Indian summer in the late fourteenth century. Monks and friars abandoned their internecine bickering to close ranks against Wycliffe, and in Thomas Netter the Carmelites, one of the four orders of friars, produced orthodoxy's most fervid champion. But a certain laxity inevitably prevailed: the king and his nobles frequented the great abbeys; eating meat outside the refectory became a common practice, and private rooms were built for obedientiaries and other officials. What had the monasteries to offer against the gathering clouds of criticism? Splendid buildings, costly plate, a lukewarm profession. The last flicker of growth came from Henry V, with his foundations of the strict orders of Carthusians at Sheen and of the Bridgettines of Syon and his attempted reform of the Benedictines in 1421; the saintly Henry VI, who might have found a better vocation in the cloister, had no will or mind to offer for the work of reform to which he might have been called. The phrase "autumn of the Middle Ages"[7] nowhere applies more aptly than to the religious orders.

[7] J. Huizinga, *The Waning of the Middle Ages* (any edition).

Schools and Universities

One type of church institution that was conceived in the Middle Ages and that has survived to today, with many miraculous changes, is education. Grammar schools and universities had their roots deep in the medieval church.

Grammar schools antedate universities; in fact, the latter were in principle (the derivation cannot always be established) a development of the former. It is probable that in the early Middle Ages schools were normally run by most cathedral and collegiate churches. Moreover, the tradition of monastic schools never died out completely. The chancellor of the cathedral or college was in charge of studies. His students were mainly sons of gentry and merchants, though occasionally an enterprising person or dean directed a few peasants into the schools. The sons of the higher aristocracy (and indeed many of the lower) were educated in the households of relatives or friends. Numbers in schools were small; discipline was harsh. Until the late fourteenth century the Latin taught in the grammar schools was translated into French, not English. Teaching was by lecture method, with the master or his assistant commenting on Priscian's grammar and the boys doing translations or composition in prose and verse. Good manners were also taught. In the fourteenth century the governing authorities of the cathedral or monastery issued "statutes" describing the forms of discipline and instruction; it is fairly clear that the senior students exercised distinctive disciplinary supervision—the power of the rod. The perpetual flogging was offset to a degree by the pantomime festivities of Christmas. A considerable number of schools were founded at various locations in most dioceses, and war was waged on the "adulterine" (unauthorized) schools that sprang up to meet the ever growing demand. Internally, there was often a struggle between choristers—those being trained for the choir (for which a modicum of Latin was necessary)—and their nonchoral fellow students, for the singing of the choir was one of the principal attractions of the cathedrals. Endowments paid the fees of poor scholars. A small number of schools grew up in association with the flood of chantry chapels founded in the later Middle Ages. Since the schools had such small enrollments, little was needed in the way of organization. A headmaster, appointed by bishop or dean or chancellor (there were legal hassles over this) and assisted by one or two masters, sufficed for the school's governance.

In addition to the church schools there were "guild" schools. Just as guilds often maintained chantries, so in the later Middle Ages they came to pay schoolmasters to teach grammar. In fact, as in the case of Ashburton Grammar School, Devon, the master was often a chantry priest as well; alternatively, as at Chelmsford or Maldon (both in Essex), the schoolmaster was a chorister or chaplain of a guild. By the fifteenth century, as in the often quoted example of Sevenoaks in Kent, a separation between spiritual and educational activity was occasionally (for practical, not intellectual, reasons) stipulated.

The universities of Oxford and Cambridge were two of the pillars of the English church, and with the Inns of Court they constituted the main foci of English scholarship. Beginning as a school of uncertain date and origin, Oxford emerged as a university probably as a result of a withdrawal of English students from Paris during the conflict between Henry II and Becket in 1167. By 1200 it is evident that a *studium generale* existed there. A similar flight from Oxford led to the founding of Cambridge in 1209. The Oxford institution had certain marked differences from the Parisian model on which it was based. First, the masters early secured the election of the chancellor (an office not clearly established until the Legatine Ordinance of 1214) from among their own number. Second, unlike the Paris chancellor, who was the representative of a bishop and often at odds with the academics, the chancellor at Oxford was the head of the academics themselves. (De jure, of course, he was the representative and nominee of the bishop of Lincoln—but Lincoln was far away, and the bishop's control was never firmly asserted.) In short, Oxford had (as did Cambridge later) the great advantage of being a "cathedral school" located far from its cathedral.

In the thirteenth century Oxford began the acquisition of a legal as against a customary constitution, and it did this largely in imitation of developments in Paris. In fact, as we shall see in surveying English thought in Chapter Five, the Oxford-Paris relationship was extremely close. By a series of statutes issued in the middle of the thirteenth century, the chancellor's powers were defined and government was entrusted to the chancellor as president of a congregation of masters regent (masters with ruling powers). At the same time, it was decreed that only regents in arts could proceed to theology. The self-determining nature of the university is reflected in the fact that the key statute was issued "by authority of the chancellor and the masters regent with the unanimous consent of the nonregents."[8] Beneath the chancellor much of the executive power lay with the proctors (legal assistants to the governing body), elected from the arts faculty. Only for a brief period (c.1228–74) were the masters divided into "nations" (north and south of Trent) after the Parisian model, which implied that foreigners should have their own organization. The model was therefore a rather artificial importation. A special feature of Oxford was the absolute dominance, including initiating, legislative, and veto power, of the masters of arts; this power was not challenged with success until

[8] The regents were the resident teaching staff; nonregents were graduates who had no university posts.

late in the fourteenth century. Of course, the "higher" faculties (theology, law, and medicine) had an important voice in the Lesser Congregation of all regents, which controlled curriculum and degrees. The nonregents had a voice in the Great Congregation, the ultimate legislating body. Not until the late fourteenth century was the complex machinery of lawmaking spelled out, in a document that embodied the priority of the arts regent and the need for a majority vote of the separate faculties.

The universities, like the other communities of medieval England, spent considerable effort in acquiring and defending wealth and privileges. Externally this meant defense against the town corporation and against episcopal or archiepiscopal discipline. In relation to the town the chancellor's court gradually acquired first immunity from and then (after about 1355) control of the town government. Not only were Oxford scholars privileged to be tried in this court, but strictly town matters, such as street paving and market practices, were put under university control. At each clash of "town and gown" the king and Council interfered in favor of the latter. Thus privilege was heaped on privilege, until the university controlled the community into which it had, in the twelfth century, intruded itself.

Relations with church authorities were less straightforward, for the very weapons used against the towns (notably excommunication) were furnished by the church to the chancellor as bishop's representative. Nevertheless, on the whole Oxford fought off ecclesiastical interference and kept it to a minimum. Against the bishops of Lincoln, who in the thirteenth century sought to assert episcopal authority, the university successfully appealed to the archbishop and convocation, just as in the conflicts with the town they had appealed to king and Council. The bishops were "licked" by 1300. This brought the university into direct relationship with the archbishop and his courts and the consequent danger of control by them. Indeed, archiepiscopal visitations were occasionally carried out, and on two occasions, in the late thirteenth century and in the period of Wycliffism, such powers were used to stamp out error or heresy. Yet by a papal bull of 1479 the university was exempted from all ecclesiastical authority: such was the reward for the great community's return to orthodox virtue.

Within the university were partially autonomous communities of students and teachers in the halls and colleges, which were gradually (and with their consent) brought under general university regulation. Yet they enjoyed a privileged and lively individuality, and the colleges developed corporate status, owning property and advowsons and authenticating acts with their own seals. A very "democratic" character prevailed in both hall and college.

Merton, founded by William of Merton, a curialist cleric, may serve as an example of the complex formation of an Oxford college, especially as it harbored some of the university's finest scholars. Begun as a foundation primarily for William's relatives, and in the unsettled times of 1264, in uncertain location, its 1270 statutes further defined the college's organization. There were to be two subwardens, one over the Surrey manor of Malden, which supplied the funds, and the other over the Oxford community of scholars. By the 1274 statutes the warden was located in Oxford, assisted by three bursars chosen from among the scholars. A *vicenarius* ("twenty-man") was appointed over every twenty scholars, and a *decanus* ("ten-man" or dean) over every ten. The disciplinary regulations produced a revolution in university life. On admission to a year's probation the scholars were to be ready for the arts course. After that the majority were to study theology, and a few canon and civil law. The senior fellows elected the warden, who was confirmed by the visitor (the archbishop of Canterbury). The system of "college livings," that is, ecclesiastical appointments under college control and peculiar to England, was established by the founder. A new dependent group of "portionists" (postmasters), servitors of individual masters, was added in 1380. At the end of the Middle Ages at Merton and other colleges the famous system of college tuition, that is, teaching by college tutors, was introduced to supplement university lectures and disputations.

Conclusion

The English church structure was serviceable and in general adaptable to changing needs. A triad of forces bore on its constituent parts— pope, king, and archbishops. Closely tied to the general structure of Christendom, it harbored not only the descending hierarchical principle but a proliferation of communal and individual interests. College and university were perhaps the most autonomous and self-governing of the many institutions we have touched upon. Yet we can never assume that the seemingly authoritarian form did not shelter within it both collegiate initiatives and proud individuals jealous of their rights.

Chapter Five
INTELLECTUAL AND CULTURAL HISTORY

England was in the mainstream of the development of Western culture. Though never so dominant in the Middle Ages as in the eighth century, England's scholars and writers contributed to European thought on a scale out of proportion to its population and wealth. It was perhaps more through certain great individuals than through schools and movements that this contribution was made. These men (and a few women) were related, in most cases intimately, to the institutions we have been following: university, monastery, parish, guild, and court. In the following pages we shall be concerned in the main with ideas rather than the milieu of those ideas. It should be kept in mind, especially when considering the university group, that we will be looking at the work of men who were educated abroad or did their teaching abroad, and who were often of non-English provenance. These men were part of a mobile and international European community. While there was much interplay between different branches of culture, it seems wise to make certain divisions. These are university thought (scholasticism), piety and mysticism, humanism, and the courtly and common culture of the laity.

University Thought

The universities of Oxford and Cambridge, particularly the former, made a significant and at times outstanding contribution to scholastic thought. It has sometimes been alleged that there was a peculiar Englishness to this contribution, a foreshadowing of Anglo-Saxon scientific empiricism. While such trends can be uncovered, it is best to consider English medieval thought as part of the general Latin thought of the West. Possibly the exceptional independence of Oxford (see p. 130) enabled some English scholars to take bolder, more extreme positions. But even this is doubtful.

Scholasticism was at once a method of inquiry and teaching and a body of ideas—the famous synthesis of Greek and Hebraic-Christian traditions.[1] This method was worked out at the very time of the founding of Oxford (c. 1167). As a method it was applicable not only to theology and philosophy but also to law and medicine—in fact, to any body of knowledge. It involved the *lectio* (exposition) and *disputatio* (disputation). Both forms were concerned with definition and classification. The exposition consisted of an explication by the master (a graduate licensed to teach)[2] of some authoritative text (e.g., in philosophy, Aristotle; in canon law, Gratian). The disputation involved the weighing of arguments for and against a certain viewpoint and interpretation, or assertion. Students posed questions against the exposition of the day, a bachelor replied, and the master summed up. Outstanding disputations on special occasions took the form of a *quodlibet* (a special free discussion), as opposed to the routine and formal *quaestio disputata* (a discussion of a set book).

The introduction of Aristotle's logic (and later his metaphysics) greatly furthered scholastic method, and of course some of his and his Arabic commentators' conclusions in metaphysics taxed the Christian mind to the utmost. The response to this challenge was the great outpouring of thirteenth- and fourteenth-century philosophical speculation and the founding of modern scientific method.

The scientific tradition in English thought antedated the founding of the schools. Perhaps Adelard of Bath (d.1140) may be singled out as the forerunner of the tradition. He traveled widely and wrote scientific books based on Arab and Greek learning. Alexander Neckham (1157–1217), who studied at both Oxford and Paris, was a monk of encyclopedic learning; he made important contributions to scientific knowledge in his book, *On the Nature of Things*. But the first and possibly greatest Oxford luminary was Robert Grosseteste (c.1168–1253), bishop of Lincoln. His contribution to the university's early institutions has been noted (see p. 112). Trained at Paris, he built up a formidable body of scientific knowledge on the basis of his Aristotelian learning (he was one of the few medieval scholastics to read Greek). He developed a metaphysic of "light" that encompassed profound inquiries into optics and mathematics. In a real sense he was the father of modern physics. This metaphysical and scientific corpus of thought was but part of a universal knowledge in which biblical studies had an important role.

Of the many English scholastics who followed in Grosseteste's footsteps we may select first the great Franciscan scholar Roger Bacon (c.1214–92) and second the fourteenth-century scientists of the "Merton school." Bacon, a

---

[1] In what follows, see especially the articles on various themes and persons in the *New Catholic Encyclopaedia* by J. A. Weisheipl, J. J. Przezdziecki, and E. A. Synan.

[2] For the stages by which one proceeded through the various degrees, the best guide is G. Leff, *Paris and Oxford Universities in the Thirteenth and Fourteenth Centuries* (New York, 1968), p. 147ff.

stormy petrel outside the mainstream of scholastic development (though he learned from fellow mendicant teachers like Robert Kilwardby, later archbishop of Canterbury), has earned fame for his vigorous championship of mathematics and languages as the basic instruments of knowledge. His contribution in these fields did not live up to his ardor in advocating them. Yet it is possible that if his ideas had been heeded many of the failings of later scholasticism would have been avoided. Enabled to pursue his individualistic path thanks to Pope Clement IV's special interest in his scientific theories, he was eventually the victim of papal condemnation when he added to his other novelties the advocacy of Joachism, the belief in the dawn of a new age of liberty and love, the "Age of the Holy Spirit."[3]

In the first half of the fourteenth century there grew up at Oxford, especially at Merton College, a group of scientists who carried on the pioneer work of the thirteenth century. Outstanding among them was Thomas Bradwardine (c.1300–49), best known for his massive attack on neo-Pelagianism, a revival of the philosophy that man is free to attain salvation through his own acts. Bradwardine's scientific work was notable for the formulation of "a dynamic law of movement that related velocity exponentially to the ratio of force and resistance and brought into prominence the concept of instantaneous velocity."[4] Other distinguished Mertonian physicists included William Swyneshed (fl.1340–55), known as "the calculator," and Walter Burley (c.1275–1344), *doctor planus*. In the story of scientific beginnings the English contribution was above all in the matter of physical laws of impetus and their application to mechanics.

Scholasticism was nothing if not disputatious, and England shared fully in the central arguments of the day. The terminology and the arguments of the schoolmen seem strange today to all but specialists and Catholic philosophers. Yet it is true that these thinkers were concerned with major issues on the nature of God, of nations, and of men, and of the relations between them. The friars for a brief while (c.1250–1330) were the leading figures in the schools, and the two friar archbishops, Kilwardby (Dominican) and John Pecham (Franciscan), entered the fray with gusto. They had a longstanding conflict on the rival achievements of their orders in the areas of preaching and poverty. Eventually, however, the two orders divided on metaphysical rather than vocational grounds. The point at issue was in general the Thomist (and therefore Dominican) acceptance of Aristotle's metaphysics as the rational basis of theology, and in particular the question of the plurality of forms (the ideas that determine a thing's nature). Both Kilwardby and Pecham condemned St. Thomas and his followers, preferring to support the official stand of the

[3] J. A. Weisheipl in *New Catholic Encyclopaedia*.

[4] J. J. Przezdziecki, "Bradwardine," *ibid*.

University of Paris against the variety of form. But the chief obstacle to the development of Thomist thought was the magisterial comprehensiveness of Aquinas' own system rather than the opposition of conservative or radical critics. St. Thomas left so little to say! However, in Thomas of Sutton, who elaborately refuted the notion of angels having a material component, and Nicholas Trivet, who modified Aquinas' views on the nature of God, Oxford contributed two significant Thomists.

The glory—or shame—of English thought lay not in these writers but in the two great Franciscans of the early fourteenth century, Duns Scotus, who became the official philosopher of the Franciscan order, and William of Ockham.

Duns Scotus (c.1266–1308), *doctor subtilis* (the acute doctor), began his education at a Franciscan friary in Scotland. He studied the arts at Oxford (c.1290) and theology at Paris. After a few years as lecturer on the Sentences (the basic Bible commentary) at Oxford, he returned to Paris in 1301, where except for a brief absence due to conflict with the French king he lectured until 1307; he spent his last year teaching at the University of Cologne. Duns was a subtle philosopher and theologian; his new blend of Aristotelian philosophy and scriptural truth has appealed more than that of St. Thomas to a great number of Catholic philosophers. His theories of the "univocity of being" (pure being as the object of the intellect) and his notion of *haecceitas* ("individual form"), one of his neologisms, as the basis of individuation have had a profound influence on modern existential theology. In his ethics Duns is notable for a new stress on the primacy of the will. In theology his insistence on the primacy of love in God's being and in particular his sophisticated Marianism—adherence to the cult of Mary—(he is also famous as *doctor Marianus*) placed him in the mainstream of Augustinian and Franciscan thought.

William of Ockham (d.1349?), *venerabilis inceptor* (honored inventor), was educated at Oxford in the Franciscan house; he may have studied under Duns Scotus. At Oxford he lectured on the Sentences but was condemned, or at least censured, for heretical opinions. His education was completed at Paris, and it was there that he worked out his revolutionary philosophical and political theories. At the same time he actively supported the champions of Christ's poverty in the debates that wracked his order. Papal opposition brought imprisonment for Ockham, followed by flight to the court of the German emperor, whom he promised to defend with his pen in return for protection with the sword. It is evident that from the first Ockham had been critical of the church's political and economic entanglements (he probably was influencing the great secularizer Marsilius of Padua in the 1320s), and as the debate on poverty became fierce and brutal he elaborated at once his ecclesiology and his political theory, in which papal power was reduced in favor of the spiritual community and royal power was checked by the need for consent. It was by his logic, however, that he effected a revolution in medieval philosophy (above all by his great influence in the university of Paris). Here he insisted on the reduction of terms and concepts to what was necessary (his "razor") and on the view that the logician's material was "terms," not "thoughts" or "objects."

Scotus and Ockham believed alike in reducing the number of metaphysical statements to which reason could attain (though in this Ockham was the more drastic) and in the corresponding exaltation of revealed truth as the basis of doctrine. They also shared an emphasis on experience of the individual object as the basis of rational knowledge. Scotus, with his many neologisms, such as the aforementioned *haecceitas,* went on to construct a system rooted in the divine will, through which alone, to the exclusion of reason, God made himself known to man. Ockham went further than Scotus in a skeptical direction and entered vigorously into the antipapalist politics of the time. For both these reasons he was condemned. Yet his influence on later medieval thought was second only to that of Scotus. Thus the English Franciscans contributed to the disintegration of the Thomist synthesis of faith and reason. The question the reader is left with is, Was that synthesis in its very universality a cause of late medieval decay, or should the blame be shared with the brilliant Englishmen who tore it to shreds? Much of what is great in modern philosophy can be traced to the outstanding analytical minds of these two English scholars. Trite as the generalization has now become, the fruitful division of faith and reason had its origins in their cunning syllogisms.

The dissolution of the Thomist schema of a hierarchy of laws under a rational God left the later medieval writers and thinkers free to speculate at length on the nature of divine and human will. The predominant question—that of grace and dominion (the right to authority and property)—became inextricably bound up in the debates of friars, monks, and seculars on the nature of property, until John Wycliffe's entry into the fray closed the ranks of the orthodox. In the middle of the fourteenth century the leading debater had been Richard FitzRalph, archbishop of Armagh, who developed the theory of dominion, which he asserted to be dependent on grace. This view could lead either to extreme ecclesiasticism (if the church was the repository of grace) or, as in Wycliffe, to a radical attack on church endowments and papal power. FitzRalph attacked the friars' privileges on this basis. Even more threatened were the immense properties of the monks. Here Uhtred of Bolton (of Durham cathedral priory), the leading monastic philosopher of the century, rushed to the defense; his argument was directed both at secularizers and at friars, in that he saw gifts to monasteries as gifts to God and therefore irreversible. He also challenged the Wycliffite thesis for disendowment.

Uhtred's position in the matter of monastic property was strictly orthodox; but in waging the attack against the friars he slipped into opinions that led to condemnation by Canterbury, after which he was silent. His "transgressions" were twofold. Principally he argued for man's autonomy in gaining salvation —in this he was ultra-Pelagian. Not only could man attain salvation by his own efforts but God himself could not decree against the moral law. In his other major "error" Uhtred was moved by a similar deep humanity: he held that man at death had a final chance to accept God, whatever his previous beliefs or acts, in a "prevision" of God as he is.

Perhaps the greatest, and the loneliest, of fourteenth-century English philosophers was Thomas Bradwardine (c.1300–49), *doctor profundus* (the deep-thinking doctor). His scientific preeminence has already been noted. Educated at Oxford, a fellow of Balliol and Merton, Bradwardine was drawn into Edward III's service as chaplain and confessor and ended his life with a brief tenure at the archbishopric of Canterbury. If his scientific work as an arts regent was influential, his massive onslaught on Franciscan Pelagianism in his theological works drew little support, except inasmuch as FitzRalph and Wycliffe used some of his arguments. For Bradwardine, God's sovereignty was fundamental: "God is the necessary co-producer of every act of the created will." Even so he argued that the will was free of necessity. Hence it is not quite correct to label him a determinist. We may conclude that the combination of Uhtred's condemnation and of Bradwardine's lack of followers did much to contribute to later sterility in English philosophy.

The philosophical basis of the best known of English scholastics, John Wycliffe, was thoroughly reactionary in its complete rejection of the then dominant nominalism. In fact, it was the very extremeness of his realism that led him to reject the cornerstone of late medieval church dogma, the transubstantiation of the bread and wine of the Eucharist into the body and blood of Christ. Extremism has been singled out as his most prominent characteristic by one of the keenest students of late medieval heresy. Wycliffe had no intelligible alternative to offer; so it was left to later reformers to deal the death blow to Roman universality.

Wycliffe's realism is less intelligible to modern minds than his intense biblicism, his new ideas about the church as the elect, his elevation of the laity, his stress on preaching, and his fierce attack on the authority of the church, notably of popes and bishops, and on the right of the church to hold property. Wycliffe was the first protestant, in that he believed in the equality of any person inspired by the Holy Spirit with the official authorities designated by the organized church.

Much has been said of the divergence between Wycliffe and his followers. Although the scholarly Wycliffites recanted after prolonged resistance, the evangelicalism of the Lollards (a term of abuse directed at heretics, increasingly applied to all who claimed to be Wycliffe's followers) of the fifteenth century was entirely in keeping with Wycliffe's thesis. The Lollards practiced his teaching, even if often in a distorted or extreme way and with no understanding of its philosophical underpinning. The monarchy responded by equating heresy with treason. This, more than the rather feeble response of ecclesiastical authority, drove Lollardy into remote and scattered places and made of it, for a while, a rather esoteric sectarian movement.

The Lollards of the fifteenth century consisted mainly of individual preachers and small groups gathered in conventicles (forbidden religious meetings), haphazardly rooted out by the diocesan and county authorities. Only rarely, and without success, did they band together in revolt. Two large-scale revolts occurred. The first rebellion, in 1414, was Oldcastle's revolt. There is little doubt that the broadening of the target of the Lollards from ecclesiastical to secular power, in the attempt to overthrow the government, ensured not only the small numbers that rallied to St. Giles' Fields but also the rapid destruction of the rebels. The second revolt, led by William Perkins ("Jack Sharpe") in 1431, was likewise aborted by the Lollards' extensive political as well as religious proposals. By now the gentry, prominent in its support of Lollardy in Henry IV's reign, had opted for conformity. The poor artisans who followed Perkins were easily dispersed. Lollardy reverted to the subterranean world of private societies and illicit preachers.

The fifteenth century produced one English church thinker of distinction, the odd and original Reginald Pecock (c.1392–1461). A graduate of Oxford in arts and theology, he moved from Whittington College, London, to become bishop of St. Asaph's in Wales (1444) and then of Chichester (1450). Because it was led by Thomas Gascoigne, Chancellor of Oxford University, his enemies worked through the Council to silence him and depose him, so that he spent his last two years in confinement at Thorney Abbey in the East Midlands. His writings in English (where his neologisms make for baffling reading) and in Latin were directed primarily at the Lollards, but his subtle defense ("clear witt," as he called it) of the church was itself branded as heretical, for he found himself defending church positions that the orthodox themselves condemned. He is an odd figure, perhaps to be noted primarily as a forerunner of vernacular philosophy and an example of the creativity latent in Lancastrian England.

The same dialectal technique that transformed the arts and philosophy was also applied to Bible study.[5] Here again formal lectures and disputations were used. The Bible never lost its position as the authoritative text for theologians in the Middle Ages, and until the age of Wycliffe the friars made it their special

[5] For what follows, see B. Smalley, *The Study of the Bible in the Middle Ages* (Oxford, 1952).

field—in fact, they established a quasi-monopoly over it. Although a master might steer his students through a book or two of the Bible (the Psalms and Pauline Epistles were easy favorites), it had already become clear in the twelfth century that a great gulf existed between the Bible and theology as a science—hence those collections of Sentences (of which the one of the mid-twelfth-century scholar Peter Lombard is most famous and was most widely used) that came to occupy a special place alongside the Bible in the schools. England's universities had a good, if not exceptional, place in the international enterprise. The great thirteenth-century archbishop of Canterbury, Stephen Langton, Robert Grosseteste, Robert Holcot (a fourteenth-century friar), and John Wycliffe can be classified with the best of other nationalities.

Grosseteste, in particular, was an attractive and profound biblicist. Apart from his technical expertise and his avoidance of dialectal subtleties, he was notable for his humane and penetrating understanding of classical and primitive errors in interpreting the Bible. For Grosseteste historical explanation was preferable to subtle dialectic (e.g., in cases where authorities differed). A glow of devotion often illuminates his comments about the sacred page. He concludes his notes on the Ten Commandments with some deeply felt words on love—"the most pleasant thing, for love only can make things pleasant, and without it all things displease."

It is significant that whereas Langton and Grosseteste were orthodox and conventional, though perceptive, expositors in the fourteenth century, the "humanist" Robert Holcot and the heretic Wycliffe began to lead the sheep astray. In general, there was a stunting of scholarship in this period—notably a loss of interest in establishing the simple meaning of the text. Erasmus of Rotterdam, the brilliant Renaissance humanist, recovered the older medieval ideal. Aristotelian science was incorporated into biblical studies, with such questions as "How could Jonah live inside a creature that didn't breathe?" There was an increase in moral judgments, particularly against corrupt worldly prelates. The distinction between "literal" and "spiritual" interpretations, with the former having a priori precedence, gave rise to very knotty problems for the professor.

The work of Wycliffe and his followers in making possible the much more general and evangelical study of the scriptures by translating them into English was an important development in the late Middle Ages. There had been translations of parts of the Bible, usually swathed heavily in interpretations, in previous centuries. But English was not a widely used literary language until the end of the fourteenth century, and authorities from the pope down (including the doctor of divinity " who said the Holy Scripture was a false heresy ") had maintained that adequate learning and ecclesiastical position orders were highly desirable qualifications for Bible study. Inevitably the new translations led to "inspirational" study by individuals and groups. The return to literal interpretation characteristic of Grosseteste would have pleased the earlier Bible critics; but the widespread use of English versions by the semiliterate, in the face of episcopal fulminations, was inevitably a breeding ground for Protestantism.

The reader should not think that the universities were entirely given over to lofty intellectual studies. There flourished an important, if unofficial, school of the practical sciences, which may have been the source of important medieval texts on such subjects as estate management farming and the masonic craft. Further, the students themselves produced a vivacious and often scandalous corpus of Latin verse, which was sung in taverns and on the road. This lively and creative activity among the scholars must have released tension, even if it sometimes spilled over into rather too vigorous horseplay.

Piety and Mysticism

Medieval men and women learned their religious views on life from two sources: the daily experience of toil and festivity and the lively representation of Christian truth in mass, sermon, penance, pilgrimage, and drama. The Mass was a sacred mystery of untold power. The centrality to the whole medieval scheme of this reenactment of Christ's sacrifice is illustrated most dramatically in the proliferation of chantries, where Masses were said for the salvation of the souls of founder or his family, in the late Middle Ages. Yet from the first, church authorities realized the importance of verbal exposition of the mysteries. Grosseteste, already encountered as a scientist and biblicist, was strenuous in seeking to ensure that preaching was adequately performed. In the long run he failed. The story told by those very sermon books on which some overeager apologists for the Middle Ages sought to build an account of a well-instructed laity is one of delinquency and ignorance. Yet sermons, whether by bishops (whose failings in the area of preaching were castigated by Gascoigne of Oxford in the fifteenth century), parsons, friars, or what Owst has called "wandering stars," did have an impact on medieval thought. What did the faithful hear? It is not always easy to find out, as the vernacular orations before laity and nuns have often survived only in Latin collections.

One clue to understanding the ideas of the laity is the minimal knowledge required by bishops of their parish clergy: usually the creed, the paternoster, the seven sacraments (baptism, marriage, extreme unction, penance, the mass, ordination, and confirmation), and the seven deadly sins (lust, pride, greed, gluttony, envy, anger, and sloth). In the sermons exposition of vices and virtues and of their respective punishments and rewards was standard fare. The leading authority has written: "Once let the medieval homilist get astride the vices, and the virtues which ever accompany them, and he may be safely trusted to gallop triumphantly to his conclusion."[6] Stories and diversions were at first frowned upon. The cycle of the Christian seasons often dictated the theme; so also did the allied lectionary (the list of daily readings) and special occasions like visitations or funerals. At first a good deal of symbolism and allegory was used, but Wycliffe and orthodox sermon compilers alike, in the English collections of the last medieval century, emphasized literal and plain exposition of the sacred texts. Frequent exhortations were made to observe church practices, such as Lenten austerities, Sunday Mass attendance, and regular confession. The various types of sermon were available in preachers' handbooks, of which probably the best known are John Myrc's works, *Festial* and *Instructions for Parish Priests* (c.1400). Myrc, unlike earlier amanuenses, reveled in storytelling. Rhyming sermons were also popular. Thus, like the minstrels who sang of Alexander and Arthur and Charlemagne, the church harnessed the mnemonic value of rhyme to teaching.

The castigation of sins (in connection with sermons dealing with the seven deadly sins) and the accompanying description of hell lacked nothing in forcefulness and yeasty examples. In this category of sermons arose a body of preaching against the mighty and the rich, both lay and clerical—a development that should dispel any notion that the medieval pulpit was an organ of propaganda for the establishment. The sermons preached at synods, usually by regular clergy, provided an occasion for the castigation of clerical sloth and backsliding. Under an umbrella of otherworldliness the preachers of medieval England attacked, criticized, and therefore molded secular and sacred institutions alike.

A word should be said about the mendicants, whose preaching aroused such hostility in secular minds. The greatest sermon collection of the Middle Ages is that of the Dominican John Bromyard (early fourteenth century). It has been said of mendicant preaching that it had "unrivalled supremacy . . . not merely in the preservation of tales and wonders, but in everything that pertains to the formal preaching art."[7]

After the Mass and the sermon, the practice of penance figured large in the late medieval church. The use of personal confession to the priest as against individual contrition was still an open question when Gratian compiled his *Decretum*[8] in the middle of the twelfth century (he adduced eighty-nine authorities for and against). Only with the Fourth Lateran Council (1215) was annual confession to a priest made mandatory. This decree echoed the words

---

[6] G. R. Owst, *Preaching in Medieval England* (Cambridge, 1926), chap. 3.

[7] *Ibid.*

[8] See p. 104.

of Alain de Lille, teacher-turned-monk, and hammer of the infidel (d.1202), who said that in hearing confession the priest should be like a physician, showing sympathy as well as skillful probing. According to the Lateran Council, the priest should "pour wine and oil on the wounds of the injured man." In the same period Hubert Walter, Archbishop of Canterbury, 1193–1205, at the Council of Westminster (c.1200) asserted that the priest should pay attention to the circumstances and magnitude of the fault and the penitent's devotion; the advice that wives' and husbands' confessions should be kept separate was a measure of his wisdom.

Penitentials (lists of sins and the appropriate penances) did not figure large in late medieval literature, or in the libraries of priests. Hence there must have been wide divergence of practice, while of course the leniancy and skill of the friars aroused the jealousy of seculars. The penitentials were developed in the Celtic church and then in England. From one widely used book, the *Penitential* of Burchard of Worms (1008–12), we can get an impression of the types of penance required for different offenses. For willful murder the offender was to fast on bread and water for forty days for seven successive years. For belief and participation in the magical powers of certain women "to turn about the minds of men" from hatred to love or vice versa penance was required for one year on appointed fast days. For defending the guilty out of friendship the penitent had to fast for thirty days on bread and water. Thus through its penitential system the church supported secular justice and combated superstition and pagan practices, as well as correcting immorality.

In the twelfth century Bartholomew of Exeter compiled a penitential that drew heavily on the books of Burchard and of the celebrated canon lawyer Ivo of Chartres. Bartholomew began with wise advice on the meaning of penance, the significance of absolution, and related matters. He also included comments on the value of silence and the art of prayer. He added to Burchard in places—for example, in describing the penance for homicide and usury. Fasting remained the major penalty, but a wider variety of abstinence was now included: thus besides the lengthy fasts prescribed for willful homicide, the misdoer was to go barefoot and unarmed, to stay in one place, and to abstain from all sexual intercourse.

Confession became the subject of learned distinctions and theory in the thirteenth century, as in Raymond of Pennaforte's influential *Summa Casuum* (c.1222–30). A theology of penance, in fact, became possible. We may note that although secrecy was enjoined in the Middle Ages, confession took place in the open church, not in special boxes.

The late Middle Ages was prolific in the production of religious handbooks and treatises and of collections of sermons for the edification of monk, secular clergyman, and layman alike. To an extent this work resulted from orders on high issued in the late twelfth and thirteenth centuries; but in the main it represented a natural burgeoning of cultural and religious interest. In fact, one may say that the episcopal and synodical legislation of the thirteenth century canalized and constricted the English Renaissance, as well as promoting it. In the fifteenth century lay religious instruction was expanded. *The Golden Legends* was translated and pious stories were collected (as in the *Alphabet of Tales*); religious instruction, probably for the bourgeois class, was imparted by such works as translations of Thomas à Kempis, the great Dutch mystic pietist, and the *Lantern of Light*. Sermon collections such as Pecock's *Donet* were given a wider public. Fourteenth-century compilations on the meaning of the mass and of the church's mysteries (e.g., *The Lay Folks Mass Book* and *The Lay Folks Prayer Book*) were circulated. With the mystery plays and religious lyrics, the average Englishman's knowledge of what the church was all about may well have been greater at the end of the Middle Ages than ever before. Given these developments, along with the circulation of Lollard tracts, it is clear that the ingredients of reform, if not of revolution, were amply present.

The less hierarchical aspects of fourteenth-century pastoral writings even penetrated into the work of a skilled canonist like William of Pagula (d.1332?); if a tenth-century penitential writer could affect the decrees of king and witan (royal council), the fourteenth-century canonist moralist might advise subjects of their rights under Magna Carta and warn kings of the dangers of tyranny.

The need for vernacular handbooks led to many translations—in fact, W. A. Pantin suggests that Edmund Rich's *Mirror of Holy Church* (early thirteenth century), one of the most seminal of these handbooks, was originally written in French.[9] Robert Mannyng's *Handling Sin,* the best known if not the most widely used of penitentials, was itself a free and expanded translation of an earlier French treatise. The same is true of the equally famous *Ayenbite of Inwit* (Remorse of Conscience), the product of a most versatile monk, Don Michael of Northgate (c.1340). It is possible to suggest that when a writer got away from his French or Latin forerunners, as in the anonymous *Prick of Conscience,* with its apocalyptic ending, he was both more popular and less enslaved by system and tradition.

At least two features that figure prominently in Huizinga's *Waning of the Middle Ages*[1] are present in both the Latin and vernacular penitentials and moralia of the late Middle Ages. These are a preoccupation with sin and death

---

[9] W. A. Pantin, *The English Church in the Fourteenth Century* (Notre Dame, 1963), p. 122. The section of Mr. Pantin's book from which this is taken is the best introduction to the whole subject here discussed.

[1] Jan Huizinga, *The Waning of the Middle Ages,* English translation (London, 1955). Huizinga's book, based largely on Burgundian and French sources, is the most lively and readable introduction to the culture of the late Middle Ages.

and the use of mnemonic devices in the form of numbers—with vices, virtues, penitential acts, and so on, grouped in sevens, fives, and threes. This "theological mathematics" must have spilled over into lay thought too, but unfortunately there is as yet no way of proving this decisively.

A more attractive feature of nonacademic literature is that "sweet piety" connected with mysticism that is popularly associated with St. Francis. It crept into the most systematic of handbooks, as when William of Pagula hymned the healing power of the contemplation of Christ's wounds or when Edmund Rich instructed his reader in the contemplation of the cold and darkness of Christ's birth. When pious contemplation passed over into ecstatic union with God, or the stages thereto, it became mysticism, and here England produced some of the most beautiful, if not profound, of late medieval writings. The peak period was the last three decades of Edward III's reign, when the greatest of England's mystical writers were at work.[2] There was also a considerable body of explanatory and imitative literature. The reader may be a little uneasy at the conclusion of W. A. Pantin that "the relentless analysis and . . . division and sub-division of every sin" and "an audience thoroughly and severely drilled in the rudiments of faith and morals" were necessary for "the exquisite flowering of the mystical literature."[3] The drill and discipline saved what we have (and no doubt their authors) from the flames, but they did not produce the flowers. The mystical light of the Middle Ages, as of St. Bernard himself, was rather the outcry of humanity in the midst of a somewhat inhuman system. By their own confession, the mystics learned their truths from "the inner voice," from scripture, and from nature. Here veritably was the dawn of the English Renaissance, the burgeoning of a tradition that had its defenders in every medieval century, and that was bound to come into conflict with a Rome resolutely committed to Aristotle and with scholastics rooted in awe of the great thirteenth-century summae of Aquinas and his followers.

The great mystical writers of the fourteenth century stood a little outside the mainstream of medieval thought and practice. They wrote in lonely places, though usually in reach of some spiritual counselor. Mysticism, "the secret knowledge of God," involved an intense self-awareness in which the purged soul was filled with the presence of God. The scriptural basis was secure; as St. Paul had written: "It is no longer I who live, but Christ who lives in me" (Galatians ii:20). Perhaps the most attractive, though not the most profound, English mystic was Richard Rolle (c.1300–49). A Yorkshireman, Rolle studied at Oxford, but he became dissatisfied with his studies and left without proceeding to a degree. He settled as a hermit near his birthplace, under the

---

[2] See W. A. Pantin, op. cit., chapter 11, and D. Knowles, The English Mystical Tradition (London, 1961).

[3] W. A. Pantin, op. cit.

protection of the father of one of his Oxford friends. Clashes with clergy, of whom he was a relentless critic, led to several moves, and he ended his days at Hampole, near Doncaster. He was a popular writer—by intention much of his work was written in English—and his writings reached a wide audience of monks, seculars, gentry, and townsfolk. Orthodox and heretic alike studied and used his major works, *The Fire of Love* and *The Melody of Love*. In fact, Rolle expressly stated that he wrote not for the disputatious scholars but for the simple, unlearned man. His popularity reflects, perhaps, his very failure to reach the higher plateaus of contemplation. His mystical experiences, which developed after an unfortunate love affair, were infused with passion and warmth. This human quality may be illustrated by a quotation from *The Fire of Love*:

> I was sitting in a certain chapel, and while I was taking pleasure in the delight of some prayer or meditation, I suddenly felt within me an unwonted and pleasant fire. . . . I learned by experience it came from the Creator and not from creature. . . . Now from the beginning of that fiery warmth . . . till the infusion of the heavenly and spiritual harmony, the song of eternal praise, and the sweetness of unheard melody . . . nine months . . . passed away. . . .[4]

After much prayer and waiting, he wrote, "I perceived within me, I know not how, a melody and most delightful harmony from heaven, which abode in my mind. For my thought was straightway changed into a song. . . ." The endearing Rolle has been denied a place among the highest mystics by the experts; his emotional experience was on a lower level of knowing, though he himself did not recognize it.

The three other leading English mystics, the anonymous author of *The Cloud of Unknowing,* Walter Hilton, and Dame Julian of Norwich, are believed to have reached the high plateaus. The anonymous mystic may have been an ex-Dominican hermit of the East Midlands; he was well versed in Thomist theology and drew inspiration from the main authorities in the mystical life— St. Augustine, the pseudo-Denis, Hugh, and Richard of Saint Victor.[5] He criticized Richard Rolle indirectly, writing of the warmth that floods the soul as a "false heat wrought by the fiend." *The Cloud,* a handbook for a novice (as were most mystical writings), drew a sharp distinction between natural and supernatural knowledge and stressed the need for a blind, "naked" act of loving attention. The author's awareness of the "dark cloud" that the soul encounters after it has rejected all carnal and creaturely ideas anticipated the thought of St. John of the Cross. He adjured his pupil: "Smite upon that cloud

[4] Translated and quoted by D. Knowles, *op. cit.,* p. 57.

[5] Respectively early church authorities, and twelfth-century scholars, all widely quoted and commented on in the Middle Ages.

with a sharp dart of longing love." Even knowledge and reasoning must be left behind. The subsequent experience of God was of course incommunicable, though as we have seen the author suspected any emotional feelings of sweetness or warmth. Yet he was no arid speculator. Of his homely phrases one may select the following: "Take good, gracious God as he is plat and plain as a plaster, and lay it to thy sick self as thou art."

Walter Hilton (probably d.1396), although he had experience as a hermit, was an Augustinian canon of the priory of Thurgarton, Nottinghamshire. He was a great teacher, in the mainstream of mystical thought, and steered a middle course between the emotionalism of Rolle and the austerity of the author of *The Cloud.* His advice was practical and graded to the stages attained by his reader. Two main steps were outlined in his *Ladder of Perfection.*[6] The first was one of active faith and ascetic practice, involving purification from worldliness and vice but no heavenly experience. The second, requiring long and tutored effort, was one of contemplation and led eventually to the mystical possession of the soul by God. Hilton accepted the warmth that Rolle experienced as legitimate, but he felt that it had to give way to a "stillness" or "spiritual silence," which truly indicated the presence of God. Like the author of *The Cloud,* Hilton recognized the "night of sense" that came between the casting off of worldly concerns and the coming of the love of God. But he was more Christocentric and stressed more deeply the primacy of love.

Dame Julian of Norwich (b. 1343) has been called the "first English woman of letters." Her experiences of suffering, her search for (and attainment of) a bodily vision of Christ's Passion, and her intense devotion to Mary give her writings a special stamp. Early in life she sought three favors from God: to see Christ and share in his sufferings, to suffer sickness in order to purify her mind, and to receive three "wounds" (sorrow for sin, suffering with Christ, and desire of God). Her teachings, as in her *Revelations,* were pungent: "Prayer oneth the soul to God . . . when our courteous God of his grace sheweth himself to our soul, we have that we desire."

The emotional overtones, but not the solid doctrine, of Dame Julian were caught up by that late incorrigible mystic Margery Kempe (fl. 1413–39). In the fifteenth century, when man seemed content to read the works of the fourteenth-century writers in the main—especially the less valuable works, if manuscript survival is any indication—Margery Kempe made a wonderful counterpart to Henry VI. Both took their mentors too literally, deserting their obligations as wife and king respectively for a rather morbid religious way of life. This was a blind alley. Margery drove her mentors almost insane; perhaps

---

[6] As it is easily available in cheap modern editions, Hilton's *Ladder* [or *Scale*] *of Perfection* is probably the best reading to suggest to a student of English mysticism. For example, Penguin Books, ed. and trans. L. Sherley-Price (London, 1957).

there has never been so emotional a response to the crucifix and other religious symbols. The very vividness of her account of her mystical experiences, which make her *Book* an important piece of literature in itself and a landmark in the history of both the English language and of individualism, can only increase our awareness of her hysteria and morbidity.[7] Thus the glories of the medieval English mystical tradition ended their short reign with more than a hint of bathos.

Humanism

Classical studies, or humanism, was the part of medieval culture that was to burgeon and become preponderant in the following centuries. A stream of humanist thought and writing ran through the whole medieval period, though it was often bound up with theological or philosophical writing. A high point was reached in the twelfth century, with the work of John of Salisbury. There was another burst among the friar scholars of the early fourteenth century. In the fifteenth century lay and clerical magnates sponsored the travels and studies of a group of English scholars who began to put England in touch with the Renaissance in Italy.

The study of grammar and rhetoric provided the underpinning of humanistic studies. Based on the works of Priscian and Donatus, as well as of such early medieval compilations as those of Alexander de Villa Dieu, John of Garland, and Eberhard of Bethune, medieval grammars and syntaxes laid the indispensable basis for classical letters.

The twelfth-century school of Chartres, with John of Salisbury (d.1180) as its greatest luminary, was a stronghold of early humanism. John, with an almost classical style of writing, argued vigorously for the study of ancient literature. His own command of Latin was classical in quality. But the triumph of the dialectic and logic of the schoolmen meant the temporary eclipse of the twelfth-century renaissance. Writers still kept the discipline alive. Men like John of Garland, Henry of Audeley, John of Wales, and Nicholas Trivet created a bridge to a more hospitable age. Encyclopedias and *mappa mundi* (world surveys), such as those of Vincent Beauvais and Bartholomew the Englishman, also served classicism well. Elegant extracts of classical authors (*florilegia*) circulated in educated circles.

The early fourteenth century brought a remarkable, if obscure and camouflaged, revival of humane letters. This revival was concealed in the biblical and homiletic writings of a group of friars. The roots had been nourished by Robert Grosseteste, who "prepared a porous soil where classicism could

---

[7] *The Book of Margery Kempe,* ed. W. Butler-Bowden (Oxford, 1954).

flourish."[8] A precise source may be sought in the Franciscan Walter Limbourne. John of Wales wrote of the pagan authors as guides to the value of natural reason and virtue and, with John of Salisbury, was much used by the fourteenth-century classicists. Nicholas Trivet (fl.1310), the chronicler, was active in commenting on Seneca, Juvenal, and the *Aeneid*. The friars who built on these flimsy foundations were not outstanding scholars. They used fake as well as real classical authorities. Thomas Waleys, who spent many years in Avignon and Italy, was perhaps the most scholarly. Robert Holcot was "the most celebrated and the most diversely gifted."[9] A Dominican who studied at Oxford and Cambridge, Holcot wrote mainly on biblical subjects. He was not without critical insight and was in advance of his time in his reflections on schooling and on the family. He took an optimistic view of man's future and was generally "liberal" in outlook. But Holcot foreshadowed a decline in the classicism of the early fourteenth-century friars. The movement left no successors, and other groups had to take up the task.

These others were the great lay and episcopal patrons of the fifteenth century —notably Humphrey of Gloucester and John Tiptoft, Earl of Worcester. Their clients did not escape the scholastic aura of English medieval thought. However, a busy traffic between England and the centers of Italian humanism was established; this activity was to bear fruit in the renaissance of classical scholarship of the Tudor period. In the productive collaboration between aristocratic patron and classical scholar two stages can be discussed. In the early fifteenth century Humphrey, Duke of Gloucester (d.1437), uncle of Henry VI and chief of the minority Council, brought Italian humanists to England to write the glories of his brother's reign and to add polish to his scriptorium. None of these humanists, who included perhaps the greatest collector of the Italian Renaissance, Poggio Bracciolini, won any following among English scholars. Yet the patronage of Humphrey was not without result; his library, which was to form the nucleus of the Bodleian Library at Oxford, was to be a great formative force when England at last produced scholars worthy of the duke's Italian protégés. Unlike Humphrey, John Tiptoft (d.1470) had been himself exposed to the Italian Renaissance, and he was able to include truly humanist Englishmen in his circle. Prominent among these was John Free (d.1465). At Oxford between 1445 and 1456 Free developed humanist yearnings that took him, under the patronage of Bishop Grey of Ely, to Italy. There he acquired Greek and engaged in typical humanist studies—notably composing letters and orations. Here the great earl of Worcester met Free and took him into his service. In the words of R. Weiss: "Just as Free was the only

[8] B. Smalley, *English Friars and Antiquity* (Oxford, 1960), p. 49. See Dr. Smalley's book for this episode in English humanism.

[9] *Ibid.,* p. 133.

Englishman who was able to assume the entire personality of the typical Italian scholar of his time, his patron, John Tiptoft, Earl of Worcester, was the English nobleman of his age who came closest to the Italian prince of the Renaissance."[1] With men like Worcester and Free, English humanism took a great step forward. Not that they should be considered isolated figures. They were supported in their interests by a gathering host of English lords and clerks —men like Bishop Grey, and John Gunthorpe (d.1498), who rose in King Edward's service as secretary and diplomat, and John Roos—who worked toward the reception of Italian humanism, with its clear style and humane outlook, into English letters.

Courtly and Common Culture of the Laity

A minority of the laity benefited from that drilling in the Latin language—in the form of the grammars of Priscian, Donatus, and Alexander de Villa Dieu—that was the basic introductory training for the clergy. In the middle of the fourteenth century English began to replace French as the medium of teaching—that is, as the language in which commentaries were written and into which Latin "set pieces" had to be translated. The innovation has been attributed to John Cornwall of Merton College and was in general use by 1400. In the last century of the period the laity increasingly obtained a grounding in grammar in the burgeoning schools founded by kings, lords, and guilds. It has been estimated that lay literacy reached a high point in the fifteenth century.

Probably the outstanding example of lay participation in the process of learning and piety was Henry of Lancaster (c.1300–61). A Knight of the Garter active in war and politics, he composed the *Livre de Seyntes Medicins* in 1354. In his book Henry compares the sins of the soul to the sicknesses of the body, working out an elaborate system of analogies. He writes with personal feeling, freely confessing many episodes of lust, gluttony, cruelty, and overfondness for outward display in his own past. This mighty duke, fully conscious of the pleasures of aristocratic life, was also capable of responding to the thunders of the clerical preachers and teachers; what is probably unique about him is that he was able to write a book about it. We may doubt that the average nobleman took the church's teaching so seriously and regurgitated it so freshly, yet to the modern man, confronted with the paradoxical spectacle of promiscuous and bloodthirsty military men possessing books of hours, having themselves portrayed in positions of humble adoration, and patronizing and promoting clergy who castigated pride and lechery, a serious writer like Henry of Lan-

---

[1] R. Weiss, *Humanism in England During the Fifteenth Century*, 2nd ed. (Oxford, 1957), p. 112.

caster comes as a delightful resolution. W. A. Pantin has written: "It is impossible to exaggerate the importance of the educated layman in late medieval ecclesiastical history."[2] He has also drawn attention to the special writings for laymen and laywomen that became frequent after about 1350, notably Walter Hilton's *Mixed Life* and the anonymous *Abbey of the Holy Ghost*, the latter written for devout laywomen. Such writings no doubt had disastrous effects on a personality like Henry VI's, in his case contributing to the catatonic schizophrenia with which he was seized, but their availability at least added prayers and attempts at moral living to the fighting, drinking, and fornication that was the usual round of lay life.

Although it is customary, and indeed justifiable, to divide medieval English literature into categories for reading or hearing by different strata of society—courtly for the nobility; fables, plays, and ballads for the townsmen and peasants; and Latin works for the clergy—there must be many modifications to such generalizations. For example, a great number of knights were never militarily inclined and must have preferred the bawdy or satirical writings of the "bourgeois" style. Henry of Lancaster is noteworthy among nobles contributing to religious literature, and certainly the historical output of the clergy was read by kings and lords. The very fact that many genres of writing were translated into English from French and Latin in the fourteenth and fifteenth centuries indicates not only the "rise of English" from its lowly position in the three centuries after 1066 but also the desire of new groups to read the works of the masters.

The "culture" of the medieval aristocracy, in the sense of the literature written both for and of its way of life, was dominated by chivalry. The roots of this idea, or perhaps one should say this congeries of ideas, go back to the heroic tales of the various peoples whose traditions were available to medieval writers and singers: the ancient stories of Greece and Rome, the lore of the Germanic forests and Scandinavian fjords, the sagas of the gods of the Germans and Celts, and the tales of Araby. The native Anglo-Saxon version of this culture, with its strong Viking overtones, was almost completely displaced after 1066 by the Norman French tradition. In fact, English courtly culture was essentially a subspecies of the French throughout the Middle Ages; this is particularly true if we remember that the dominant French culture was itself both highly varied and open to many influences, including those stemming from the isles of Britain. Broadly speaking, the originally dominant theme of heroic warfare was transformed by the softening influence of courtesy during the twelfth century.

The Early English Text Society has filled eleven volumes with the matter of

[2] W. A. Pantin, *op. cit.*

Charlemagne, little related to the actual deeds of Charlemagne (ruler of Francia from 768 to 814). Like the matter of Britain, these themes, originally military and masculine, were influenced by courtly love in the twelfth century. Indeed, the romantic influence was already at work in the *Chanson de Roland* (c.1000), the greatest of the early epics, centering on the heroic rearguard action of Roland, one of Charlemagne's commanders in the Pyrenees. In the later stories the predominant "crusading" spirit was overlaid by romantic adventures of individual nobles. Examples of Carolingian stories in English verse are *Sir Otuel, Roland and Vernagu,* and *Sir Ferumbras,* which survive in fourteenth-century manuscripts. In the second of these Roland takes on in singlehanded combat the giant black champion of the sultan of Babylon. In the others the Saracen opponent is invariably converted to Christianity. Magic was not lacking, but it was a subordinate note.

Native English stories, however, did not die out with the coming of the Normans. In *Havelock the Dane* and *Bevis of Hamtoun* (also only surviving in late medieval versions), for example, the English-speaking subjects of the Angevins could read of the wars against the Danes, now transformed by French influence into crusading adventures against the infidel. In *Guy of Warwick* Northumbria is saved for King Athelstan from the assaults of a fierce dragon, for both love and nobility are involved. Thus was the heroic age of the tenth century transformed in the minds of the twelfth- and thirteenth-century English.

The magic of King Arthur and his court was bound to prevail. Perhaps the Arthurian stories had a certain advantage in that there was no tradition of military sagas; or rather that the war hero Arthur was so quickly overtaken by the story of a king who presided over a court of chivalry that the adventures of the queen and of the individual knights could be developed in a galaxy of romances. Yet the home of the real Arthur and of the earliest mentions of him, Britain, was not as zealous as the continental nations in developing the erotic aspects of the romance; these aspects, so closely debated and expounded in the twelfth-century courts of France, received relatively slight attention in the works of English translators and imitators. In the Middle Ages as in the nineteenth century, one had to read French to enjoy the most probing psychological studies of love.

Already, by 1170, Arthur was of European stature. As a contemporary wrote: "Whither has not flying fame spread and familiarised the name of Arthur the Briton, even as far as the empire of Christendom extends?" The legends of Arthur and his knights originated in the Celtic areas of Britain and were gradually refined and changed by Breton storytellers in the years after 1066 to suit the tastes of the Anglo-Norman and French aristocracy. The magic and mystery of the tales provided relief from the rather excessive military concerns of the Carolingian cycles. It was Geoffrey of Monmouth (d.1155), a highly educated clerk who rose to the rank of bishop and had powerful court patrons, who wove the stories into a national epic of alleged historical veracity in his immensely popular and influential *History of the Kings of Britain*. This work may be considered a literary counterpart, perhaps even an "ideology," for the new Plantagenet realm. A hint of the "love interest" that was to dominate later Arthurian legend is already present. In Geoffrey's words: "The women . . . deemed no one worthy of their love but such as had given proof of his valour in three several battles."

The subsequent history of Geoffrey's inventions is strange indeed. Frenchi-fied by Wace in his *Brut,* a copy of which was presented to Henry II's queen, Eleanor, the Arthurian tales were given a new audience. Thus when the English speakers received them back (c.1200) at the hands of Layamon, a Worcestershire priest, a new strain of imagery and emotion was to be detected.

It was not from Wace but from a far greater writer, perhaps the greatest of epic romanticists, Chrétien de Troyes (fl. 1170), that the West received the fully sophisticated tales of Arthur, Lancelot, Cliges, and others. Written to the order of French princes and princesses, his tales already had a touch of the satire that was eventually to be the undoing of romance. Here the transforming power of love, the adventures and humiliations enjoyed for its sake, and the magical themes of Celtic myth were presented in high literary style for the delectation of the upper classes in the centuries to come. Themes like "the perilous bed," "the unknown champion," and "the magic talisman" abound. In twelfth-century romances such as the *Lai of the Horn,* composed in the same French courts, "Celticity" was even more predominant.

Middle English poetic romances abounded after 1300. Only rarely did they attain high art. These romances, by the very nature of their rhyme and allitera-tion, were intended for recitation by minstrels, principally in the halls of nobles but also no doubt often in humbler circles. The tales were the culmina-tion of a long oral tradition. The fact that they were written down indicates a growing literacy and also an increasing Anglicanization of courtly culture in England. One great masterpiece—England's greatest chivalric poem—was produced. This was, of course, *Sir Gawain and the Green Knight,* with its three themes of "the beheading game" (Irish), "temptation" (Welsh), and "the exchange of winnings." Despite his preeminence, the late fourteenth-century author of this great work, who also wrote *Pearl,* the heart-rending story of love and death, is unknown. A reading of *Sir Gawain* and of Chaucer's "Wife of Bath's Tale" is probably the best way into the mind of the late medieval nobility. The coarser patriotism of the earlier *Alliterative Morte d'Arthur,* with its heavy debt to Geoffrey of Monmouth, represents the emerg-ing national pride of the middle of the fourteenth century.

At the end of the Middle Ages Sir Thomas Malory, who has not been positively identified from among several fifteenth-century knights of that name, but was probably a soldier and something of a rascal, wrote the *Morte d'Arthur*. This best known of medieval romances drew from a wide variety of sources. It is a patchwork of often contradictory tales of romance and war. While retaining the magic themes of Celtic myth, it reflected the new nationalism already detected in the previous century. Moreover, Malory drew on actual events and on his own experiences and wove the whole into a brilliant prose story. Here was a handbook for the edification and amusement of lords and ladies in the twilight of chivalric England.

The so-called literature of the bourgeoisie offers a startling contrast to that of courtly love. The high ideals of chivalry are mocked: love is seduction, the cuckold is pilloried, and the morality (as in the fables) is of an earthy and "prudential" variety. Such observations apply to the bulk of this literature, but against *Dame Sirith*, with its Boccaccian flavor, in which a clerk achieves adultery by a ruse, must be set the tender devotion of the religious lyrics. In fact, judged by the literature that has survived (and the stress must be on *survived*), the medieval Englishman grew increasingly religious as the centuries progressed. The farcical element in the popular drama, for example, is vastly outweighed by the dramatic religiosity of both the mystery and miracle plays and by the fifteenth-century flowering of the religious carol. The church, indeed, seemed to absorb and make good use of the classical and folk traditions that threatened its dogmas.

The last quarter of the fourteenth century and the opening years of the fifteenth witnessed a remarkable outpouring of literature that almost deserves the title of English Renaissance. This "movement," if one may dare use the term, was loosely related to the royal court and to the patronage of high nobility. But it was as varied in this respect as in its subject matter. What is clear is that a new, much wider English-speaking audience had emerged on the scene during the previous century, as witnessed by the encyclopedic *Cursor Mundi* (c.1300), the English manuals of devotion, and the early English romances.

The author of *Piers Plowman*, William Langland (born c.1362), combines moral earnestness with a superior literary talent, an imaginative grasp of human nature, and a strong indignation. Here the traditional chivalric writer's technique of measuring the rottenness of present times against a visionary past is transposed to an essentially noncourtly setting. The Plowman, a symbol of hard-working secular Christianity, at times of Christ himself, shows the way out of the social morass. We can see here some of that spirit of peasant pride that brought a new class onto the stage of English culture. A poor priest himself, Langland was the epitome of the serious, morally upright, and loyal peasantry of the late Middle Ages.

Geoffrey Chaucer (c.1343–1400), who also wrote in French, was the greatest of the Middle English writers. This is partly because, like all men of genius, he transcended his age. Yet even in so doing, with his joint inheritance of court and marketplace, his vast erudition, his combination of classical and medieval themes and of French and Italian idioms and ideas, he was able to comment on his age with a sophistication never before and rarely since achieved. Romance, satire, and devotion can all be found in Chaucer, even in the confines of his magnum opus, *The Canterbury Tales*. Of course, social historians find in him a gold mine second in importance only to, among literary sources, the fifteenth-century collections of letters. The sublime heights that he occasionally attains, his ability to write in terms of both tragedy and comedy, his sheer literary brilliance, and the universality of his outlook all stamp him as the genius of English medieval culture. In short, Chaucer provides us with a vast range of cultural and social insights, adding to them a brilliant grasp of character. There is room here for only a brief mention of some of these insights.

Chaucer expresses the cult of the knight and of courtly love and the mundane interests of the upper class with all seriousness—notably in the matter of Rome of *Troilus and Criseyde* and in the " Wife of Bath's Tale." The follies of the church are exposed in *The Canterbury Tales* in the pictures of friar, summoner, and prioress, while its aspirations shine through in the characterization of the poor parson and in passages in *Troilus* and *The Legend of the Good Women*. Yet it is the material concerns and " bourgeois " bawdy of Chaucer's writing that appeal most to the modern reader, and they can lead the unwary student to see him as a " liberator " from medieval allegory and otherworldliness. This is a mistake. Chaucer's greatness lies precisely in his ability to reflect, as no one else could, the whole range of medieval attitudes, not in his rejection of the dominant concerns of the Middle Ages. More truly than Petrarch or Eustace Deschamps, the French poet and friend of Chaucer, he testifies to a complex and variegated society, and if his tangy humor discredits rather than elevates as often as not, such is the price any serious civilization pays for nurturing genius. The celestial vision, the earthy materialism, and the values and dreams of various social groups all receive justice from this master of prose and verse, who wrote from the secure stance of a successful businessman, soldier, diplomat, and highly placed administrator (as clerk of the King's Works, for example) at the height of medieval Englishry.

Certain works—such as Aquinas' *Summa Theologia* and Dante's *Divine Comedy*—seem to sum up the ethos of medieval thought. The great exemplar in courtly and bourgeois literature is the *Roman de la Rose* of Guillaume de Lorris and Jean de Meung, composed in the thirteenth century, a poem that spans the gulf between what is frequently called " courteous " and " bourgeois " attitudes. The impact of this great Janus-faced work was not felt in England until the era we have called the English Renaissance. But with Chaucer's translation it became part of the English heritage.

Though Chaucer towers above other English writers, he does not stand alone. He is the great star in a constellation of late medieval writers. Others also shed light on the ideas and life of the times. In the trilingual writings of John Gower (fl. 1390) moral criticism, ever present in medieval writings, is carried further in a denunciation of private and public wickedness. Gower's plea for peace rather than war as a goal for the nobility is new. The conjunction of ability, seriousness, and loquacity in a series of poems that are perhaps to be read by the specialist rather than by the ordinary reader makes Gower a valuable guide to the more solemn and restless spirit of an uneasy age. His *Confessio Amantis* belongs at once to penitential and chivalric literature.

Hoccleve, a clerk in the privy seal office (1378–1425), also offers an interesting series of comments on the manners of his age, though his poetic ability leaves a great deal to be desired. He depicts at once the drudgery of a minor civil servant (on which he waxes tearfully eloquent) and the roisterous round of drinking, gaming, and whoring available to the London lower middle class, a round that brought Hoccleve to debt and insanity. Perhaps few writers of the golden age were more assiduous in the cultivation of noble patrons, from royal princes to aristocratic ladies (from whom Hoccleve sought an increment of his exiguous salary). His verse, though didactic in tone, is well sprinkled with observations on both the ecclesiastical and lay abuses of his age.

While the fifteenth century witnessed a decline in the rich achievement of English letters, the post-Chaucerian lyricists and playwrights and the compilers of handbooks of behavior maintained a reasonably high level of English civilization. At Bury and in London the interminable monk John Lydgate (c.1370–1450) wrote a series of epics—largely unreadable today—that delighted the late medieval audience. Lydgate also published a great variety of allegorical and occasional verse. The moral of his *Fall of Princes,* for instance, drills into the reader in endless reiteration the ghastly fate that has befallen, over the whole range of classical, biblical, and modern history, those rulers who have been too treacherous, lecherous, and above all proud. The effect of such moral exhortation on his patron, Humphrey of Gloucester, may well be questioned; indeed, while assiduously read and admired by fifteenth-century men, Lydgate appears to have had more effect in encouraging works of penance than in furthering a way of life.

English drama came of age with the mysteries and moralities that grew out of the austere Latin miracle plays of the early Middle Ages. As the drama moved from church to churchyard, and from churchyard to street and marketplace, it lost some of its moving, if somber, austerity. Drama may be characterized as the culture *par excellence* of town and guild, just as the ballad was

A PORTRAIT OF CHAUCER.
From a fifteenth-century edition of Thomas Hoccleve's poem De Regimine Principum. *Courtesy The Bettmann Archive.*

exemplary of the culture of shire and village. Whether one regrets it or not, the introduction of human portraiture and low comedy must surely be seen not only as part of the transition to the glories of Tudor drama but also as a bridge between clerical ideals and the spirit of tavern and common. If this is true of the miracle plays, it is even more true of the moralities. From the sublimity of *Everyman* to the vulgarity of *Mankind,* the moralities of the fifteenth century represent a splendid means of entry into the minds of ordinary English men and women. In *Everyman* the personified Good Deeds alone saves the hero from the devil when all his other achievements (also personified) desert him. In *Mankind* a salacious coarseness is added to the story of the triumph of virtue, no doubt to the delectation of the artisan audience.

The medieval ballads probably carry us closer to the feelings and outlook of the people than any other source. It is still a matter of dispute whether they were the direct creation of the folk or the products of individual authors. They were created in the milieu of the folk by individuals or groups. They therefore reflected and molded the sentiments of nation, border, and shire. They are by definition anonymous, but they may be related in spirit to the known writings of such political rhymesters as Laurence Minot, who celebrated the early victories of Edward III. Originally a ballad was a brief song intended for dancing, but was early transformed into a narrative poem telling of heroic or brave deeds. Snatches of ballads survive from the eleventh century, but it is not until the fourteenth and fifteenth centuries that full versions are extant.

Some of these poems were a reflection of English patriotism in the wars against the French and Scots. The poems celebrating the victories of Agincourt and the Siege of Calais were products of later stages of the Hundred Years' War. Much more significant were the border ballads, which England shared with Scotland. In the English versions the English leaders, notably the Percies, in the forefront of the wars with the Scots, were the heroes; in the Scottish versions it was their opponents who figured heroically. In any case, these ballads told of the heroism, courage, and loyalty of a nation in conflict with its enemies.

Ballads reflected the outlook of the people. Some were patriotic, as noted. Others underlined filial devotion ("The Marchand and His Son"), moral rectitude ("A Father and His Son"), the mass ("A Lady That Was in Dispayre"), devotion to Mary ("The Knight and His Wyfe"), love of animals ("The Mourning of the Hare"), and anticlericalism ("How the Plowman Learned His Pater Noster"). The king's devotion to his subjects was frequently celebrated ("King Edward and the Shepherd," "King Edward and the Hermit"), and chivalry was burlesqued ("The Tournament of Totenham," "The Cuckold's Dance"). From these popular themes we can build up a picture of the late medieval mentality.

Reflecting both the social unrest and the loyalty of late medieval men were the various ballads of Robin Hood. These stories tell us a great deal about the life and social attitudes of the well-to-do yeomen who were such a vigorous part of late medieval society. A recent study has examined the Robin Hood ballads as an expression of social discontent. M. Keen has suggested that the "matter of the Greenwood" should be added to the "matter of Britain, France, and Rome" as a guide to medieval attitudes.[3]

The first outlaw to be celebrated in legend was a national hero, Hereward the Wake, leader of the Anglo-Saxon resistance to William the Conqueror after 1066. In his legend many of the stories of forest life, of ruses and disguises, that figured in later legends were anticipated. His outlawry, his dependence on humble men against the rich, and his resistance to unjust rule anticipated later themes. An element of "romance"—of magic and spectacular heroism— clung to Hereward and was later shed by the ballads of Robin Hood. Bridging the gap between the eleventh-century hero and later legend were the romances of Fulk Fitzwarin and Eustace the Monk. The robbing of rich merchants was now added to the common stock of themes. The rescues by Fulk's magician assistant, John de Rampayne, anticipated in detail the episodes of the Robin Hood ballads. Fulk was the prototype of the resister to royal tyranny, and his legendary opposition to King John was the basis of later deeds performed against the oppression of the sheriff of Nottingham. In the tale of Eustace the Monk the ordeals and achievements of a dispossessed lord were elaborated. The protest against injustice was advanced, with stories of magic and stratagem, as a part of medieval folklore.

Unlike later outlaw heroes Hereward, Fulk, and Eustace were genuine historical figures, and their tales were trapped out with chivalry and magic. Eustace, for example, is known to have left his monastery to claim his inheritance; he entered King John's service and was an effective sea captain; when John allied with his old enemy the count of Bologne, Eustace entered the service of King Philip and Prince Louis of France. He died at the naval battle of Sandwich in 1217 in the course of his service to the latter. His historical career was turbulent and romantic enough, but the romancer tricked it out with all manner of marvels. Eustace used his magic to trick surly landlords who insisted on payment and to throw the monks into confusion, causing them to fast when they should be eating and to mutter curses when they should have been saying the hours. As an outlaw he performed deeds later ascribed to Robin Hood, such as releasing the truthful and keeping prisoner those who lied.

Another heroic outlaw whose deeds were sometimes incorporated in the

[3] M. Keen, *The Outlaws of Medieval Legend* (Toronto, 1961).

Robin Hood legends was William Wallace, the Scottish guerrilla leader who successfully resisted Edward I's invasion of his country. The historic tale of Wallace's resistance to English oppression also anticipated the border ballads, both English and Scottish, that were to form a large part of ballad literature. Wallace was associated with Robin Hood by later Scottish writers. His story advanced the ballad tradition in the manner of that of Hereward, by an association of the hero with the humble who remained loyal after the great lords had gone over to Edward I. Among Wallace's disguises was that of a potter, a device also used by Hereward and of course destined to make the gist of one of the Robin Hood ballads. The forest setting was also typical of this genre. True, marvelous episodes (e.g., Wallace's overcoming a lion) continued the ethos of romance lacking in the Robin Hood stories. But in these early tales of Hereward, Fulk, Eustace, and Wallace are found many of the ingredients—outlawry, guile, disguises, and clever ruses—later incorporated in the ballads of Sherwood and Barnesdale.

Another romance, the mid-fourteenth-century *Tale of Gamelyn,* effects the transition to the peasant outlaw. Here we move from the national to the local scene, with a setting in the shire. Gamelyn is the son of a knight, and his story is not in ballad form; but the paraphernalia of the Robin Hood tales is now present: the wicked sheriff, the sympathy with oppressed peasants, the hero as king of the outlaws, the corrupt churchman, the king's pardon. It is worth noting that in some of the Robin Hood tales the hero is also given a noble origin.

With the tales of Robin Hood we come to the greatest and most significant of the English ballads. Robin Hood's claim to historicity is very flimsy; if he must be located in history at all he probably belongs in the early years of Henry III. But like his chivalric counterpart Arthur, his legends, not his historical deeds, are what give him importance. These legends were already current in the late fourteenth century and were first set down in writing in the fifteenth, with new ones added in the sixteenth and seventeenth. Quite apart from their entertainment value, they afford valuable insights into the mentality of the wealthy yeomen who emerged as key figures on the English social scene after the decline of feudalism. The tales are told in ballad form—that is, there is a lack of evidence of individual authorship; they grew up in the milieu of song and recitation in marketplace and tavern. Originating in single episodes of perhaps not more than one stanza, they were for the most part full-fledged narratives by the time they were written down. Something of the old form often persisted in the repetition of the last line of a verse in the first line of the next.

One of the oldest and most famous of these ballads, "The Littel Geste of Robyn Hode and His Meiny," probably written (according to linguistic evidence) about 1400, may be used to give the flavor of the tales. It consists of four interwoven episodes, each probably representing an earlier ballad. In the first story Robin's men bring before him a poor knight, Sir Richard atte Lee, who had been traveling through Sherwood Forest (a favorite *mise en scène* of these stories). Sir Richard is honest and has been wronged (like Gamelyn). Freed because of his truthfulness and befriended by the outlaw band, Sir Richard is loaned £400 to pay off the abbot of St. Mary's, who holds his lands "in pawn." Little John becomes Sir Richard's valet. In the second episode, Little John is taken in disguise into the sheriff's service because of his prowess at a shooting match.[4] He lures the sheriff into the forest with a tale of hunting opportunities. Made prisoner by Robin and his men, the sheriff has to dine off his own poached venison. Later Robin captures the abbot's treasurer, and with him the money needed by Sir Richard, which is duly handed over to the poor knight when he comes to repay Robin's loan.

In the third episode Sir Richard, who has become a wealthy and powerful protector of Robin from the sheriff's wrath, is taken prisoner by a ruse. A last-minute rescue is staged by the outlaws as Sir Richard is unlawfully led to execution. The king (Edward), disguised as an abbot, now falls into Robin's hands. But his physical strength and his features give him away. In the end Robin and his men ask pardon of their royal captive and enter royal service as liveried retainers. The fourth episode, a brief and mutilated story, tells of Robin's death at the hands of the prioress of Kirklees, a kinswoman, who uses Robin's request for "bleeding" to bleed him to death, an end hastened by a fight with her lover, Red Roger.

Other medieval ballads of Robin Hood—"Robin Hood and the Potter," "Robin Hood and Guy of Gisborne," and "Robin Hood and the Monk"— tell of the worsting of the sheriff by either Robin or Little John, making heavy use of disguises and ruses. The skill and hospitality of the outlaws are always in the forefront.

Such were some of the tales that entertained squires and yeomen of the shire, much as Arthur's romances embellished the life of the court. What do they tell us of the prosperous county communities? They reveal, above all, a passionate love of justice and a corresponding hatred of the unjust way in which the law was administered. The forest laws, designed to keep out of the extensive royal forests all poachers, wood-gatherers, and would-be settlers by imposing penalties on the infringers, were particularly abhorrent. The sheriff was the villain. They also tell of a deep sympathy with the underdog, with oppressed peasantry and the disinherited knight. Wealthy churchmen are pilloried. Yet the king is often seen as above the social struggle; he appears to give pardon and to take into his service those who have tricked, defied, or even

---

[4] Shooting matches organized by the county sheriffs were part of fourteenth-century monarchs' successful attempts to build up the formidable fighting force of archers who did so much to win the battles of Crecy, Poitiers, and Agincourt.

killed his officers. It is against this background of culture, as well as in the context of sermon literature, that one must place the attitudes of peasant rebels in the late Middle Ages. Wronged knight and sturdy outlaw combined to defeat the wickedness of forester and sheriff. So on a larger stage, the occasion of revolt in 1381 and 1450 and at other times, would the people rise in the cause of justice against unjust royal servants. This was the code of the country, just as Arthurian chivalry was the code of the royal court. However far removed from reality—and we have enough information about late medieval outlaws to know that they were often cruel and ruthless—the very fact that the enemies of the law and local authority became the heroes of the marketplace gives us a vital insight into the mentality of the prosperous middle classes of the period of the Hundred Years' War.

In our effort to understand the minds of medieval Englishmen, we should not overlook the rich, varied folkways that have been painstakingly reconstructed by folklorists, anthropologists, and students of ecclesiastical laws. It is clear that many pagan practices connected with fertility, especially at the times of sowing, harvest, and New Year, persisted in the guise of games, festivals, and dancing. From these there emerged a lower-class culture of drama, carol, and music, some of which was accepted by the church and included in its liturgical life, some of which was stamped out, and some of which persisted in spite of repeated condemnations by bishops and councils.[5]

Manuals and handbooks of instruction and etiquette, never absent from medieval literature, give valuable direct evidence of the codes of behavior that, if not obeyed in all respects, were at least aspired to in the late Middle Ages. Walter of Henley's *Husbandry,* written in the thirteenth century, sustained its popularity until well into the modern period. It is an important supplement to the direct records of rural life discussed in Chapter Two. Books on knighthood —its privileges, duties, training, and aspirations—began to abound. Forerunners of Emily Post and Benjamin Spock produced vernacular treatises on etiquette and child rearing—though it is highly doubtful that our modern mentors would find much to approve of in these fifteenth-century tutors. One may mention the widely popular *Babees Book* and *The ABC of Aristotle.* These works of instruction were all part of that new self-consciousness that at a higher level produced books on kingship, studies of maritime policy (*The Libel of English Policy*), and reflections on the English constitution and legal achievement and need for reform. The best known of this last genre are the works of Chief Justice John Fortescue.[6] In brief, the fifteenth century was an age of reflection, of education, and of self-improvement, though the works that embodied those goals (at the end given a wider public by William Caxton's printing press) only rarely achieved literary merit.

[5] E. K. Chambers, *The Medieval Stage* (Oxford, 1903), vol. I.
[6] Notably *The Governance of England,* ed. C. Plummer (Oxford, 1885).

Appendix One:
INTRODUCTION
TO SOURCES

This appendix gives a brief and very selective account of the sources on which English medieval history is based. It serves two purposes. First, it should help the student to realize with what materials a historical account must be constructed. Second, it offers to the more advanced undergraduate an introduction to the sources on which a research essay should be based. The fuller guides to such an undertaking are mentioned in context.

The sources of English medieval history have traditionally, and rightly, been divided into two main categories: narrative and record. There are also a number of valuable supplementary sources, including the various disciplines that may be grouped under the term "archeology"—ranging from the study of architectural forms to the aerial photography of field systems and lost villages—and those literary products of the age that cannot be classified as either narrative or record—homiletic writings, penitentials, scholastic treatises, romances, plays, popular ballads and political satires, handbooks of "applied science," and so on. Only a start has been made at studying these various types of evidence as historical sources. Most of what has been written on them is of a technical or editorial nature. What they might tell us of the outlook of classes and individuals has only rarely been investigated.

Of the two basic sources, narrative and record, much use has been made and much has been said. The narrative sources, for a while disparaged, are beginning again to claim the serious historian's attention: witness two recent books on the early and late Middle Ages respectively, John Beeler's *Warfare in England* and J. R. Lander's *Wars of the Roses*. Both works rely largely on narrative—Beeler's because there is practically no other documentation for most of the period, and Lander's because the documentation is intolerably tedious and complex and therefore of little use for his purpose. But apart from such special reasons for reliance on narrative, in these books and in others like them one can discern a certain reaction against the overdependence on records.

Many notable examples of the skillful interleaving of record and narrative are to be found in the *Constitutional History of Medieval England* of B. Wilkinson —this in contrast to the tendency of early twentieth-century constitutional histories to distrust narrative sources to an excessive degree.

The twelfth century was particularly rich in monastic chronicles. The aim of the chroniclers, inasmuch as they set it forth, was to enlighten by example of virtue and to warn by example of vice; the whole, of course, was sustained by a strong sense of an overshadowing, and at times dramatically intervening, providence. The judgments of William Stubbs, in his introductions to several of the chronicles, have been modified and corrected by subsequent scholars; but they remain of great value.

The late twelfth century was a high-water mark for the chronicle. It was partly under the influence of the brilliant court of Henry II that the early chroniclers labored. Yet it was William of Newburgh, in his *Historia rerum Anglicorum,* written in faraway Yorkshire, who exposed the fictions of Geoffrey of Monmouth (not that this exposure did anything to lessen Geoffrey's subsequent popularity). Apart from this critical flight, William compiled but a modest account of the reigns of Stephen and Henry II; nevertheless, his very distance from court enabled him to achieve a modicum of objectivity, and he had a somewhat precocious concern with cause and effect. Other chroniclers of the late twelfth century include Richard of Devizes, Ralph of Diceto, and the so-called Benedict of Peterborough, whose text is valuable for the documents it contains. In the absence of record evidence we are unusually dependent on these writers and on contemporary commentators, critics, and geographers such as Walter Map (*De Nugis Curialium*) and Gerald of Wales[1] for our knowledge of the period; of outstanding human and local interest is Jocelyn of Brakelond's chronicle of Bury St. Edmunds (*Chronica*). These twelfth-century writers not only had access to court documents; they were also imbued with a critical acumen and lively interest in personality not matched in later works.

In the early thirteenth century a new group of English chroniclers emerged known as the school of St. Albans, which was to reign supreme until the early fifteenth century. These writers, very different in temperament and method, established the tradition of constitutional, proaristocratic bias in the treatment of the period that has influenced historical scholarship to the present day. The first of the line, Roger of Wendover, who wrote *The Flowers of History,* has been rightly criticized for his unquestioning acceptance of the stories about King John's atrocities current in his day. Some of these stories, it should be noted, may have recorded a genuine historical tradition; but it is for his account of the early years of the reign of Henry III that Roger is most valuable. His

[1] Gerald of Wales was a prolific writer; two works of outstanding value are his *Itineraries* and his *Gemma Ecclesiastica.*

successor, Matthew Paris, not only produced a mammoth account of Henry III's reign (1235–59) but also showed lively interest in European and Oriental affairs. He had access to government documents, many of which he published as an appendix to his *Cronica Majora*. No historian can ignore the judgments and recorded events of these two luminaries of the St. Albans school; moreover, since they coincided with the beginning of the age of record, it is possible to check their baronial sympathies against the official documents of the period. It is time to acknowledge our indebtedness to writers who were not overawed by the majesty of the monarchy. It is not unimportant that the major work of Matthew Paris has been called " the high-water mark of medieval historical writing in England,"[2] and that Paris is considered by many to be the greatest of medieval chroniclers. Neither opinion comes from scholars noted for Whig sympathies.

Although lesser men like William Rishanger continued the St. Albans tradition, the late thirteenth century is notable for another group of authors— among them Bartholomew Cotton of Norwich, who is especially valuable for his work on episcopal history and on the critical years when Edward I was confronted by church and lay leaders (1291–8); Thomas Wykes of Oxford, whose writings are invaluable as expressions of the royalist point of view; and Nicholas Trivet, whose *Annales* were but part of the output of a man of European stature. These writers enliven and enlighten our insight into the events of the later years of Henry III and the reign of Edward I. A great number of more modest monastic chronicles help to fill out not only religious but general history in the thirteenth century. London too began to produce annals of both local and national significance, notably Arnold Fitz Thedmar's chronicle of mayors and sheriffs, *Chronica majorium et vicecomitum Londoniarum*.

The great age of monastic writing was over by the fourteenth century. Nevertheless, in Henry Knighton of St. Mary's Leicester a worthy upholder of the tradition was active, and at the end of the century Thomas Walsingham revived the St. Albans school in all its glory. For a while, however, Westminster rather than St. Albans led in historical production. But secular and lay writers were now coming to the fore. Thus Geoffrey Baker, a clerk of Osney, wrote informedly about the early years of the century, while the *Vita Edwardi Secundi,* which can be read in modern translation, is thought to have been written by a clerk of the earl of Hereford. At the end of the century Adam of Usk, an ecclesiastical lawyer, produced a particularly valuable account of the deposition of Richard II and the accession of Henry IV, events in which he was a privileged participant.

A new note creeps into reporting with the onset of the Hundred Years' War.

---

[2] V. H. Galbraith, *Historical Research in Medieval England* (London, 1951).

Chivalric interest and concern with details of military events first make their appearance, with the work of such writers as Sir John Chandos (*The Life of the Black Prince*). Of course, the greatest of the new chivalric historians was John Froissart, better considered as founder of a distinguished Burgundian school of history than as a writer in the mainstream of English prose. Diversification was another important feature of fourteenth-century writing. At one extreme there emerged the local London histories, at the other the universal history, or *Polychronicon,* of Ralph Higden, who not only wrote on a world scale but also was deeply interested in geography. His work probably shaped all late medieval men's view of the universe. Thus in spite of the decline the fourteenth century made a valuable contribution to historical writing.

After Walsingham and Froissart, deterioration—manifested in fragmentation and localization—set in fast. Yet there were also signs of revival, as has been well shown by C. L. Kingsford, whose book on fifteenth-century historical literature makes this the best-analyzed aspect of the most chaotic of English centuries.[3] Moreover, with the work of J. R. Lander, already mentioned, the real achievement of fifteenth-century historians can better be assessed by a wide public. Perhaps the dominant feature of the time is the triumph of the vernacular city chronicle over the earlier tradition of Latin monastic annals (though the *Croyland Annals* and the *Register of Whethamstede* forbid too simple generalization). Although the chronicle tradition of medieval England must, at least after 1200, take second place to the record evidence, no serious student can ignore the stories, comments, and explanations contained in the numerous chronicles. Even more important, the chronicles often record lost documents (e.g., Walter of Guisborough's copy of the *De Tallagio Non Concedendo* [Concerning the Withholding of Tallage], important for understanding the opposition to Edward I in 1297), report on events otherwise unrecorded (e.g., the commons debates of 1376 in the *Anonimalle Chronicle*), and correct official versions of events (e.g., the deposition of Richard II). Used with discrimination, they tell us how medieval men regarded their own activities and occasionally how they viewed their past.

It would be presumptuous, even if possible, to do more than indicate the vast variety of record evidence that has for many years displaced the chronicle as the staple source for medieval English history. The volume and continuity of English records not only give England an indisputable lead in the study of politics; they also bear witness to the advanced state of English government in the medieval period.

While original (or recipients' copies of) royal documents are to be found in profusion in the Anglo-Saxon period, the official enrollments that constitute the historian's main source do not survive in continuous series until the be-

[3] C. L. Kingsford, *English Historical Literature in the Fifteenth Century* (Oxford, 1903).

ginning of Henry II's reign. The first rolls are the famous Pipe Rolls, or records of shrieval accounting at the Exchequer; with their offshoots they constitute a principal source of information on royal finances.

The variety of public records can best be grasped by reading through M. Giuseppi's two-volume *Guide to the Public Records*; from there one must go on to the indexes and calendars of the Public Record Office. A small part of the vast archives listed there have been published in extenso or in calendar form. Such publications, both of the Public Record Office and of various other bodies, are listed in E. L. C. Mullins' indispensable *Texts and Calendars*. On the nature of records, and on their interpretation, the most readable and subtle of comments are those of V. H. Galbraith, notably in his *An Introduction to the Use of Public Records*. For a general guide to both record and narrative sources, one must still go back to C. Gross' *Sources and Literature*, published in 1915.

The systematic study of English politics becomes possible only with that revolution at the end of the twelfth century whereby Chancery began enrolling the letters that were sent out in the king's name. Quickly differentiated into charter, patent, and close rolls, these records enable us to follow the operations of government with some sense of certainty. Very broadly, the three categories of letters reflected the importance and permanence of the documents in descending order. Allowance has to be made for mistakes, for deliberate tampering, and for misdating. Most of the medieval patent and close rolls have been published in calendar form (the early rolls were published in extenso). These rolls were the product of Chancery. As time went on special rolls dealing with Scotland, Gascony, and foreign relations (the Treaty Rolls) were added to the basic series.

Behind and above Chancery were those offices closer to the king; hence a chain of command between king and chancellor emerged. Unfortunately, only part of this hierarchy can be reconstructed, for the more intimate offices did not keep rolls. On the king's order the secretary (from the fourteenth century) sent a warrant sealed with the signet to the keeper of the privy seal. On this authority the keeper sent a privy seal warrant to the chancellor, and it was only at that point that the business of Chancery authorization (by the great seal) and enrollment began. Sometimes the hierarchy of command was short-circuited by direct commands to the chancellor. But it should be clear that the reconstruction of government operations is no simple matter. The beginning student may proceed by observing the notes of authority—"By the king," "By the Council," and so on—that were entered in the enrolled writs and that are usually recorded in the printed calendars.

The financial side of government had its own collection of documents. We have referred to the Pipe Rolls, the earliest of these to survive. Closely duplicating these records were the Chancellor's Rolls, which were supplemented by other enrollments from an early time. It was not until the very end of the Middle Ages that the treasurer began to keep systematic records in the Treasury of Receipt at Westminster Palace. The Receipt Rolls date back to the twelfth century and were almost duplicated by the Issue Rolls. The Memoranda Rolls—in two series, those of the lord treasurer's Remembrancer and those of the king's Remembrancer—date from early in the thirteenth century.[4] The Exannual Rolls (from Edward I's reign) and foreign accounts (from the late fourteenth century) filled out the series. For the late Middle Ages there survive a vast number of particular accounts (e.g., of war leaders, diplomats, and various household officers); these were entered in abbreviated form on the enrolled accounts. Only a tiny fraction of the financial records have been printed or calendared. Hence the student will have to rely on secondary work in his study of financial history. The workings of the financial machinery in the early Middle Ages can be studied in the *Dialogues de Scaccario* and the early Pipe Rolls and Memoranda Rolls, if the student gives special care to reading the introductions. Of the many specialized studies of later medieval finance, it would be well to read K. B. MacFarlane on loans, E. B. Fryde on public finance, and A. B. Steel on the Receipt Rolls.[5] An attempt to tabulate the various royal revenues was made by J. H. Ramsay, but his conclusions must be used with the greatest caution.

The judicial records are even more complex than the financial ones. The general working of royal justice at the beginning of the Middle Ages can be studied in the printed Curia Regis Rolls. Pleas before itinerant justices have been edited for some counties over limited periods, notably by Lady Stenton for Lincolnshire. Bertha Putnam's edition of proceedings before justices of the peace is a gold mine for later medieval social history. The introductions to these publications and to the Selden Society volumes (e.g., G. O. Sayles on the King's Bench) are essential supplementary reading to the extensive monographs of Maitland and Holdsworth. Even with the considerable number of *Year Books* (unofficial accounts by lawyers of cases for teaching purposes), the student of legal matters can gain only the slightest knowledge of the judicial practices of medieval England from what is in print.[6]

---

[4] The Remembrancers' duties overlapped extensively. It included a wide range of financial and judicial work arising from the king's financial activities—so wide that all Exchequer records are today subsumed under these two titles. For the attempt to rationalize their respective duties in the fourteenth century, see J. F. Willard, "The Memoranda Roll and the Remembrances," *Essays in Medieval History Presented to T. F. Tout* (Manchester, 1925).

[5] K. B. MacFarlane, "Loans to the Lancastrian Kings," *Cambridge Historical Journal,* IX (1947); A. B. Steel, *The Receipt of the Exchequer* (Cambridge, 1954). See also E. B. Fryde, "Public Credit with Special Reference to North-Western Europe," *The Cambridge Economic History of Europe,* vol. III (Cambridge, 1965), chap. 7.

[6] For a selection of these writings, see the Bibliography of this volume.

Parliament had its own records. The Rolls of Parliament are in print, though the student should be warned that they are largely filled with parliamentary petitions and contain little about political activity. The parliamentary writs of summons have been collected by Francis Palgrave and offer a useful corrective. The activities and composition of the Council from the late fourteenth century can be studied in part in the memoranda of its meetings collected by N. H. Nicolas. A selection of the Council's judicial work has been published by the Selden Society.

Church history has survived in a wide variety of records, in spite of the appalling destructiveness of the Reformation. Cathedrals and monasteries kept records much more substantially than lay landlords, and quite a few of their chartularies (records of charters and deeds) have survived and been printed. Bishops' registers and monastic annals (which often include bits of national news) are essential sources. Two early scholars made important collections of diocesan and monastic material respectively—William Dugdale in his *Monasticon Anglicorum* and Henry Wharton in his *Anglia Sacra*. Parish history has left no such documents and must be reconstructed largely from records of higher authorities or from the wills of parish priests.

Local history, one of the latest and most vigorous of disciplines, is likewise hampered by the absence of all-encompassing records. From the thirteenth century extensive materials in the form of court rolls (records of the decisions of manorial officials), account rolls (financial documents of manorial auditors and treasurers), and extents (legal documents verifying the boundaries and contents of manors) make it possible to study representative localities in some depth. These local documents, a few of which have been published by local record societies, must be supplemented by royal documents that shed light on local affairs. The latter run the gamut of the national archives discussed previously, but especially valuable are the Subsidy Rolls, which record local tax assessments, and the *Inquisitions Post Mortem*, which gives information about the land held by tenants in chief. The local historian is also aided today by a keen scrutiny of the landscape, on foot or from the air, from which he can learn so much about the layout of medieval villages, even those that have disappeared.

Perhaps the saddest gap in our knowledge of medieval England is in the area of county records. We know from the national materials that the shire was a living and vital element in the life of the people, a community that gave meaning to the daily intercourse of baron, knight, and peasant. But the sheriff's records, incomplete in the first place, have largely vanished, and we have to guess at the life of these communities from reports of coroners, J.P.s, justices in eyre, and taxcollectors, or from the activities of their representatives at the central courts. Most county histories have been written by members of local families proud of their local associations and achievements rather than by professional scholars.

Town records have survived more fully, though our knowledge of them is very spotty. Diligent town law officers often compiled accounts, since printed, of urban proceedings—such as the Bristol *Red Book* and the London *Letter Books* and *Memoranda Book*. If the town was a port, customs records are available to supplement our information, and even records of internal tolls have often been preserved. In some cases towns, like monasteries, had their own chroniclers to supplement the rather dry information of official documents. Here again, county and urban record societies have made available in print a portion not only of local but also of pertinent national material.

Appendix Two:
SELECTED
READING LIST

1. Bibliographies

BROWN, C., and R. H. ROBBINS (eds.). *Index of Middle English Verse*. New York, 1943.

FARRAR, C. P., and A. P. EVANS (eds.). *Bibliography of English Translations from Medieval Sources*. New York, 1946.

GROSS, C. *The Sources and Literature of English History from the Earliest Times to About 1485*. 2nd ed. London, 1915.

HARDY, T. *Descriptive Catalogue of Materials Relating to the History of Great Britain and Ireland*, 3 vols. Rolls Series 1862–71.

Historical Association. *Annual Bulletins of Historical Literature*. London, 1911–.

HOYT, R. S., and P. H. SAWYER (eds.). *International Medieval Bibliography*. Minneapolis, 1967–.

Modern Humanities Research Association. *The Annual Bibliography of English Language and Literature*. Cambridge, 1920–.

Oxford History of England. Bibliographies.

WELLS, J. E. *A Manual of Writings in Middle English, 1050–1400*. New Haven, Conn., 1916. With supplements.

2. Sources and Collections

CHRIMES, S. B., and A. L. BROWN (eds.). *Select Constitutional Documents*. London, 1961.

DOUGLAS, D. (ed.). *English Historical Documents*. Vols. II and IV. Oxford, 1952, 1969.

LODGE, E., and G. THORNTON (eds.). *English Constitutional Documents*. London, 1935.

Oxford Medieval Texts (in process of publication). Oxford.

STEPHENSON, C., and F. G. MARCHAM (eds.). *Sources of English Constitutional History*. New York, 1937.

STUBBS, W. (ed.). *Select Charters*. 9th ed. Oxford, 1929.

3. Guides, Handbooks, and Aids

CHENEY, C. R. (ed.). *Handbook of Dates*. Royal Historical Society, London, 1961.

Handbooks and guides published by the Historical Association.

MULLINS, E. L. C. (ed.). *Texts and Calendars: An Analytical Guide*. Royal Historical Society, 1958.

POWICKE, F. M., and E. B. FRYDE (eds.). *Handbook of British Chronology*. Royal Historical Society, London, 1961.

4. General Works and Periodicals

a. Essential periodicals in English

Cambridge Historical Journal, Church History, Economic History Review, English Historical Review, History, Journal of Ecclesiastical History, Medium Aevum, Past and Present, P.M.L.A., Speculum.

b. Short general accounts

CAM, H. M. *England Before Elizabeth*. London, 1967.

CANTOR, N. *The English*. London, 1968.

POWICKE, F. M. *Medieval England*. Oxford, 1931.

c. Basic general works

A History of England in Ten Volumes. Vols. 3 and 4. London, 1961, 1969.

The Oxford History of England. G. H. Clark (ed.). Vols. 3–6.

The Oxford History of English Literature. Vol. 2, parts 1 and 2. Oxford, 1945, 1947.

The Pelican History of England. Vols. 3 and 4. London, 1953, 1962.

The Political History of England. Vols. 2–4. London, 1904–6.

d. Reference works and encyclopedias

The Cambridge Economic History of Europe.

The Cambridge History of the Bible.

COCKAYNE, G. E. *Complete Peerage.* 13 vols. London, 1910–49.

The Dictionary of National Biography.

The Encyclopaedia Brittanica (11th ed. and latest ed.).

The New Catholic Encyclopaedia.

The Victoria History of the Counties of England.

5. Approaches to English Medieval History

CAM, H. M. "Stubbs Seventy Years After," in her *Lawfinders and Lawmakers.* London, 1962.

DOUGLAS, D. C. *English Scholars.* London, 1939.

EDWARDS, J. G. *William Stubbs.* London, 1952.

FINBERG, H. P. R. *Approaches to History.* London, 1965.

FISHER, H. A. L. *F. W. Maitland.* Cambridge, 1910.

LEVY, F. J. *Tudor Historical Thought.* San Marino, Cal., 1967.

POWICKE, F. M. *Modern Historians and the Study of History.* London, 1955.

6. The Monarchy and the Community of the Realm

a. CONSTITUTIONAL AND ADMINISTRATIVE ACCOUNTS

CHRIMES, S. B. *English Constitutional Ideas in the Fourteenth Century.* Cambridge, 1936.

————. *An Introduction to the Administrative History of Medieval England.* Oxford, 1952.

JOHNSON, C. (ed. and trans). *Dialogus de Scaccario.* London, 1950.

HOLT, J. C. *Magna Carta.* Cambridge, 1965.

LYON, B. *Constitutional and Legal History of Medieval England.* New York, 1960.

MAXWELL-LYTE, H. *Historical Notes on the Use of the Great Seal.* London, 1926.

POWICKE, M. R. *Military Obligation in Medieval England.* Oxford, 1962.

ROSKELL, J. S. *The Commons in the Parliament of 1422.* Manchester, 1954.

————. *The Commons and Their Speakers, 1376–1523.* Manchester, 1965.

SCHRAM, P. *A History of the English Coronation.* Oxford, 1937.

STUBBS, W. *The Constitutional History of England.* 4th and 5th eds. Oxford, 1903, 1906.

TOUT, T. F. *Chapters in Medieval Administrative History*. 6 vols. Manchester, 1923–35.

WILKINSON, B. *Constitutional History of Medieval England*. 4 vols. Toronto, 1952–66.

WILLARD, J. F., *et al*. *The English Government at Work*. 3 vols. Cambridge, Mass., 1940–50.

b. LEGAL ACCOUNTS

GLANVILL, R. *The Treatise on the Laws and Customs of the Realm of England*. G. D. G. Hall (ed. and trans.). London, 1965.

HOLDSWORTH, W. S. *History of English Law*. Vols. 1–3. London, 1922–3.

PLUCKNETT, T. F. T. *A Concise History of the Common Law*. 5th ed. London, 1956.

POLLOCK, F., and F. W. MAITLAND. *History of English Law*. 2nd ed. Cambridge, 1899.

PUTNAM, B. (ed.). *Proceedings Before the Justices of the Peace*. London, 1938.

THORNE, S. E. (ed. and trans.). *Bracton: On the Laws and Customs of England*. Cambridge, Mass., 1968.

Selden Society publications:

BATESON, M. (ed.). *Borough Customs*. Vols. 18, 21 (1904, 1906).

LEADAM, I. S., and J. F. BALDWIN (eds.). *Select Cases Before the King's Council*. Vol. 35 (1918).

MAITLAND, F. W. (ed.). *Select Pleas in Manorial Court*. Vol. 2 (1889).

SAYLES, G. O. (ed.). *Select Cases in the Court of the King's Bench*. Vol. 55 (1936); Vols. 5, 6 (1938); Vol. 58 (1939).

——, and H. G. RICHARDSON (eds.). *Select Cases of Procedure Without Writ*. Vol. 60 (1941).

TURNER, G. J. *Select Pleas of the Forest*. Vol. 13 (1901).

c. BIOGRAPHICAL WORKS

BEMONT, C. *Simon de Montfort*. Oxford, 1930.

FOWLER, K. *The King's Lieutenant: Henry de Grosmont*. London, 1969.

JONES, R. H. *The Royal Policy of Richard II*. Oxford, 1968.

KENDALL, P. M. *Richard III*. London, 1955.

——. *Warwick the Kingmaker*. London, 1959.

LANDER, J. R. "Edward IV: The Modern Legend and a Revision," *History*, Vol. 41, 1956.

PAINTER, S. *William the Marshal.* Baltimore, 1933.

POWICKE, F. M. *King Henry III and the Lord Edward.* Oxford, 1947.

SCOFIELD, C. L. *The Life and Reign of Edward IV.* London, 1927.

TOUT, T. F. *The Place of the Reign of Edward II in English History.* Manchester, 1936.

VICKERS, K. *Humphrey, Duke of Gloucester.* London, 1907.

WARREN, W. L. *King John.* London, 1961.

7. Local Communities

BENNETT, H. S. *Life on the English Manor.* Cambridge, 1937.

BERESFORD, M. W., and J. K. ST. JOSEPH. *Medieval England: An Aerial Survey.* Cambridge, 1958.

CAM, H. M. *The Hundred and the Hundred Rolls.* London, 1930.

CARUS-WILSON, E. M. *Medieval Merchant Venturers.* London, 1956.

DU BOULAY, F. R. H. *An Age of Ambition.* London, 1970.

GREEN, J. R. *English Town Life in the Fifteenth Century.* London, 1894.

GROSS, C. *The Gild Merchant.* Oxford, 1890.

HILL, J. W. F. *Medieval Lincoln.* Cambridge, 1948.

HILTON, R. H. *The Decline of Serfdom.* London, 1969.

HOMANS, G. C. *English Villagers of the Thirteenth Century.* New York, 1941.

HOSKINS, W. G. *The Making of the English Landscape.* London, 1956.

―――. *Local History in England.* London, 1959.

KOSMINSKY, E. A. *Studies in the Agrarian History of England.* Oxford, 1936.

LABARGE, M. W. *A Baronial Household.* London, 1965.

POOLE, A. L. *Obligations of Society.* Oxford, 1946.

POWER, E. *The Wool Trade in English Medieval History.* Oxford, 1942.

―――, and M. POSTAN. *Studies in English Trade in the Fifteenth Century.* London, 1933.

RAFTIS, J. H. *Tenure and Mobility.* Toronto, 1964.

STEPHENSON, C. *Borough and Town.* Cambridge, Mass., 1933.

TAIT, J. *The Medieval English Borough.* Manchester, 1936.

THRUPP, S. *The Merchant Class of Medieval London.* Chicago, 1948.

UNWIN, G. *The Guilds and Companies of London.* London, 1908.

WILLIAMS, G. A. *Medieval London: From Commune to Capital.* London, 1963.

8. Church Structures

BROOKE, Z. N. *The English Church and the Papacy*. Cambridge, 1931.

EDWARDS, K. *The English Secular Cathedrals*. Manchester, 1949.

HEATH, P. *The English Parish Clergy*. London, 1969.

KNOWLES, D. *The Monastic Orders in England*. Cambridge, 1940.

————. *The Religious Orders in England*. Cambridge, 1948–59.

LAWRENCE, C. H. (ed.). *The English Church and the Papacy*. London, 1965.

LEACH, A. F. *The Schools of Medieval England*. London, 1915.

LUNT, W. E. *Financial Relations of the Papacy with England*. 2 vols. Cambridge, Mass., 1939, 1962.

MAKOWER, F. *Constitutional History and Constitution of the Church of England*. London, 1895.

MOORMAN, J. R. J. *Church Life in England in the Thirteenth Century*. Cambridge, 1945.

PANTIN, W. A. *The English Church in the Fourteenth Century*. Cambridge, 1955.

RASHDALL, J. H. *The Universities of Medieval Europe*. Rev. ed. Oxford, 1936.

THOMPSON, A. H. *The English Clergy and Their Organisation in the Later Middle Ages*. Oxford, 1947.

WESTLAKE, H. F. *The Parish Gilds of Medieval England*. London, 1919.

WOOD-LEGH, K. *Church Life Under Edward III*. Cambridge, 1934.

9. Intellectual and Cultural History

CALLUS, D. A. *Robert Grosseteste, Scholar and Bishop*. Oxford, 1935.

CHAMBERS, E. K. *The Medieval Stage*. Oxford, 1903.

CHILD, F. J. *The English and Scottish Popular Ballads*. 5 vols. Boston, 1882–98.

CRAIG, H. *English Religious Drama*. Oxford, 1955.

CROMBIE, A. C. *Medieval and Early Modern Science*. New York, 1959.

FERGUSON, A. B. *The Indian Summer of English Chivalry*. Durham, N.C., 1960.

GILSON, E. *History of Christian Philosophy in the Middle Ages*. New York, 1955.

JACOB, E. F. "Reynold Pecock," *Proceedings of the British Academy*, Vol. 40, 1953.

KEEN, M. *The Outlaws of Medieval Legend*. Toronto, 1961.

KER, W. P. *English Literature: Medieval*. Oxford, 1955.

KNOWLES, D. *The English Mystics*. London, 1927.

————. *The Evolution of Medieval Thought*. London, 1962.

LEFF, G. *Bradwardine and the Pelagians.* Cambridge, 1957.

———. *Heresy in the Later Middle Ages.* Manchester, 1967.

LOOMIS, R. S. *The Development of Arthurian Romance.* London, 1963.

MACFARLANE, K. B. *John Wycliffe and the Beginnings of English Nonconformity.* London, 1952.

MATHEW, G. *The Court of Richard II.* London, 1968.

OWST, G. R. *Preaching in Medieval England.* Cambridge, 1926.

———. *Literature and the Pulpit in Medieval England.* Cambridge, 1933.

POWICKE, F. M. *Stephen Langton.* Oxford, 1928.

ROBBINS, R. H. *Secular Lyrics of the Fourteenth and Fifteenth Centuries.* Oxford, 1952.

———. *Historical Poems of the Fourteenth and Fifteenth Centuries.* New York, 1959.

SMALLEY, B. *The Study of the Bible in the Middle Ages.* Oxford, 1941.

———. *English Friars and Antiquity.* New York, 1960.

VINAVER, E. *Malory.* Oxford, 1929.

WEISS, R. *Humanism in England During the Fifteenth Century.* 2nd ed. Oxford, 1957.

WORKMAN, H. B. *John Wyclif.* Oxford, 1926.

Glossary

ad scaccariam: "at the Exchequer."

advowson: the right to nominate a cleric to a benefice.

appanage: the office and land granted to a younger member of the royal family.

appeal: a private accusation; the normal way of beginning a lawsuit.

appropriations: the acquisition of a benefice by an outside body (typically, by a monastery).

assigned tally: a tally (receipt) given to a creditor.

assignments: grants of revenue in advance of a collection.

assize: a legal document; also a court session.

arts regents: active teachers in university faculties of arts.

benefice: the holding designed to support a cleric.

benefit of clergy: the right of a cleric to be tried in a church court.

benevolence: a supposedly voluntary tax.

boon: theoretically voluntary service.

borough: a town with certain privileges and a degree of self-government.

bot: payment to the injured party in law case.

burgage: a free form of tenure in boroughs.

canons regular: secular clergy living by a rule.

chantry: a church endowment for prayers for the dead.

chapter: the governing body of a cathedral, monastery, or monastic order.

charter, original and confirmed: formal grant or regrant of land or privileges.

carucage: an early tax based on the carucate, a small land unit.

cathedral: the principal church of a diocese.

college: a chartered university residence.

convocation: the assembly of the clergy of a province (viz., York, Canterbury).

county (shire): the basic local administrative unit.

curialist: a cleric engaged in royal administration.

Danegeld: the earliest English tax.

darrein presentment **(writ of):** an inquiry into the rights over a church.

decanus: a dean, head of a group of ten.

Decretals: the official collections of church laws.

dilapidation: decay of church building.

diocese: the basic unit of church government, headed by a bishop.

dona: a form of church taxation.

escheat: reversion of land to overlord, in case of lack of heirs or forfeiture.

eyre: a traveling judicial inquiry.

fabric: buildings (usually of a church).

farm: a lump sum paid in lieu of detailed accounting.

fee farm: land held by a fixed rent.

fee simple: land held directly of the crown.

feed retainer: a follower (usually military) receiving annual payments.

fief (fee): a unit of military land holding.

forestalling: the purchase of goods before they reach market.

frankpledge: a judicial review of local police arrangements.

free alms: tenure by prayer alone.

Grand Assize: the jury available to defendant in place of trial by battle.

hall (at a university): a residence, usually of masters and students.

heusire: a form of peasant rent.

heriot: a payment (usually of the best beast) to a lord on the death of a tenant.

high farming: cultivation of the demesne by paid labor.

honor: a lord's holdings.

hundred: a subdivision of a shire (county).

in consimili casu **(writs):** "in a similar form of legal action."

in partibus infidelium: "in heathen parts."

Justice of the Peace (J.P.): the principal local justice in the late Middle Ages.

leasehold: the land held by a lease of one or more years.

legate *a latere :* a papal representative (usually a cardinal).

liberties: lands free of some royal control.

Lollardy: the heresy of Wycliffe's followers.

magister scholarum: "school master" or professor, usually at a cathedral.

manor: the basic land holding, centered on a manor house.

mark: 13s. 4d. (i.e., two-thirds of a pound).

marshalsea: disciplinary office (or prison) of a household.

marrow: plowing partnership.

mooting: a discussion of imaginary law cases.

mortuary: a payment to a church (usually of second-best beast) on the death of a tenant.

mort d'ancestor (writ): an inquiry into the dispossession of an heir.

novel disseisin (writ): an inquiry into recent dispossession.

obedientiary: a monastic official.

opus dei: "the service of God," especially by prayer.

oyer et terminer: a form of judicial inquiry.

palatine, palatinate: a county or larger unit free of royal intervention.

pallium: the insignia of an archbishop.

papal nuncio: a legate of lower standing.

patent and close writs: letters with seals pendant (patent) or closing letter (close).

plaint: a legal action.

pluralism: the holding of more than one church appointment by one individual.

possessory writs: inquiries by a jury into the possession of land or a right.

praemunire (statutes of): law against taking (church) cases out of England.

prebend: the land supporting a cathedral cleric.

priory: a monastic foundation, usually subordinate to a "mother" house.

profer: a sum offered by an official in discharge of obligations, *or* an offer of military service by a feudal tenant.

proficua: "profits."

prolocutor: a legal spokesman.

recognition: inquest by oath of a jury.

refectory: an eating place.

rotulus pullorum: a small roll of bad debts at the Exchequer.

Saint Benedict, rule of: the principal guide to the duties of a monk.

scriptorium: a writing office.

scutage: a money payment in lieu of military service.

seizin: legal possession.

sequestration: the custody of lands in case of vacancy or default.

sheriff's tourn: legal session by sheriff.

suffragan bishop: a subordinate bishop assisting the diocesan bishop.

suit of court: the obligation to attend a court.

synod: an assembly of the clergy of a diocese.

synodals: the acts of a synod.

tallage: a tax, usually at will, on demesne.

tally: a receipt in the form of a stick notched and split down the middle.

tenement: a holding.

tithe: a tenth of produce owed to church.

tithing: a group of ten for police purposes.

title: the legal right to own.

trailbaston: a form of judicial inquiry into acts of violence.

trespass: the invasion of another person's land or rights.

trial by battle: the settlement of a lawsuit by a judicial duel.

use: a form of holding land on behalf of another.

vill: village.

virgator: a small tenant with about thirty acres.

warrant: a form of authorization, such as by a seal.

wer: the value of a man's life at law.

wite: payment by way of punishment.

Index

THE COMMUNITY OF THE REALM
BY MICHAEL R. POWICKE

MICHAEL R. POWICKE was born in Manchester, England. He received his B.A. and M.A. from Oxford University, then moved in 1946 to the University of Toronto, where he is now Professor of History. A specialist in the history of late medieval England, he served as a Councillor of the Medieval Academy of America from 1967 to 1970. He is a Fellow of the Royal Historical Society of Great Britain.

A NOTE ON THE TYPE

THIS old face design, BEMBO 270, has such an up-to-date appearance
that it is difficult to realize this letter was cut (the first of its line)
before A.D. 1500. At Venice in 1495, ALDUS MANUTIUS ROMANUS
printed a small 36 pp. tract, *Petri Bembi de Aetna ad Angelum
Chabrielem liber*, written by the young humanist poet PIETRO BEMBO
(later Cardinal, and secretary to Pope Leo X), using a new design
of type which differed considerably from that of Jenson's. The
punches were cut by FRANCESCO GRIFFO of Bologna the designer
responsible six years later for the first italic types. A second roman
face followed in 1499 and this type design, based on the first, and
used to print the famous illustrated *Hypnerotomachia Poliphili*, was
the one which, after adaptation by Garamond, Voskens and others,
resulted finally in Caslon Old Face.

62627